ALTRUISM
IN WORLD
RELIGIONS

ALTRUISM IN WORLD RELIGIONS

Jacob Neusner
and
Bruce D. Chilton
Editors

Georgetown University Press/Washington, D.C.

Georgetown University Press, Washington, D.C.
© 2005 by Georgetown University Press. All rights reserved.
Printed in the United States of America

10 9 8 7 6 5 4 3 2 1   2005

This book is printed on acid-free paper meeting
the requirements of the American National Standard
for Permanence in Paper for Printed Library Materials.

As of January 1, 2007, 13-digit ISBN numbers will replace
the current 10-digit system.
Paperback: 978-1-58901-065-9

Library of Congress Cataloging-in-Publication Data
Altruism in world religions / Jacob Neusner and Bruce D. Chilton, editors.
        p. cm.
    Includes bibliographical references and index.
        ISBN 1-58901-065-5 (pbk. : alk. paper)
    1. Altruism. 2. Conduct of life. 3. Religions. I. Neusner, Jacob, 1932– II.
Chilton, Bruce
        BJ1474.A475 2005
        205—dc22

                        2005008369

Contents

Preface

The task of defining religion and making sense of diverse religions in the context of that definition requires a labor of comparison and contrast. To sustain comparison, things must be alike and not-alike: alike to validate treating them as comparable, not-alike to yield consequential difference in a common continuum. Hence, comparing religions requires identifying a topic treated by all religions—a shared category. Only when we establish grounds for comparison will exercises of contrast take on consequence. Finding shared categories, however, is the first step.

For that purpose the contributors to this volume have taken up the matter of altruism. All world religions concur that altruism—unrewarded action for the sake of another person—is virtuous. All world religions encourage sacrifice of one's own interests for those of another—a stranger, an outsider. Each religious tradition frames altruism in its own context, however. The challenge to the specialists who participate in a project of generalization—comparison and contrast—is to determine whether the religious tradition in which they specialize addresses the category-formation under discussion at all. The solutions to that problem animate this discussion, from *philia* in Greco-Roman philosophy to the canonical statements of Judaism, Christianity, Islam, Buddhism, Hinduism, and the philosophical and religious traditions of China and Japan.

The first task requires a definition of altruism. William Scott Green's introduction to this volume surveys the scene and finds a compelling definition. He emphasizes that the act of altruism must be gratuitous; the one who performs it cannot hope to find compensation for sacrifice. In the chapters that follow, each contributor tests that tradition's treatment of altruism against Green's definition. For some—for example, Greco-Roman philosophy, with which we begin—that task requires an imaginative process of identifying the category-formations of philosophy that relate to altruistic conduct. The philosophical and religious traditions of China pose a similar problem of defining category-formations that pertain and also work for the canonical evidence. For other traditions, Green's definition points to data ready at hand. In the epilogue, however, Green calls into question whether altruism is a category that serves religion or philosophy at all. As the explorations in these chapters demonstrate, it is difficult to find a religion or philosophy that does not reward goodness (however defined) done for others without hope of compensation, though the venue of the reward may be postponed beyond this life—and may take supernatural form. Thus, whether altruism is a *religious* category or in context a purely *secular* one remains an open question.

Introduction: Altruism and the Study of Religion

William Scott Green

As an academic field of learning, the study of religion depends almost entirely on its theoretical underpinnings. In critical ways, religion as a field of study is newer to the secular academy than the rest of the established humanities, such as literature, art, and philosophy. Moreover, because religion in the post-Enlightenment West is so easily associated with faith and evangelism, its native categories do not translate easily into critical academic analysis or discourse. Terms such as "sin," "salvation," and "forgiveness" seem more appropriate to the pew than the lecture hall. Thus, university scholars of religion have worked to maintain distance between themselves and their subject to establish for the study of religion the same standards of analysis and argument that, in principle, characterize professional research in most other subjects across the academy. The long-established distinction between "theology" and "religion" or between "theological studies" and "religious studies" as academic fields—and perhaps between religiously sponsored and secular universities as contexts for scholarship on religion—has marked the difference between those who self-consciously represent, advocate, and advance the religion they study and those who do not.

As Walter Capps observes, "Disciplines put searching questions before a subject in a rigorous manner, then exercise cultivated memory and practiced intelligence over the inquiries that are formulated as well as the responses that are evoked, elicited, and prove stubborn and troublesome. To call religious studies an intellectual discipline is to recognize that it employs established rules and methods of inquiry to address such issues and to record responses."[1] The field of religion has worked very hard to establish neutral analytical definitions and categories for its study. Some of these definitions and categories seem to be particular to the subject itself, such as "sacred space" and "sacred time"; others, such as "myth" and "ritual," derive from and are used in other fields as well. These theoretical tools have at least two goals. First, they establish a set of parameters that allow scholars to classify a broad array of data as "religion." Definition is central to the study of religion because it clarifies the focus of analysis. No reader of the writings that intellectually ground the field—the works of Rudolph Otto, Mircea Eliade, Max Weber, Emile Durkheim, William James, Sigmund Freud, and others—can suppose that all of them mean the same thing by the term "religion." Absent some definition, it is impossible to explain how teachings from the Bible and the Buddha should be studied together as exemplars of the same phenomenon—that is, which parts of them allow these texts and teachings to be classified together. Second, the definitions and categories establish a set of preliminary questions that the study of the subject aims to answer. As Capps suggests, the purpose of an academic discipline is to make the subject it studies "intelligible." The definitions and categories it uses are the means by which it accomplishes that goal.

This book was written to answer a single, straightforward question: Is "altruism" a useful and appropriate category for the academic study of religion? Does altruism provide a distinctive perspective, raise questions otherwise unasked, or freshly illuminate aspects of religion? In short, does altruism make religion more intelligible by exposing it in a way that no other category does or has? Does it add value to our academic work?

Providing a common answer to this question requires some limitations on the terms of the question. Minimally, we need a degree of shared understanding about the meaning of the terms "religion" and "altruism." Because each of these terms is contested, it will help us to work with definitions that are broadly plausible, methodologically inclusive, and analytically useful. We ought to avoid definitions that are too narrow or too broad or are otherwise not well framed.

For "religion" I propose that we adopt the well-known definition of Melford Spiro: "an institution consisting of culturally patterned interaction with culturally postulated superhuman beings."[2] Spiro uses the concept of "superhuman being" as the variable that distinguishes religion from not-religion—from politics or philosophy, for instance. Spiro's notion of cultural patterning and cultural postulating allows the definition to attend to the distinctive "otherness" of discrete cultures, so that even unfamiliar religious actions can have the integrity to which they are entitled. The definition's focus on "interaction with a superhuman being" allows it to be expansive because "interaction" can include a wide range of activities: obedience, prayer, social action, and intention, among others. In terms of the definition, whatever human beings do in response to the superhuman beings their culture postulates would constitute part of what the study of religion would seek to make intelligible. To Spiro's conception we may add a note of historical and phenomenological description. Religions exhibit a tendency to totalize—to extend their reach. The religions of the world come to expression not only in speech and writing but also in art, music, and dance; in smell and taste; in ethics and intellect. They have cosmologies (stories of the origin of the world) and eschatologies (stories of the end of the world), as well as theories of nature, birth, morality, sexuality, marriage, suffering, and death. The comprehensiveness of religion allows it to touch all the transition points of life, collective and individual, and thus to make definitive claims on the total human being.

It is well known that "altruism" (from the Latin root *alter*, "other") was invented by Auguste Comte in the 1830s as a general term to designate care for others. In the contemporary academy, altruism is a category that transcends disciplines. It is used in evolutionary biology, sociology, psychology, economics, philosophy, and religion. None of these disciplines denies that human beings act to benefit others. Because of their diverse theoretical orientations, however, they differ sharply on how to explain this behavior and the motivations behind it. Debates about altruism entail the following sorts of questions: Do humans really have the capacity to act for the benefit of others, or are such actions actually forms of self-interest? What are the mechanisms—genetic, biological, psychological, cognitive—that shape or determine behavior directed toward the welfare of others? Is other-directed behavior innate or learned?[3] Although these questions are important and interesting, they are not the primary focus of the present inquiry. Our task is more modest. It is not to explain altruism but to determine if and how it advances the study of religion. To perform that task, we need to find a minimal definition of altruism.

To be analytically useful, a definition of altruism must distinguish it from alternative forms of other-regarding attitudes and behaviors. Kristen Renwick Monroe rightly observes, "In our scholarly discussions of altruism . . . we must take care to distinguish between altruism and closely related prosocial acts, such as giving, sharing, cooperating, and deep, generous love."[4] Using altruism as a general synonym for care or concern for others makes it too broad to help make religion intelligible or to provide a distinctive perspective.

To find a definition of human altruism it will be useful to examine several possibilities to see if we can identify some common elements among them. These common elements can serve as the foundation for specific questions the authors can bring to their sources.

A standard dictionary definition describes altruism as "unselfish concern for the welfare of others: opposed to egoism."[5] The four components of this definition distinguish altruism from other kinds of care for others. "Unselfish" carries with it the notion that the altruist acts for the sake of the other rather than himself or herself. "Concern" suggests that altruism entails a motivation as well as an action. "Welfare" means that the goal is to benefit, rather than harm, the other. And "others" implies that the altruist is capable of seeing the object of concern as someone distinct from himself or herself. All of these elements appear in the definitions that follow.

Kristen Renwick Monroe elaborates these components in her comprehensive definition:[6]

Traditionally, altruism refers to action intended to benefit another, even when such action risks possible sacrifice to the well-being of the actor. This conceptualization entails several critical points: (1) Altruism must involve action. Good intentions or well-meaning thoughts are not enough. (2) The action must have a goal, although the goal may be either conscious or reflexive. (3) The goal must be designed to help another person. If another person's welfare is affected as an unintended or secondary consequence of behavior motivated primarily to further one's own welfare, the act is not altruistic. (4) Consequences are less important than intentions. (5) Altruism sets no conditions. The purpose of the altruistic act is helping another person; there is no anticipation or expectation of reward for the altruist. In addition to these five points, conceptualization of altruism often contains a sixth: (6) Altruism must carry the risk of diminution of the actor's well-being. Acts that improve both the actor's and another's welfare usually are considered collective action. This aspect is more widely debated in social science, however, and is not always considered critical.

In this conception, altruism is intentional behavior the ultimate goal of which is to improve the welfare of another. The behavior is neither designed nor intended—consciously or reflexively—to benefit the altruist. Thus, the effect of the altruist's behavior on the altruist is intended to be either neutral or negative.

Other scholars focus on different aspects of Monroe's definition. The definitions of C. Daniel Batson and of Eliott Sober and David Sloan Wilson focus on the motivation of the altruist. In Batson's terms, "Altruism is a motivational state with the ultimate goal of increasing another's welfare."[7] For Sober and Wilson, altruism "attributes to people ultimate desires concerning the welfare of individuals other than themselves." They suggest that "altruists have ultimate desires concerning what they think will be good for others."[8] In these definitions, the use of the word "ultimate" to describe the altruist's goal or desire matches Monroe's notion that the primary purpose of altruistic behavior is the benefit of others. Thus, their definitions imply that the altruist intends to derive no benefit from the action on behalf of others.

On the other side, Samuel P. Oliner and Edith Wyschogrod both make the possibility of loss to the altruist a feature of their definitions. Oliner describes altruism as follows: "We characterize behavior as altruistic when it is (1) directed toward helping another, (2) involves a high risk or sacrifice to the actor, (3) is accompanied by no external reward, and (4) is voluntary."[9] Wyschogrod's definition is characteristically precise and concise: "Altruistic behavior may be minimally defined as action favoring other individuals at the expense of the altruist."[10] For these definitions, the possibility of a loss or cost to the actor appears as one of altruism's distinguishing variables.

Although these definitions emphasize different aspects of altruism, they do not appear fundamentally to conflict with one another. On the assumption that, taken together, these definitions of altruism represent a reasonable scholarly consensus, it is plausible to suggest that a minimal conception of altruism would take it to mean intentional action intended ultimately for the welfare of others that entails at least the possibility of either no benefit or a loss to the actor. If the consequences of action on behalf of others in principle can never be either neutral or negative, it is unclear how this understanding of altruism could apply. If this understanding is reasonable, a minimal discussion of altruism would need to pay attention to the following topics: the understanding of "the other," the assessment of intention or motivation, and the possibility that action to benefit others can be at least inconsequential for the actor.

On this basis, the following chapters on discrete religions and philosophical traditions address these questions to their primary texts:

1. In the sources of the religion you study, what are the major categories of behavior for the welfare of others? What does the religion mean by "others," both doctrinally and historically? For example, in the classical texts do "others" include people outside the religious community? If so, does historical practice follow the guidance of the texts?
2. How does the religion assess the meaning of behavior for the welfare of others? For instance, does it assess such behavior in terms of its impact on the recipient, in terms of the action itself, in terms of the motivation or intention of the actor, or in terms of some combination of these factors? If the actor's intention or motivation is a factor in determining the action's meaning, how is intention or motivation known and assessed? Does the actor determine what motivated the action, or is there some other source that makes such a determination?
3. Does the religion create a context in which it is possible that intentional action for the welfare of others can have only a neutral or negative consequence on the actor? Is it possible for action on behalf of others to have no beneficial consequence for the actor?

These questions provide a consistent lens through which to read the classical texts of the traditions under study in this book. Ultimately, they will help us determine the value of altruism as a category for the study of religion.

Notes

I am grateful for constructive conversations with Th. Emil Homerin, Edward Wierenga, Paul Muller-Ortega, Richard Feldman, Gerald Gamm, and Rebecca Fox.

1. Walter Capps, *Religious Studies: The Making of a Discipline* (Minneapolis: Fortress Press, 1995), xiii–xiv.
2. Melford E. Spiro, "Religion, Problems of Definition and Explanation," in *Culture and Human Nature: Theoretical Papers of Melford E. Spiro,* ed. Benjamin Kilbourne and L. L. Langness (Chicago: University of Chicago Press, 1987), 187–222. I have drawn the remainder of this paragraph from William Scott Green, "Introduction," in *God's Rule: The Politics of World Religions,* ed. Jacob Neusner (Washington, D.C.: Georgetown University Press, 2003).
3. For a sample of the range and intensity of these debates, see, for example, Howard Rachlin, "Altruism and Selfishness," *Behavioral and Brain Sciences* 25 (2002): 239–96. The article itself comprises pp. 239–50; the remainder consists of extensive "peer commentary" by scholars from various disciplines. See also Colin Grant, *Altruism and Christian Ethics* (Cambridge: Cambridge University Press, 2001), which suggests that altruism is a secularized concept that originates in Christianity. David Konstan, "Altruism," *Transactions of the American Philological Association* 130 (2000): 1–17, suggests that "altruism is not, in the first instance, a question about behavior but about the interpretation of behavior" (p. 2).
4. Kristen Renwick Monroe, "Explicating Altruism," in *Altruism and Altruistic Love: Science, Philosophy, and Religion in Dialogue,* ed. S. G. Post, L. G. Underwood, J. P. Schloss, and W. B. Hurlbut (Oxford: Oxford University Press, 2002), 106–22, at 107.
5. *Webster's New Universal Unabridged Dictionary* (New York: Simon and Schuster, 1983), 53.
6. Monroe, "Explicating Altruism," 107. Also see Kristen Renwick Monroe, "A Fat Lady in a Corset: Altruism and Social Theory," *American Journal of Political Science* 38, no. 4 (1994): 861–93.
7. C. Daniel Batson, "Addressing the Altruism Question Experimentally," in Post et al., *Altruism and Altruistic Love,* 89–105, at 90.
8. Eliot Sober and David Sloan Wilson, *Unto Others: The Evolution and Psychology of Unselfish Behavior* (Cambridge, Mass.: Harvard University Press, 1998), 229–30.
9. Samuel P. Oliner, "Extraordinary Acts of Ordinary People: Faces of Heroism and Altruism," in Post et al., *Altruism and Altruistic Love,* 123–39, at 123.
10. Edith Wyschogrod, "Pythagorean Bodies and the Body of Altruism," in Post et al., *Altruism and Altruistic Love,* 29–39, at 29.

Chapter 1

Altruism in Greco-Roman Philosophy

Robert M. Berchman

This chapter has as its goal a general definition of altruism in Greco-Roman philosophy. Because the religious sources of these traditions are fragmentary, largely secondary in nature, and almost impossible to fit into any definition of altruism, I focus on philosophical sources that offer theories of friendship and concern for others. Even here, however, my analysis is limited to the writings of Aristotle, Epicurus, the Stoa, the Pythagoreans, and selected neo-Platonists.[1]

All this should set us thinking: Were the "pagans" in fact quite so blind to the importance of "selfless factors" in human experience and behavior? This study grew out of that question. Answering this question completely clearly would involve a survey of the whole cultural achievement of Greco-Roman antiquity. What I attempt here is much more modest: merely to try to throw some light on the origin of Greco-Roman notions of friendship and the amplification of these into theories by Aristotle, Epicurus, the Stoa, the Pythagoreans, and neo-Platonism.

I do not suggest that the pagan tradition has little to offer in general on our subject. There also is little evidence of theories of altruism emerging *sui generis* out of the sources of any of the religious traditions of Mediterranean antiquity. When and where there is such evidence, a solid argument could be made, at least at the theoretical level, that much of that evidence depends on Aristotle, Epicurus, the Stoics, the Pythagoreans, and the neo-Platonists.

Two words need to be bracketed, which nonetheless prove useful in any analysis of friendship in Greco-Roman paganism. The problem is that no ancient sources use the terms "altruistic" or "egoistic" to describe ethical thoughts, intentions, or actions. I use these terms only because they are not only conventional modern terms but also a convenient heuristic device for characterizing the differences between what Greco-Roman theorists regarded as two types of friendship. These two categories reflected primarily a difference in the intentions of the friends. In an "altruistic" friendship, both friends act for the sake of each other: Each one intends to benefit the other. In an "egoistic" friendship, both friends act for the sake of themselves. Nonetheless, in each case the primary intention is to benefit the other as an extension of oneself.

This point raises another, perhaps problematic, issue, to which I return at the end of this chapter. There is little to suggest that contemporary definitions and theories of altruism summarized by William Scott Green in the introduction to this book fit Greco-Roman definitions of "selfless activity" at all. Indeed, there is little in the definitions provided by Batson, Monroe, Sober, Wilson, Oliner, Wyschogrod, or Green that helps to make sense of what is called altruism in Greco-Roman paganism.

There are three basic reasons for this difficulty. First, the ethical theories of Aristotle, Epicurus, the Stoics, and the Pythagoreans are politically, socially, and consistently rationally grounded. Hence, they do not fit modern theories of the emotivist (Hobbes) sensationalist (Hume), duty (Kant), or utilitarian (Bentham/Mill) varieties. Second, Greco-Roman theories of the soul have a social if not political dimension that is far more variegated than Descartes', Hobbes's, Hume's, or Kant's theories of the self.[2] Third, the Aristotelians, Epicureans, Stoics, and Pythagoreans claim that the joint presence of intelligence and rational choice (*prohairesis*) is the basis for human friendship (or altruism)—that the other person is another self because my true self and your true self ultimately are one and the same, which is the presence of love for the rationality present in each other human being. Such a claim leaves little room for modern emotivist, sensationalist, utilitarian, or even rationalist theories of altruism.

Here the difference between altruistic and egoistic friendship is not necessarily a difference between a self-sacrificing relationship and a non–self-sacrificing relationship. In an altruistic friendship, one need not sacrifice himself or herself for the sake of the other, although one may choose to do so. The difference between these kinds of friendship is simply one of intention. What we moderns call altruism has its "pagan" origins in the social commitments and political obligations of friendship. Greco-Roman notions of community friendship as a common project are largely alien to modern understandings of altruism. Greco-Roman philosophical views of friendship also carry with them a rejection of modern notions that we have banded together in friendship for selfless advantage, emotions, or out of moral duty. The Greco-Romans also evince a rejection of modern theories of the self with their appeals to an emotional, desiring, or duty motivation for altruism. This observation suggests that "pagan" understandings of "altruism" and friendship mean much more than merely a type of emotional state and motivational disposition. Friendship refers to a type of social and political relationship that is based on the excellence of reason. Reciprocal social and political relationships define the terms of friendship.

Moreover, Aristotle, Epicurus, the Stoics, and the Pythagoreans regard excellence of character and intelligence as inseparable—a view that is characteristically at odds with that dominant in the modern world.

Modern theories of altruism follow Kant rather than Aristotle. Thus, in the words of Alasdair MacIntyre, "Those characters so essential to the dramatic scripts of modernity, the expert who matches means to ends in an evaluative neutral way as a moral agent has no genuine counterpart within the classical tradition at all."[3]

This judgment is central as we turn to Green's three topics of altruism. Greco-Roman philosophical theories of friendship have little in common with modern theories of altruism. The two traditions have radically different views of the soul or self; the other; assessments of ethical intention and motivation; and the notion that action to benefit others is inconsequential for the moral agent. In brief, Greco-Roman understandings of friendship are not driven by an unselfish concern for the welfare and care of others. Friendship is not based on the concept of regarding the object of concern as someone distinct from the self, nor are bonds of friendship designed to help another or increase the welfare of another. Friendship does set conditions, which minimally are a reasoned political and social reciprocity that is based on justice. Friendship does not involve a high risk or sacrifice to the agent, unless one rationally chooses to assume such risks and sacrifices. Hence, friendly behavior does not involve favoring other individuals at the expense of the self.

In this context, two other terms also require definition: "monistic" and "pluralistic." In contemporary moral theory, both words indicate how many goods a moral theory recognizes. A monistic theory recognizes only one good; a pluralistic theory recognizes several goods. Greco-Roman sources generally advance a pluralistic theory of goods. There are happinesses of more than one kind, there are many human activities that we may perform for their own sakes, and there are activities we may perform in accordance with good habits.

The Origins of Altruism

Any consideration of altruism in the Greco-Roman traditions must begin with a central concept: *philia*. Although the conventional translation of *philia* is friendship, this one word covers every type of attachment from kinship relations to membership in a *polis*. The Greeks of the Archaic Age understood friendship largely sociologically. When friendship is mentioned at all in Homer, it is generally in connection with the word *arete*—which translates as any excellence and, later, as virtue.[4]

This concept of virtue or excellence is more alien to us than is commonly recognized. What is alien to our conception of virtue is the intimate connection in classical society between the concept of courage and its allied virtues, on one hand, and the concepts of friendship, fate, and death on the other. To be courageous is to be someone on whom reliance can

3

be placed. Thus, courage is an important ingredient in friendship. The bonds of friendship are modeled on those of kinship. Hence, I define who my friends are by who my kinsmen are. The other ingredient of friendship is fidelity. A friend's courage assures his or her will and power to aid me and my household. My household's fidelity is the basic guarantee of its unity. Hence, Andromache and Hector, Penelope and Odysseus are friends as much as Achilles and Patroclus. Friendship cannot be divorced from social structure. As the etymology of the word *ethos* suggests, ethics and social structure are one and the same. Ethics as something distinct does not yet exist.

The Greek words for alien and guest are the same. A stranger has to be received with hospitality—limited but well defined. When Odysseus encounters the Cyclopes the question is whether they possess *themis*, or customary law shared by all civilized peoples. The answer to this question is discovered by how they treat strangers. Because the Cyclopes eat strangers, they have no *themis* and have no recognized human identity as strangers.

There is a contrast between the man who not only possesses courage and its allied virtues but also has kinsmen and friends, on one hand, and the man lacking all these, on the other. Death waits for both alike, however. Thus, life is the standard of value. If someone kills my friend, I assume the right of their death. The more extended my system of kinsmen and friends, the more liabilities I incur—which might end in my death. Moreover, there are powers in the world that no one can control. Human life is invaded by passions, which appear as impersonal forces and sometimes as gods. These forces and the rules of kinship and friendship constitute patterns of an ineluctable kind. Neither willing nor cunning will enable one to evade them. Fate is a social reality.

The person who does what he or she ought moves steadily toward death. Defeat, not victory, lies at the end. To comprehend this reality is a virtue. It is a necessary part of courage to understand this. What is involved in such understanding, however? What would we understand if we grasped the connections between courage, friendship, fidelity, the household, fate, and death? We would understand that human life has a determinate form, with *philia* at its core.

Definitions of Altruism

Plato asserts that concern for the good of others promotes the just person's own interests. He does not say much, however, to connect my interest with the good of others. Aristotle's discussion of friendship argues for a connection. Aristotle distinguishes three kinds of friendship: that concerned with advantage, pleasure, and goodness. The first two kinds are easy to understand from a purely self-interested point of view. Often we can advance our own interests more efficiently if we can rely on help from others for mutual advantage. We also might take an interest in other people because we enjoy their company. In this case our concern depends on what we enjoy, not on any concern for the other person. The third kind of friendship involves concern for the other because of himself or herself and for his or her own sake, not as a source of advantage or pleasure. Aristotle also argues that this concern for others promotes one's own good.

Aristotle argues that we can see how love of self requires concern for the good of others once we understand what we mean by self-love and self-interest. What we think is in our self-interest depends on what we think the self is and what sorts of desires need to be satisfied to achieve its interests. Aristotle argues that the self is naturally social, so something is missing from our good if all our concerns are merely self-interested.[5] In our concern for other people, we become interested in aims and activities that otherwise would not interest us and become capable of activities that otherwise would be beyond us. This what Aristotle means when he says that for the virtuous person a friend of the best sort is "another self."[6] If we are virtuous, we care about the friend in the way we care about ourselves. In doing so we take an interest that we would not otherwise take in what the friend does. Thus, concern for others does not interfere with our interests but expands them.

The type of friendship Aristotle has in mind embodies a shared recognition and pursuit of several goods. This sharing is essential and primary to the constitution of any form of self and community, whether household (*oikos*) or city (*polis*). The social nature of human beings is the basis of justice. Justice is another's good.[7] In this sense, justice is not a separable virtue but the whole of virtue insofar as it is practiced toward other people. Because virtuous people value the good of other people for the sake of the other people themselves, they also choose virtuous actions for their own sakes. Aristotle describes this attitude to virtuous actions by saying that virtuous people choose them "because they are fine" or "for the sake of the fine."

Without friendship there is no justice—which is the rewarding of desert and the repair of failures within a relationship or community. Thus, friendship is the sharing of all in the common project of creating and sustaining the life of the *polis*—a sharing incorporated in the immediacy of an individual's particular friendship. As such, friendship involves affection. Such affection arises within a relationship defined in terms of a common allegiance to and a common pursuit of goods.

Aristotle claims that human beings have a function, which is "an active life that has a rational principle"—one part obedient to a rational principle, the other part possessing reason and exercising thought.[8] Aristotle states further that the *polis* is concerned with the whole of life—not with this or that good but with the good as such.

Charles Kahn has taken passages from *Nicomachean Ethics* 8 and 9 to develop a theory of Aristotelian altruism.[9] In brief, the basis for the friendship of human beings with one another is the presence in each rational human being of the principle of the active intellect (*nous poietikos*). The joint presence of intelligence is the basis of human friendship; the other person is another self because my true self and your true self are identical—which is the *nous poietikos* shared by a rational community. Altruism is the principle of respect for the community, for the rationality present in each other's rational being (*ousia*). According to such a theory, the principle of respect for persons is a special instance of a more general rational principle of love for the rationality present in each other rational being.

Performance of this rationality function is the basis for a happy life (*eudaimon*) for each human being. Aristotle asserts that freedom is a necessary condition for achieving one's *telos*. Slaves, unlike free persons, have their tasks determined for them because they have less of an understanding of what they ought to be doing.[10] Free persons, however, as rational agents, are more likely to have their activities determined by their concepts of the good life and their commitment to it. Thus, it is appropriate for each of us to maximize the fulfillment and contribute to the maximization of human friendship in others. "The end of the good state is the good life ... the state is the union of families and villages in a perfect and self-sufficing life, by which we mean a happy and honorable life.... Political society exists for the sake of noble actions ... those who contribute to such a society have a greater share in it than those who have the same or greater freedom or nobility of birth but are inferior in political virtue."[11]

There are several reasons for thinking that Aristotle did not have—and could not have had as Kahn suggests—a principle of "respect for persons" as a central part of his ethical theory. The primary reason is historical. The modern principle of "respect for persons" owes much to Kant's ethical theory, which depends on a double universalization of moral maxims as embodied in the formulation of the categorical imperative: Act so that you always treat humanity, whether in your own person or in the person of any other, never simply as a means but always at the same time as an end.

Aristotle's ethical theory turns primarily on what the citizen is and does, the sort of life he or she leads—which end in the various moral states of character, or activity of soul, developed. Aristotle says, "He who participates in rational principle (*koinonon logou*) enough to apprehend is a slave by nature."[12] On the contrary, one who has a rational principle and who is concerned about the well-being of one's *genos*—as a rational community or *polis*, is a friend.

Aristotle asserts a communal commitment to the achievement of human happiness within a community or state. He adds that because free persons are the most rational members of the household, they are more conscious of the duties they must impose on themselves to achieve such a kingdom of ends. On the other hand, the less rational, less responsible members of the household are not conscious of their moral duties and are far more likely to perform random actions. In brief, the nonrational members of society are the source of political instability, if not a model for the explanation for the indeterminacy of the material elements in the universe.

Definitions of Friendship

Aristotle's definition of friendship is essentially good friendship, and friendship of this type is altruistic. Persons who are good friends act with the intention of advancing the happiness of one another. This friendship plays out in two ways: as an activity and as a virtue. When Aristotle defines friendship as an activity he does so as one defines a friend: "Friends must bear good will and good wishes for one another, not without recognition, for the sake of one of the objects discussed."[13] "Friends must bear good will and good wishes, and they must do so for the sake of their goodness, their usefulness, or their pleasantness because these three qualities distinguish the lovable objects under discussion."[14]

Aristotle begins with the object of love: "Not everything seems to be loved but only the lovable, and this seems to be either good, or pleasant, or useful. But the useful would seem to be that by means of which some good or pleasure comes to be so that the good and the pleasant would be lovable as ends."[15] Love is for the sake of the lovable, and the lovable can be divided into the good, the useful, and the pleasant. Moreover, the useful is a means, whereas the good and pleasant are ends.

Aristotle also considers the elements of good wishes and their reciprocity. He shows that friendship requires good wishes and their reciprocity: "Love for a lifeless object we do not call friendship. For there is no reciprocal love nor is there a good wish for the other. To bear a good wish for wine would be ridiculous. If anything, we wish that it may keep so that we may drink it. But we say that it is necessary to wish the good for a friend for his sake."[16]

Another example of reciprocity would be the distinction between good will and friendship: "To those who wish to be good we ascribe only good will, if the same wishes do not arise from another. For friendship lies in reciprocal good will."[17] Thus, even if we wish good will for another, we cannot say we are friends unless the good will is reciprocated.

Aristotle also argues that friends must recognize their good wishes for one another: "Or must we add that they do so without recognition?

For many people bear good wishes for those whom they have not seen but suppose to be good or useful. And someone among these may feel the same toward them. These people seem to bear good will for one another. But how could some one call them friends when they do not recognize how they feel about themselves?"[18]

These passages convey the sequence of events in the development of friendship: affection, good will, and reciprocity. They also suggest a distinction between essential and accidental friendship, which allows for definitions of altruistic and egoistic friendship that are based on the loves exhibited in them. Such loves are distinguished by their objects: "The lovable objects differ as species from one another, and therefore so do their loves and friendships. There are therefore three species of friendship equal in number to the lovable objects. For in accordance with each object there is reciprocal love and it is recognized. Those loving one another wish what is good to one another in the respect in which they love one another."[19]

Because of these qualifications in lovable objects, some friends bear good will for others altruistically, and some friends offer good wishes to others egotistically. The former act for others essentially, advancing the good of others as an end; the latter act accidentally, advancing the good of another as a means to some other end. That is, altruism consists of good will and good wishes, reciprocated and recognized, for the sake of the goodness of another. "Perfect friendship is the friendship of good men and of men who are similar according to their virtue. For they wish things that are good similarly to each other as good men they are essentially good."[20] Hence the distinction between good friends and useful and pleasant friends. Only with good friends does one friend love the other for the sake of the other. "Those who wish the good to their friends for the sake of them are the most friends, for they do this for their sake and not accidentally."[21]

Aristotle also claims that we may have good will for the sake of another or for the sake of ourselves. He distinguishes altruistic good will from egoistic good will; ultimately, however, good will of either kind is the beginning of friendship. Altruistic good will consummates in good friendship, whereas egoistic good will ends in either useful or pleasant friendships. Of the three, good friendship is the more stable because it lasts as long as men are good and their virtue endures.[22]

Aristotle further proposes that friendship is a habit (*hexis*) or activity of the soul, in accordance with a mean, and that it concerns an emotion. Here, however, he is careful to make the point that practical wisdom (*phronesis*) determines this emotional mean. This is why friendship as a habit is virtuous. If friendship were based merely on emotions, it would lack requisite rationality, or rational choice (*prohairesis*), and thus would not be virtuous.[23]

Because love is a passion and friendship is a habit, it follows that love divides into two species: a passion and a habit.[24] Of these two species, only love that is reciprocal and for the sake of another qualifies as a habit because friends love what is lovable in each other.[25] The quality of being for the sake of another is crucial because it relies on rational choice (*prohairesis*): "Friends love each other reciprocally from choice and their choice springs from a habit."[26]

In *nuce*, for Aristotle friendship includes three species. Moreover, good friendship is the essential species, good friendship is altruistic, such good friendship is a habit that is based on rational choice according with virtue, and happiness defines the end of good friendship in that good friends act with the intention of advancing the happiness of their friends.

Friendship as Another Self

Why does someone enter into a good friendship and acquire virtue? The answer to this question takes us into the center of Aristotle's theory of friendship or altruism.

The mark of a good friendship begins with a good friendship with oneself.[27] The reason is that it is a short step from being a friend to oneself to being a friend for others. Significantly, in being a friend for others one acquires, becomes, is another self (*allos autos* or *heteros autos*). What one comes to acquire as another self are the rational marks of good or excellent friendship, which include the reflective, controlling, discriminating center of one's considered attitudes, thoughts, actions, and decisions. It is appropriate to love not only that self in us but that self in others because it is admirable and wise. This is reasoned love, not a love driven by vulgar opinion.[28]

The importance of acquiring another self ultimately rests on two principles: Man is a political being, whose nature is to live with others,[29] and being alive is good and pleasant in itself.[30] Aristotle argues that the happy individual needs a certain kind of friend because the living-together that is distinctively human is not simply living in proximity to others of one's kind (like herd animals) or in a mutual arrangement designed for human protection and economic advantage but a living-together as rational beings—sharing talk and exchanging thoughts. Indeed, the activity of thought is a vital functioning for humans. It is every bit as much of what we are as respiration, pulse, and metabolic changes or as memory, imagination, desires, emotions, and motor activity, but even more. Intellectual activity is the *telos* of being human.

Such an end is only optimally possible in friendship with another, in friendship as another self. Thus the desirability of a good person of a good friend's existence and being aware of it through intellectual activity. If one lacks good friends, one forfeits happiness. We need friends if we are to be happy.[31]

Aristotle further argues that a man and his friend choose to spend their days together doing whatever activities they enjoy most: "And therefore some drink together, and some dice together. Others exercise together and hunt together, and others philosophize together. The individuals spend their days together in whatever they are most fond of in life."[32]

Philosophizing together is primary happiness; the other activities are secondary happiness. We establish friendships, however, because we humans mutually find the happiness of other people to be choice-worthy and the primary and secondary happiness of others choice-worthy.

One can argue that Aristotle's ethics is decidedly self-centered. Man aims—and should aim—at his own *eudemonia* (happiness). Traces of this egoistic view are ample in Aristotle's account of friendship. Friendship demands a return. Yet loving is said to be more essential to friendship than being loved;[33] a man wishes well to his friend for his friend's sake, not as a means to his own happiness.[34] Indeed, the various forms of friendship that Aristotle mentions are illustrations of the social nature of man. Friendship is a virtue; it even implies virtue and is necessary for life.[35]

The most controversial part of Aristotle's theory is that friendship is based on the love of the good man for himself. Yet Aristotle warns against supposing that self-relation can be an accurate term: "By a metaphor we may say that there is justice—not between a man and himself but between two parts of him."[36] Here Aristotle is criticizing Plato's view that justice is essentially a relation within the self. Ultimately, for Aristotle, justice is a relation to another self. The good man wishes and does the best for the intellectual element in him, which is most truly himself. Because the harmonious relation called justice exists within the good man, and because his friend is another self to him, friendship possesses the characteristics of goodness and justice.[37]

Aristotle's moral theory has significance for our inquiry. As Sir David Ross notes, Aristotle's theory is an attempt to break down the antithesis between egoism and altruism by showing that the egoism of a good man has the characteristics of altruism.[38] Ross argues that Aristotle's attempts to argue that one can be interested in and sympathize with the other are a failure because it requires two distinct selves. Although this point is valid, Ross argues it too radically. Aristotle also speaks of treating the other as another self [39] or as part of oneself.[40] Aristotle is making the point that a woman may so extend her interests that the welfare of another becomes as direct an object of concern as her own well-being. A mother feels pain from her child as if it were the pain of her own body.[41] Here egoism is not only the necessary, it is also the sufficient condition for altruism. The question is what sort of self you love. Here the mother finds her interest in the welfare of her child as a friend or as the friend as another self.

> The excellent person is related to his friend in the same way as he is related to himself, since a friend is another self. Therefore, just as his own being is choice-worthy for him, his friend's being is choice-worthy for him in the same or similar way. We agreed that someone's own being is choice-worthy because he perceives that he is good, and this sort of perception is pleasurable in itself. He must, then, perceive his friend's being together <with his own>, and he will do this when they live together, and share conversation and thought.... If then, for the blessedly happy person, being is choice-worthy, since it is naturally good and pleasant, and if the being of his friend is closely similar to his own, then his friend will also be choice-worthy. Whatever is choice-worthy for him he must possess, since otherwise he will to this extent lack something. Anyone who is to be happy, then, must have excellent friends.[42]

This sort of concern for others promotes not only one's own good but the good of others—as another self.

Aristotle subsequently argues that a human being is naturally social, so something is missing from our good, and the good of others, if all our concerns are merely self-regarding. Thus, personal friendships set the conditions for the possibility of a more divine friendship—political friendship, which is an extension of friendship as another self.

Aristotle is eager to argue that the social nature of human beings also is the basis of justice. Here he agrees with Thrasymachus that justice is another's good.[43] Hence, justice is not a separable virtue but the whole of virtue insofar as it is practiced toward the other as another self. Because virtuous people value other people for the sake of the others themselves, they choose virtuous actions for their own sakes, and thus for the sakes of others as other selves.

Friendship as Other Selves

Aristotle discusses political friendship most explicitly when he discusses unanimity. Unanimity is political friendship, a friendship among other selves: "Unanimity appears to be political friendship.... For it concerns our interests and things pertaining to our life."[44]

By acting in unanimity, friends act altruistically, rather than egoistically. They act for the sake of the happiness of one other. Unanimity is not similarity of opinion or agreement about just any matter. It is agreement about moral matters: "Unanimity of such sort occurs among good men.

For they are unanimous both with themselves and with one another, being of the same intellect, so to speak. The wishes of such men are steadfast and do not shift like the currents of Euripos. They wish for what is just and for what is in their interests, and they seek these things by common consent."[45]

There is insufficient space here to explain how Aristotle defends this claim politically, through his analysis of a variety of constitutions. Suffice to say that political friendship is a type of kinship that is based on justice: "Friendship appears to exist in accordance with each of the consitations to the extent there is justice."[46]

Justice is a mark of political friendship. It is the wish to do what is good for the sake of another:[47] "The best of justice seems to be a mark of friendship."[48] This is so because Aristotle conceives of justice as both a virtue and an activity. Justice is a habit (*hexis*) that produces just wishes and actions.[49] What actions are just actions? Does a just individual act for the sake of others or for the sake of himself or herself? Does the just individual act for the sake of happiness or not? A brief answer is that because justice appears to have the same end as political friendship, someone who is just aims at happiness when he or she abides by the law. Moreover, because the law aims at the common good in a political community, and the common good is happiness, the just individual acts to achieve both his or her own happiness and the happiness of others. Ultimately, however, Aristotle implies that someone who is just acts for the sake of another: "Justice is also complete because someone possessing it is able to exercise virtue in relationship with another and not only in relation to himself. For many are able to exercise virtue in their own actions, but they are unable to exercise it in a relationship with another."[50] Thus, justice is the exercise of virtue for the sake of another: "And because of this, because it is in a relationship with another, justice alone of the virtues seems to be another's good, for it does what is in the interest of another, either someone ruling or someone in the community."[51]

Aristotle's argument is that whatever is in the interest of another is another's good. Because justice is in the interest of another, justice is another's good. Hence, justice is wishing and doing what is good for the sake of another. Here Aristotle divides justice into two kinds: distributive and corrective justice. Both are the resources necessary for social and political happiness. Distributively, as one person is to another so what one person receives is to what another person receives. Correctively, as one person is to another so what one person receives is equal to what another person receives. Aristotle goes on to say that the worth of persons serves as the principle for determining both the distribution of things[52] and the proportion of things.[53]

Significantly, such a conception of worth implies for Aristotle that the motives for distributive and corrective justice are not only altruistic but also egoistic. Nonetheless, justice as the lawful and the fair is the fundamental mark of political friendship. Lawful and fair individuals wish for and act for the happiness of themselves and others. Here political friendship and personal friendship have as their goals the happiness of oneself and other selves based on justice. As such, justice of both kinds entails degrees of reciprocity.

This notion of reciprocity is why Aristotle's conceptions of friendship and justice are similar. Justice is acting for the sake of the happiness of self and others; it is reciprocal, and it involves a rational mean similar to friendship. Where they differ is in the nature of the relationship. Those who are friends and those who are just do what is good for one another. However, friends do so out of love whereas just people do so out of good will.[54]

Friendships can arise out of justice when they arise out of good will.[55] People who are friends concern themselves with the same actions that just people do. They both wish for and do what is good for one another.[56] Justice and friendship occur together to the extent that people have things in common.[57] The difference is that friends act out of love, and just people act out of good will.

Finally, Aristotle argues that friendship with oneself occurs with justice for oneself. We do wish for and do what is good for the sake of ourselves.[58] Hence, we act as someone who is a friend and as someone who is befriended. We are another self to ourselves. This self-relation leads to a motivation and activation of political justice as a mark of political friendship. This political friendship occurs because justice is wishing and acting for the sake of the happiness of other selves. Thus, Aristotle's conception of personal friendship and political friendship is ultimately egoistic, altruistic, and pluralistic; we have two kinds of friends with a plurality of goods appropriate to each if we are to attain happiness.

The Pleasures of Friendship

Aristotle argues that the virtues are parts of happiness that are based on the claim that we have sufficient reason to be virtuous, and a virtuous person must choose virtuous action for its own sake. Hence, our virtuous choices and actions result in friendship and justice. If it cannot be proven that virtue is not a part of happiness, it cannot be proven that virtue really deserves to be chosen for its own sake, and it cannot be proven that we have sufficient reason to be virtuous, friendly, or just.

Epicurus rejects this argument[59] because he regards the ultimate good as pleasure—understood as the absence of pain and anxiety—any other good is only instrumentally valuable.[60] Friendship, for example, is a good only because it promotes or maintains the condition of *ataxaria* (tranquility). Epicurus argues that we can defend the virtues even if we take a purely instrumental attitude toward them. He defends his argument by advising regulation of desires so that we do not depend on external conditions for happiness. Here temperance and friendship are valued very highly—temperance because Epicureans do not fear the loss of worldly goods; friendship because in a society of friends they find mutual aid and pleasure in their pursuit of tranquility.

Epicurus's arguments for the pleasures of friendship suggest that he offers no positive reason to care about the good of others for its own sake, as a good in itself. Here friendship is a means to some other good, and this good is egoistic because it is a means to the pleasures of tranquility. The Epicurean is indifferent to the interests of others as a good in itself; he or she has no reason for doing any good for others except when it offers some further benefit to himself or herself and his or her own pleasure.

The highest form of social life for Epicurus is friendship—a view that is distinctive in a philosophy that regards the individual as the atom of society. By friendship, however, Epicurus meant personal friendship, not political friendship. Political life is a prison from which the sage will steer clear.[61] Only a quiet life in retirement from public affairs ensures the pleasures of happiness.[62] Hence, friendship for Epicurus arises out of a notion of justice understood as a compact not to harm or be harmed.[63] In this sense, "The just man is most free from trouble, but the unjust man abounds in trouble."[64]

This concept of justice is not akin to Rousseau's social contract.[65] People have no obligation to act justly because of any moral or social obligation. Respect for the rights of others rests solely on an egoistic calculus that is based on self-interest and self-protection. One abjures harming others if they agree not to harm oneself. In brief, justice is desirable for the freedom and pleasure it brings from fears of mental distress and physical harm. Moreover, one acts justly because doing so ensures tranquility (*ataxaria*).

Epicurus's concept of justice readily explains his theory of friendship. Friendship is useful and beneficial because of its instrumental value. It ensures that the pleasures of happiness are requited: "Friendship dances round the world, announcing to us all that we should bestir ourselves for the enjoyment of happiness."[66]

Friendship is unconditionally the highest of earthly goods.[67] With whom we eat and drink is far more important than what we eat and drink.[68] Although Epicurus claims that friendship is desirable for its own sake,[69] that philanthropy is to be pursued, and that one can attain pleasure from helping a friend without hope of any benefits, the reason one has friends has as its basis the pleasures of self-interest.[70] Cicero reports that one portion of the Epicurean school—the least consistent—maintained that friendship is pursued for the sake of its own use and pleasure as a kind of unselfish love.[71] These Epicureans proposed that among the wise there is a tacit agreement requiring them to love one another as much as they love themselves.[72] Yet even here altruistic friendship has as its source egoistic motives that are based on self-interest.

The Epicureans argued that friendship grounded on utility is not inconsistent with holding such friendship in the highest esteem because friendly associations with others afford a feeling of security that results in the most pleasurable of circumstances. Cicero notes that this connection optimally exists when friends love one another as themselves. Thus, it follows that self-love and love of a friend must be equally strong.[73] In an emergency, the sage will not shrink from suffering the greatest pains, even death, for a friend.[74]

Critics such as Cicero claimed that such a view is inconsistent with Epicurean hedonism—that Epicurus has united under the term *pleasure* two very different kinds of desire: positive enjoyment and absence of pain.[75] It is difficult to square the notion that absence of pain entails pleasure or, even more, that absence of pain brought on by friendship may bring with it the greatest pains, including death. If the latter principle holds, Epicurean friendship is altruistic after all.

Scholars have often noted that the Epicurean philosophy is deficient in coherence and consistency. This objection is not without foundation. Epicurus did not approach philosophical problems with a complete scientific groundwork, logical development, or ethical cogency. Epicurus's strongest plea is a path to happiness. Here we take our cue.

Epicureanism offers us almost a thoroughgoing egoistic, hedonistic, and utilitarian ethic encountered in Greco-Roman antiquity. The memory of past pleasures and anticipation of future pleasures can mitigate present sufferings.[76] Epicurus says, "For the virtues are naturally linked with living pleasurably, and living pleasurably is inseparable from them."[77]

Cicero's Torquatus puts it very succinctly: Pleasure is the only thing that is good in itself, so prudence, justice, moderation, and courage have value only if they are a means to pleasure.[78] This association between virtue and pleasure results in the pursuit of friendship and the claim by Epicurus that "[F]riendship is an immortal good."[79]

Here Epicurus is keen not to suggest that the interests of others should be preferred to or evaluated independently of the interests of the agent. The thrust of his hedonism is thoroughly egoistic and self-regarding.

Critics of Epicurus and Epicureanism abound in ancient sources—pagan, Jewish, and Christian—and such criticisms offer a fruitful way into an analysis of the topic of altruism.[80] First, can an egoistic ethic form a valid basis for theories of friendship and perhaps even egotistic friendship? Second, can the wise person find pleasure in the company of his or her friend apart from any further instrumental benefits? Third, can friendship be treated differently from justice? The general response to these questions, as exemplified by Cicero, is that it is difficult to see how such pleasures can be justified.[81]

If an Epicurean's happiness consists in pleasure taken in friends, for which no other means to tranquility can be substituted, a strictly hedonist conception of happiness must be false. Furthermore, the love of friendship, adumbrated by Aristotle, may bring fears and anxieties about the welfare of friends that an Epicurean rejects. Therefore, if we have no such fears and anxieties, we do not have the attitudes that are expected of and by friends. Finally, if we work out the consequences of the Epicurean case for the instrumental value of friendship, is it not clear that we would find objections to the Epicurean view that every good other than pleasure has only instrumental value? If so, Epicurus would have to abandon his argument against Plato's and Aristotle's claim that virtue is to be chosen for its own sake apart from its effects on pleasure and pain.

Reason and Friendship

Cicero tells us that a society for which all rational beings are intended will be found to exist among those who have become alive to their rational nature and destiny. This community was among the wise; specifically, it was the society of the Stoic sage. The wise and virtuous are friends because they all agree in their views of life and because they all love one another's virtue.[82] Plutarch claims that every action of a wise man contributes to the well-being of every other wise man in that if a wise man only makes a rational movement with his finger, he does a service to all wise men throughout the world; he is useful to deity as deity is to him.[83]

Seneca mentions that because only a wise man knows how to love properly, true friendship exists only among sages.[84] Thus, only the wise man possesses the art of making friends because love is won only by love.[85] Cicero also reports the Stoic view, however, that "we have been bound together and united by Nature [Reason] for civic association."[86] Thus, social principles are derived from a rational impulse implanted by Nature to form familial and friendly relationships.[87] Moreover, the principle that determines such behavior is not different in kind from the principle that activates self-regarding actions.

If this synopsis correctly describes the Stoic view, the starting point of justice is *oikeiosis*—an attitude of attraction toward things that belong to oneself.[88] Because *oikeiosis* determines an animal's relationship to its environment, but the *oikeiosis* to which it is primarily disposed is itself, it follows that the attraction to form any civic relationship has as its root an innate capacity to recognize things that belong to itself.[89] If this is so, the development of friendships is the recognition that community life and virtue are preeminently things that belong to human nature.

The crucial question is this: Is this disposition to family, friends, and social associations egoistic or altruistic? This question is difficult to answer with any certainty. According to the careful analysis of Sextus Empiricus, however, good is a concept of wider extension than virtue, but every good thing other than virtue or virtuous action has virtue as one of its parts. Whereas virtue and virtuous action are wholly defined by "benefit," benefit is intrinsic to but not exhaustive of good things such as a virtuous man and friend.[90] This is because friendship exists only among the virtuous.[91] Stobaeus muddies the waters by reporting a more complex classification of goods. He opens the door to a much more diverse set of items and drops the essential connection between benefit = virtue/virtuous action and good. He does this apparently to exhibit differences between goods in ways that are fully compatible with this principle. In any case, friends are classified as purely "instrumental goods": "Of goods, some are final, others instrumental, and others good in both respects. The prudent man and the friend are only instrumental goods. Joy, cheerfulness, confidence, prudent walking about are only final goods. But all the virtues are instrumental and final goods. For they both generate happiness and they complete it, since they are its parts."[92]

In other words, friends share with the virtues the property of generating happiness but are not its actual constituents, as is the case with the virtues of joy, cheerfulness, and the like. If this is a correct reading of Stoic theory, the acquisition of friends is purely instrumental. That is, friends are a means to happiness and its virtues, not an end in themselves.

If this conclusion is correct, the sages' disposition to acquire friends is egoistic, not altruistic. One makes friends so that one can perfect one's human nature and thereby attain happiness. This reading is suggested further by the claim that in the ideal world the state withers away because each Stoic sage is self-sufficient and his own authority.[93] All the sage possesses is the bond of friendship with other self-sufficient, self-authoritative wise men. All sages are friends to each other, and friendship in its true sense exists only between them.[94] In this communal life, in this "blessed" pattern of social behavior, all distinctions based on sex, birth, nationality, and property are dispensed with.

On this point, how can the need of society be reconciled with the sage's freedom from wants? If the wise man is self-sufficient, how can another help him? Why would he want to assist others? Seneca offers a series of answers. Chief among them is the following: "The wise man does not wish to be without friends, but still can be without friends."[95]

The question is not whether one can be without friends but whether one can be without friends without loss of happiness. If the answer is negative, the wise man is not self-sufficient and happy; if the answer is affirmative—as Seneca affirms—a sage will bear the loss of a friend in calmness because he can have another in a moment. If this is the case, friendship is hardly important at all for the self-sufficient wise man.

Seneca attempts to salvage what he can of Stoic friendship, however. It has its value in itself alone: Every wise man must wish to find those like himself; the wise man needs a friend—not to have a nurse in sickness and a helper in trouble but to have someone whom he can tend and assist and for whom he can live and die.[96] Even here, however, friendship is egotistically self-referential. It is an object for the sage's moral activity, however altruistic it may be. Ultimately, friendship belongs to external goods, and the wise man is largely indifferent to such goods. Unlike Aristotle, the Stoic sage does not even expect or need the reciprocity of friendship from the friend. Nor does friendship make the wise man dependent. Such is the absolute independence of the *spoudaios*.

The Kinship of All Life

It might strike the reader as odd that this study concludes, rather than opens, with a consideration of the Pythagorean life. I undertake this approach to avoid the *Truemmerfeld* of reconstructing the teachings of the historical Pythagoras and early Pythagoreanism. Because many of our sources about Pythagoras and the Pythagorean *bios* are late and historically problematic, it is prudent to focus on what Greco-Roman writers said of the Pythagorean life, thereby bracketing claims that any of these practices go back to Pythagoras himself.[97] I follow the example of Porphyry, whose language shows unusual caution in an attempt to confine himself to what he may regard as certain.[98]

Porphyry writes of Pythagoras as follows: "What he said to his disciples no man can tell for certain, since they preserved such exceptional silence. However, the following facts in particular became universally known: first that he held the soul to be immortal, next that it migrates into other kinds of animal, further that past events repeat themselves in a cyclic process and nothing is new in an absolute sense, and finally that one must regard all living things as kindred [*homogene*]. These are the beliefs which Pythagoras is said to have been the first to introduce to Greece."[99]

The doctrine of the kinship of all living things is foundational to Pythagorean teaching. Without it the general view of the transmigration of souls would not be possible. The basic claim is that the souls of humans and animals are of the same family (*homogenos*), which makes it possible for a singular soul to enter the bodies of a human, an animal, or a bird. Closely connected to this doctrine is the teaching of abstinence from animal foods, eggs, and beans.[100]

At any rate, what we know is that the Pythagorean community was a kind of religious order that followed a rule of life that was determined by the expectation of lives to come. In this sense, to be a Pythagorean involved an *askesis*—the practice of a special way of life. Abstinence from animal and some vegetable foods is a corollary to transmigration: The animal or vegetable you kill may be the dwelling place of a human soul or self. Behind this view is the horror of spilt blood and the blood guilt associated with the dismemberment, boiling, roasting, and eating of Dionysus Zagreus by the Titans.[101]

One question remains: Is the Pythagorean teaching of the kinship of all living things an example of altruism—an understanding of the other with the intention of welfare for others—with the consequence of such moral actions the cleansing of the moral agent? A provisional answer would be no.

If the Pythagorean teachings regarding the kinship of all living things and prohibitions against the eating of animal and some vegetable foods go back to a belief in an inherited blood guilt, the motives for believing and acting on these principles would be to expiate the penalty of an ancient grief. Plato quotes Pindar in the *Meno* that there is human responsibility for the slaying of Dionysus.[102] If this is so, the Pythagoreans maintained a notion of "original sin"—which explains the universality of guilt feelings.

The Titan myth explained why the Pythagoreans thought themselves both god and criminal.[103] They shared the view that life is trouble and punishment: "Good are the troubles, but the pleasures are evil at all events; for whatever has come in for punishment must be punished."[104]

As Walter Burkert notes, when this view becomes the permanent mark of a group an opposition appears between a common, despicable world and the special, self-chosen life. The self-chosen life is a protest against the established *polis*. Instead of the communities of family, tribe, and city there is now a self-chosen form of association.[105] In this sense, the Pythagorean community and *bios* surely constitute a *philia,* an *arete* based on kinship. Only the Pythagorean, however, possesses *themis*—customary law shared by civilized peoples. The other is a Cyclopes who eats animals. Thus, the other has no recognized human identity.

If misanthropy characterizes this elitist movement, then egoism does as well. An individual is motivated to choose the Pythagorean way out of self-interest alone. In doing so, he or she purges his or her soul of blood-guilt and, over cyclical time, purifies himself or herself so that he or she becomes divine. Any "altruistic" allegiance to life and community is purely instrumental. Reverence for life is a means to an end, not an end in itself.

The tradition of Pythagoras was associated with dietetic medicine, which is a method of protecting health through a regulated way of life on the basis of individual decision (*diaita*). Cynics were characterized similarly, in a negative way.[106] Thus, until the close of antiquity Pythagoreanism remained a marginal movement. As Burkert reminds us, however, a self-imposed *bios* can become the basis for a new religious *polis*—in this case, the neo-Platonic community.[107] Hence, Pythagorean teachings were brought back into the mainstream by later Platonists such as Porphyry, Iamblichus, and Proclus. Indeed, by the third century of the Common Era (CE) we have not only Pythagoreans but also Essenes favorably characterized by Porphyry, as Pythagorean in life and customs.[108]

Friendships Divine

T. H. Huxley noted that one of the virtues or excellences of friendship is that one cannot do as one likes to the other. This principle is clear from readings as diverse as those of Aristotle, Epicurus, Cicero, Seneca, and Porphyry. Social, political, and ethical considerations and constraints preclude such extravagances. The important question is: Why?

E. R. Dodds offers the insight that in Greco-Roman antiquity the individual began to use the tradition rather than being used by it.[109] This development is most obvious in Greco-Roman philosophy. Aristotle's uses of Homer, Sophocles, and Plato; Epicurus's use of Democritus; the Stoic uses of Heraclitus and Empedocles; and Pythagorean appropriation of Orphic myth are cases in point. Yet in the words of Charles Kahn, the basis for human friendship with oneself and one another also is the presence in each human being of intellect (*nous*).[110]

In a stunning—indeed, thundering—statement, Aristotle advises us to reject the old rule of life that counseled humility, bidding humans to think in mortal terms, because humans have within them a divine thing: the active intellect; insofar as one can live on that level, one can live as though one were not mortal.[111] Epicurus did not make such a bold claim, but he argued that through reflection on the truths of philosophy one could live "like a god among men."[112] The Stoic Zeno of Citium went further still. The sage's intellect was not merely in the image of God, it was God—a portion of the divine substance in its active state.[113] Finally, the claim that the soul is immortal and divine is attributed to Pythagoras.[114]

Ordinary human living is not like that. Aristotle knew that no one can sustain the life of active intellect for more than very brief periods.[115] In the wake of such limits, Aristotle and Epicurus found refuge in friendship. Only the Stoic and Pythagorean sages still aimed to sustain intellect and claims to divinity perfectly, within one's own rationally grounded self-reliance and within an ascetic community of friends.

As much as Aristotle tried to study friendship as it is, the Epicureans, Stoics, Pythagoreans, and Platonists of the Hellenistic-Roman period concentrated their attention on a portrait of friendship as it might be: the ideal *sapiens* or sage. Attainment of moral perfection was independent of natural endowment and of habituation; it depended solely on the exercise of reason. For Epicureans, passions were driven by superstitions, and morbid judgments were based on such superstitions. Eliminate superstition and disturbance will cease, leaving the mind in tranquility. For the Stoics, passions were merely errors in judgment or morbid disturbances resulting from errors of judgment. Correct the error and disturbance will cease, leaving the mind untouched by hope or fear. For Pythagoreans, a fallen soul polluted by guilt continually makes errors in judgment and habit. Purify the soul and disturbance will cease, leaving the mind hopeful of eventual divinization.

This psychology maintained itself throughout Greco-Roman antiquity because it was considered necessary to a moral system that aimed at combining egoistic intention with altruistic action with complete inward detachment. Unlike Plato or Aristotle, the Epicureans, Stoics, and Pythagoreans made the claim that without philosophy there can be no goodness.[116] In broadest outline, such were the relations within a psychology of friendship as articulated in the Greco-Roman philosophical schools.

However distinct the friendship theories of Aristotle were from those of the Epicureans, Stoics, and Pythagoreans, all shared a common thread: that *egoistic* intentions form the basis for *altruistic* actions. Without the former, the latter are impossible. No attempt is made to give an impression of a complex situation by oversimplifying it. Altruistic activities are undertaken. Although such actions are an accepted part of public life, they are largely a kinship expression of religious custom and thus the practice of age-old familial and civic virtues.

Among later Romans, the progressive decay of traditional religious and civic traditions undermined the needs of self-reliance, self-sufficiency, tranquility, and apathy, which in turn promoted the will for a new philanthropy. The anonymity and loneliness of life in the great new cities, where one was a cipher, reinforced the need for a community of divine friends and helpers. What the individual did with the solitariness in this age was to form small private clubs devoted to the worship of individual gods, old and new, or to join philosophical schools dedicated to the common bond of friendship. These associations replaced the inherited local community of the old closed society. Such associations formed the basis for new relations in late antiquity; *philia* is replaced by *philanthropia*, egoism by altruism.

One could argue that the tide of rationalism begins to ebb between the first century before the Common Era (BCE) and the second century CE.

Many of the philosophical schools, other than the Epicureans, began to take a new direction at this time. A new dualism appeared in Posidonius. In the middle Stoa, there was a tension of opposites between sensible and intelligible fracturing of the unified cosmos and the human nature of the old Stoa.[117] At the same time, an internal revolution within the Academy put an end to the skeptical phase in the development of Platonism. Platonism became a more speculative philosophy that culminated in the neo-Platonisms of Plotinus and his heirs. Significant as well was a revival of Pythagoreanism under Platonic auspices as a cult and way of life. Pythagoras was presented as the inspired sage—a counterpart of Zoroaster, Ostanes, and Manes. What is taught in his name is a detachable theurgic, rather than rational self; once this theurgic was activated, it allowed an escape from this world of darkness and penance to one of light and salvation. In such *katharsis,* the soul becomes one with the divine. Here we enter the world of neo-Platonism, with its novel notions of *philia.* Friendship takes on the aura of a divine rather than human constellation of kinship, familial, and civic relationships.[118]

The thoughts of men and women became increasingly preoccupied with the techniques of individual salvation through holy books, prophetic inspiration, and revelation or by oracles, dreams, and waking visions. Others found salvation in ritual by initiation in esoteric *musteria.* In brief, we encounter the starting point for a new and entirely different kind of *philosophia* and *religio.* The philosopher becomes, in the words of Marcus Aurelius, "a kind of priest and minister of the gods."[119]

In the words of Justin Martyr, "The aim of Platonism is to see God face to face."[120] Here the agent does not determine what motivates ethical action, higher authorities do: divinities and their interpreters—the philosopher-theurgist.[121] Intentional action can have either beneficent, neutral, or negative consequences on the agent. This intentional action depends on the efficacy of an agent's divine knowledge of moral *praxis.*

As for the later Platonists, their positions on friendship largely mirror those of Plato—but with a fundamental shift in emphasis. A theory of divine friendship is articulated; this theory is based on grace, where divine souls are conceived as each dependent on a transcendent intelligence enjoying eternal contemplation of the Forms. Even here, however, a distinction is maintained between different orders of souls; human souls are not consubstantial with those of the gods.

What accelerates at the close of antiquity is the practice of the theological virtues. Aristotle's egoistic condition for the possibility of altruism has its origins in a reasoned egoism in both personal and political friendship; that such relationships find expression in friendships of self as another self in relation to other selves drop away, to be replaced by the new virtues of charity and forgiveness.

In considering the nature of friendship, Aristotle concludes that a good person cannot be the friend of a bad person. This conclusion is not surprising because the bond of friendship is a shared allegiance to justice. On the other hand, the virtue exhibited in forgiveness is charity. Yet there is no word in the Greek or Latin of the Aristotelians, Epicureans, Stoics, or Pythagoreans for charity.

A new term—grace—appears in later Platonists such as Porphyry, Iamblichus, and Proclus. This new term symbolizes a new shift in emphasis. Here, we are already within a late Roman rhythm. Iamblichus proposes that Soul is a separate, self-subsistent Hypostasis, dependent on and inferior to Intelligence.[122] Proclus goes on to argue that although Soul's essence is eternal, her activities take place in time.[123] This understanding leads both Iamblichus and Proclus to emphasize that human souls contain only the *logoi* operative within Universal Soul, but not within Intelligence, because no human soul can know the Forms as long as he or she remains a fallen soul.

Here divine grace (and providence) come into play. Iamblichus and Proclus argue that both exist under an appropriate mode on successive levels of reality.[124] Union between the divine and the human occurs only through appropriate ritual actions, however. The rituals that invoke the gods are a voluntary bestowal of divine power.[125] The human soul blessed by such power gains salvation. This claim resulted in claims by Iamblichus and his heirs that theurgy, not philosophy, leads to divine union.[126] Hence, there is an emphasis in later neo-Platonism of the need for divine grace, combined with a new human receptiveness toward such grace. Without it, salvation of the soul is impossible.

Plotinus describes the One as will and as love of itself.[127] Significantly, divine grace is regarded as the product of divine will, or "undiminished giving," which is the nature of divine activity.[128] Within the intelligible world will, giving, and order imply one another. Thus, unaffected and unconcerned, the One wills reality as a spontaneous outflowing (*prohodos*) of itself throughout the totality of Being. Then, at the levels of Intellect and Soul, there is a turning back (*epistrophe*), wherein Soul and Intellect contemplate the One and so receive form and order. Here we encounter for the first time the notion of a divine, nonreflective, selfless altruism. Here, for the first time, a metaphysics of the will, rather than of reason alone, emerges.[129]

Conclusion

In his introduction to this book, William Scott Green proposes that the contributors address three considerations: the understanding of the "other," the assessment of intention or motivation for the welfare of others, and the consequences of moral actions on the agent of moral actions. I conclude my analysis with this charge.

Greco-Roman philosophical sources make a variety of consistent claims:

- The major category of welfare for others is *philia*, friendship. This tradition means by "others" the "other" as an extension of oneself. "Others" include people outside the philosophical community because *philia* is understood in terms of political, social, and ethnic kinship. Consequently, historical practice follows the guidance of the texts.
- The meaning of behavior for the welfare of others is assessed in terms of *reciprocal* impact, action, intention, and motivation. Intention and motivation are known and assessed by criteria established on the basis of rational choice (*prohairesis*). Hence, actor and recipient, as rational beings, make such a determination. Consequently, no superhuman agent determines the efficacy of the impact, action, intention, or motivation of *philia*.
- There is no context in which intentional action for the welfare of others can have a neutral or negative consequence on the actor. Nor is it possible for action on behalf of others to have no beneficial consequence for the actor. Intentional action for the welfare of others is undertaken on the premise that in acting for the welfare of others, one is also acting for the welfare of oneself. Consequently, egoism is the condition for the possibility of any altruistic act.

This change has significant importance for the study of altruism. It is a harbinger of what emerges in the modern period: either an emotivist, sensationalist duty or a consequationalist theory of altruism, which is then read back into Greco-Roman philosophical sources—with dubious results.

Attitudes toward these issues begin to shift, however, in the later Roman period, beginning in neo-Platonism. The basis of this shift is a metaphysical "turn" from a metaphysics of reason to a metaphysics of the will. Contemporary definitions of altruism have much to do with will, and little to do with reason.

The explanation for this shift is complex and cannot be addressed in this chapter. One might suggest, however, that although "altruism" had its ancient philosophical origins in Plotinus, Iamblichus, and Proclus—with their emphasis of divine grace and *philanthropia*—it has its modern philosophical origins in Hume and Kant, who radically truncated the role of reason in moral affairs. Briefly, Hume reduced ethics to sentiments, and Kant, in the shadow of Hume, limited ethics to a categorical imperative based on willful duty, not friendship based on rational choice (*prohairesis*).

Green's principles of altruism are an extension of a late-Roman rhythm that finds consummation in Kant's moral law and eventually in Comte's notion of altruism. That is, an unselfish concern for the welfare of others motivated by virtues such as charity and forgiveness and a motivational state with the goal of increasing another's welfare are products of a metaphysics of the will. The crucial difference between ancient and medieval concerns and motivational states, on one hand, and modern approaches, on the other, is that moderns have taken upon themselves the altruistic activities of the divine. This approach is very different from the Greco-Roman rationalisms of the Aristotelians, Epicureans, Stoics, and Pythagoreans, who see the virtues of friendship, love, and justice as making rational choices to live a certain kind of life; who claim that virtue is a choice that issues in right action; and who argue that excellence of character and intelligence cannot be separated.

In *nuce*, this "pagan" view is characteristically at odds with the view that is dominant in Green's principles of altruism, which rest primarily on Kant's distinction between good will—possession of which alone is both necessary and sufficient for moral worth—and what Kant took to be a distinct natural gift: that of knowing how to apply general rules to particular cases.

Alasdair MacIntyre calls the lack of this gift stupidity: "So for Kant one can be both good and stupid, but for Aristotle stupidity of a certain kind precludes goodness . . . modern social practice and theory follows Kant rather than Aristotle at this point—not surprisingly. Hence, those characters so essential to the dramatic scripts of modernity, the expert who matches means to end in an evaluative neutral way and the moral agent who is anyone and everyone who is not actually mentally defective, have no genuine counterpart in Aristotle's scheme or indeed within the classical tradition at all. It is indeed difficult to envisage the exaltation of bureaucratic expertise in any culture in which the connection between practical intelligence and moral values is firmly established."[130] Thus the great divide between Greco-Roman theories of friendship and later ancient and modern theories of altruism.

If MacIntyre is correct, the triumph of good will over reason in accordance with excellence, as well as the triumph of charity over justice, is nearly complete. The aforementioned symptoms that resulted in the triumph of will over reason, altruism over egoism, can be regarded as progressive. They were a reflection of that present age. Yet they also were regressive, in another aspect, as portents of things to come. They point to what would become characteristic features of the modern world.

To avoid misunderstanding, I emphasize three points. First, Greco-Roman culture is too complex to be explained without residue in terms of any simple formula, whether historical, sociological, anthropological, or philosophical. Second, to explain the origins and developments of friendship is not to explain away values. Thus, we should beware of underrating the significance of this "shift" from egoism to altruism and from *philia* to *philanthropia* in late antiquity.[131] Third, we also should resist the temptation to simplify what is not simple.

There is, however, the Archaic problem of *ate* that persists through the close of antiquity. In the *Iliad*, Agamemnon ascribes three agents of *ate*: Zeus; *moira*, or fate; and the Erinys, who walk in darkness. *Ate* is not merely a punishment leading to physical disasters but a deliberate deception that draws the victim on to fresh error, intellectual or moral, whereby he or she hastens his or her own ruin. Closely akin to this agent of *ate* are the irrational impulses or passions warily condemned by Euripides and Plato. Among the *atai* is will. As Aristotle reminds us in the *Poetics*, Sophocles above all expresses the full tragic significance of such themes in the overwhelming sense of human helplessness in the face of the *ate* that awaits all human achievement, including the triumph of the will—whether it is Kant's good will or Nietzsche's will to power:

> Hope goes fast and far: to many it carries comfort,
> To many it is but the trick of light-witted desire—
> Blind we walk, till the unseen flame has trapped our footsteps.
> For old anonymous wisdom has left us a saying:
> "Of mind that god leads to destruction
> The sign is this—that in the end
> Its good is evil."
> Not long shall that mind evade destruction.[132]

I leave with what has become a problem. There are consequences of any "turn"—in this case, the turn from reason to will and from egoism to altruism. There is a loss here, but Aristotle and his heirs would not agree that it is the loss Green's theorists outline. It is what moderns motivationally, and thus altruistically and philanthropically, sanction—which is, in our age, the loss of rational choice and thus friendship.

Notes

1. If circumstances permitted, studies also would have been devoted to Platonic, Skeptic, and Cynic theories of friendship. The omission of these traditions may be excused, given the purview of my assignment. I focus on Greco-Roman traditions in which one could possibly argue for an altruistic theory of friendship. Plato's views of friendship are decidedly egocentric. He asserts that concern for the good of others promotes the just person's own interests. Nor are the attitudes of Skeptics and Cynics different. Both argued for the ideal of radical self-reliance. This ideal was to be achieved in the Skeptic's case by holding no opinions at all and in the Cynic's case by having no obligations at all.

2. As Preus notes, the exception may be Hegel, who like Aristotle posited an ethical "community of the active intellect." See Tony Preus, "Aristotle and Respect for Persons," in *Aristotle's Ethics Essays in Ancient Greek Philosophy,* vol. 4, ed. John Anton and Tony Preus (Albany: State University of New York Press, 1991), 215–26.

3. See Alisdair MacIntyre, *After Virtue* (Notre Dame, Ind.: University of Notre Dame Press, 1984), 146–64, esp. 155.

4. *Iliad,* 15.642. See Karl D. Alpern, "Friendship and Self-Sufficiency in Homer and Aristotle," *Journal of the History of Philosophy* 21 (1983): 303–15.

5. *Iliad,* 1097a28–b21; *Politics,* 1252a1–1253a39.

6. *Iliad,* 1170b3–19.

7. Ibid., 1129b11–1130a5.

8. Ibid., 1097b25.

9. Charles Kahn, "Aristotle and Altruism," *Mind* 90 (1981): 20–40.

10. *Metaphysics* (hereafter *Met.*), 12.10.1075a20–23.

11. *Politics,* 1280b39.

12. Ibid., 1254b22.

13. *Nicomachean Ethics* (hereafter *NE*), 1156a3–5.

14. Ibid., 1155b18–19.

15. Ibid., 1155b18–21.

16. Ibid., 1155b27–31.

17. Ibid., 1155b32–34.

18. Ibid., 1155b34–1156a3.

19. Ibid., 1156a6–10.

20. Ibid., 1156b7–9.

21. Ibid., 1156b9–11.

22. Ibid., 1156b11–12.

23. Ibid., 1106b36–1107a2; 1105b25–28.

24. Ibid., 1157b28–29.

25. Ibid., 1155b17–19; 1156a3–5.

26. Ibid., 1157b30–31.

27. Ibid., 1166a1–2.

28. Ibid., 166a16–17; 1169a2; 1178a2–6.

29. Ibid., 1169b18–19.

30. Ibid., 1170a19–20.
31. Ibid., 1170a13–b19.
32. Ibid., 1172a3–6.
33. Ibid., 1159a27.
34. Ibid., 1155b31.
35. Ibid., 155b3–5.
36. Ibid., 1138b5–7.
37. Ibid., 1166a1–b29.
38. See David Ross, *Aristotle* (London: Metheun, 1948), 251.
39. *NE*, 1161b28; 1166a32; 1169b6; 1170a6.
40. Ibid., 1161b18.
41. Ibid., 1159a28; 1161b27; 1166a5, 9.
42. Ibid., 1170b3–19.
43. Ibid., 1129b11–1130a5.
44. Ibid., 1167b2–4.
45. Ibid., 1167b4–9.
46. Ibid., 1161a10–11.
47. Ibid., 1166a2–5.
48. Ibid., 1155a28.
49. Ibid., 1129a6–9.
50. Ibid., 1139b31–1130a1.
51. Ibid., 1130a3–5.
52. Ibid., 1131a25–29.
53. Ibid., 1132a6–10.
54. Ibid., 166b32–1167a2.
55. Ibid., 1167a3–12.
56. Ibid., 1161a10–11.
57. Ibid., 1159b29–31.
58. Ibid., 1166a14–17.
59. Plutarch, *Against Colotes*, 1108c.
60. Epicurus, *Diogenes Laertius* (hereafter *Diog. Laert.*), 10.140.
61. Epicurus, *Sentences* [Vat.], 58; Epicurus, *Diog. Laert.*, 10.19. *cf.* Lucretius, *De Rerum Natura*, 2.59–77.
62. Epicurus, *Principle Doctrines*, 7,14.
63. Ibid., 33.
64. Ibid., 17.
65. See A. A. Long, *Hellenistic Philosophy: Stoics, Epicureans, Sceptics* (London: Duckworth, 1986), 70.
66. Epicurus, *Sentences* [Vat.], 52.
67. Epicurus, *Diog. Laert.*, 148.
68. Seneca, *Epistles* (hereafter *Ep.*), 19.10.
69. Ibid., 23.
70. *Epicurea* [Usener], 138; 544.
71. Cicero, *De Finibus* (hereafter *Fin.*), 1.20,69.
72. Ibid., 1.70.
73. Ibid., 1.20,67.
74. Ibid., 1.20,65.

75. Ibid., 2.20.
76. *Epicurea* [Usener], 437.
77. *Epistle ad Menoeceum*, 132.
78. Cicero, *Fin.*, 1.42–43.
79. Epicurus, *Sentences* [Vat.], 78.
80. Cicero, *Fin.*, 2.69–71.
81. Ibid., 2.66–69.
82. Cicero, *ND*, 1.44.121. *cf.* Stobaeus, 2.184.
83. Plutarch, *On Common Notions Against the Stoics*, 22.2; 33.2.
84. Seneca, *Beneficius*, 7.12.2; *Ep.*, 81.11; 123.15; 9.5.
85. Seneca, *Ep.*, 9.5.
86. Cicero, *Fin.*, 3.66.
87. *De Officileus*, 1.12.
88. *Stoicorum Veterum Fragmenta* (hereafter *SVF*), 1.197.
89. *Diog. Laert.*, 7.85.
90. Sextus, *Against the Professors*, 11.22–26.
91. *Diog. Laert.*, 7.124.
92. *Stobaeus*, 2.7115–72.6.
93. *SVF* 2.617.
94. Ibid., 3.625.
95. Seneca, *Ep.*, 9.5.
96. Ibid., 109.13; 9.8; 10.12; 18.
97. The sources Guthrie cites for reconstructing Pythagorean teachings all derive from Hellenistic and Roman sources. See W. K. C. Guthrie, *History of Greek Philosophy I* (Cambridge: Cambridge University Press, 1962), 187–88.
98. This is not to suggest that a cautious reconstruction of Pythagoras and early Pythagoreanism cannot be cobbled from these sources. See, e.g., Guthrie, *History of Greek Philosophy I*, 146–340; Walter Burkert, *Lore and Science in Ancient Pythagoreanism* (Cambridge, Mass.: Harvard University Press, 1972); Walter Burkert, *Greek Religion* (London: Blackwell, 1985), 296–304.
99. *Vita Pythagoriae* = DK fr. <14.8a>.
100. This teaching is controversial. For sources, see Guthrie, *History of Greek Philosophy I*, 186–91.
101. Pausanius, 8.37.5.
102. Pindar, fr. 127b = Plato, *Meno*, 81bc.
103. Here see E. R. Dodds, *The Greeks and the Irrational* (Berkeley: University of California Press, 1951), 155–56.
104. Iamblichus, *Vita Pythagoriae*, 85.
105. Burkert, *Greek Religion*, 303.
106. Burkert, *Lore and Science*, 293, 202–4.
107. Burkert, *Greek Religion*, 304.
108. Porphyry, *On Abstinence*, 4.11–14. See Robert M. Berchman, "In the Shadow of Origen: Porphyry and the Origins of New Testament Criticism," in *Orgeniana Sexta*, ed. Georges Dorival and Alain Le Boulluec (Leuven, The Netherlands: Leuven University Press, 1995), 657–73.

109. Dodds, *The Greeks and the Irrational*, 236–69.
110. Kahn, "Aristotle and Altruism," 20–40.
111. *EN*, 177b24–1178a2.
112. *Ep.*, 3.135; cf. *Sentences* [*Vat.*] 33; Lucretius, *De Rerum Natura*, 3.332.
113. *SVF* 1.146.
114. Porphyry, *Vita Pythagoriae*, 19 = *DK* fr. <14.8a>.
115. *Met.*, 1072b14.
116. For the Stoics, see Seneca, *Ep.*, 89.8; for the Epicureans, see *Papyrus Herculeneum* 1251, col. xii.6; for the Pythagoreans, see *Diog. Laert.* 8.8.
117. See John Dillon, *The Middle Platonists* (London: Duckworth, 1977), 107-13.
118. See Robert M. Berchman, "Rationality and Ritual in Neoplatonism," in *Neoplatonism and Indian Thought*, ed. Parker M. Gregorios (Albany: State University of New York Press, 2002), 229–68.
119. *Med.*, 3.4.3.
120. *Dial.*, 2.6; cf. Porphyry, *Epistle ad Marcellam*, 16.
121. See Peter Brown, "The Rise and Function of the Holy Man in Late Antiquity," *Journal of Roman Studies* 61 (1971): 80–101.
122. *De Animae apud* Stobaeus, 1.365.5–22ff.
123. *ET*, 191.
124. Proclus, *Platonic Theology*, 1.19, p. 91.16–21.
125. Iamblichus, *De Mysteriis*, 1.12; 1.14; 3.16–18.
126. Ibid., 2.11.
127. *En.*, VI.8.13.5ff.; 15.1.
128. The source of this doctrine is Plato's account in *Timaeus* 29e–30a of the divine motive for creation.
129. Jean Trouillard, John Rist, and Arthur Lovejoy have traced the metaphysical trajectories of this metaphysics of the will through their notions of the "Doctrine of Divine Love" and the "Principle of Plenitude." These notions subsequently became normative in the metaphysical systems of medieval Judaism, Christianity, and Islam. See Jean Trouillard, *La Procession Plotinienn* (Paris: Presses Universitaires de France, 1955); John Rist, *Eros and Psyche Studies in Plato, Plotinus, and Origen* (Toronto: University of Toronto Press, 1964), 76ff.; Arthur Lovejoy, *The Great Chain of Being* (New York: Harper and Row, 1960).
130. MacIntyre, *Beyond Virtue*, 155.
131. Wilhelm Nestle referred to this shift as "vom *muthos* zum *logos* zum *muthos* wieder"; see Wilhelm Nestle, *Vom Mythos zum Logos* (Stuttgart, Germany: Kroener Verlag, 1941 [1975]), 539–50.
132. *Antigone*, 588ff.

Chapter 2

Altruism in Classical Judaism

Jacob Neusner and Alan J. Avery-Peck

We begin with a rough-and-ready definition of altruism, which permits us immediately to turn to the concrete data of classical Judaism. The definition is simple: Altruism is unselfish, unrewarded behavior that benefits others at a cost to oneself. The many refinements and complexities of the matter enter in due course. It is difficult to imagine that a critical position for altruism will present itself in a religious tradition that takes as its watchword, "You will love your neighbor as yourself" (Lev. 19:18)—meaning, not more than yourself—and teaches, "Your life takes priority over the life of another." In Judaism one is expected to give up one's life for God, "for the sanctification of God's name"—which means to accept death as a martyr rather than publicly commit idolatry, murder, or sexual impropriety. Accepting martyrdom under less exalted auspices than God's is difficult to validate. For example, the law assigns priority to the life of a woman in childbirth over that of the fetus until the baby is born:

Mishnah Yebamot 7:6
A. The woman who is in hard labor—they chop up the child in her womb and they remove it limb by limb, because her life takes precedence over his life.
B. If its greater part has gone forth, they do not touch him, for they do not set aside one life on account of another life.

At the very critical transaction of childbirth, an act of self-sacrifice is not demanded of the mother, even as it cannot be demanded of the fetus. We should not anticipate that altruism—meaning more than just a generous spirit toward others—will form a dominant motif in the religious system represented by these rulings and comparable ones. A more systematic account of Judaism is required, however, to characterize the normative position. For systemic theological reasons, altruism in any rigorous definition—meaning anything beyond mere philanthropy in a broad sense—does not apply. If it finds a natural home in Christianity, that too is for systemic reasons particular to the theological narrative of Christianity, not to the generic religiosity that is characteristic of all religious traditions (if we may speak of the generic in the context of religion at all).

Identifying Normative Doctrine in Law
and Theology of Judaism

When we want to identify the normative doctrine of a particular religion, we first must explain how we go about the task. Like the other enduring religions that appeal to the authority of canonical documents, Judaism sets forth a mass of opinions, in law and theology alike, and over time these opinions change. Moreover, matters of context and proportion demand consideration because interpreting data demands attention to the circumstance in which an opinion registers and the importance, relative to the religious system as a whole, of a particular ruling. Issues of taste and judgment also enter in the conversation, therefore, when we wish to describe, analyze, and interpret particular laws and doctrines of a given religious tradition.

In Judaism, moreover, the absence of central institutions (e.g., an authority comparable to the papacy) and reliance on consensus of the faithful form massive obstacles to defining normative doctrine. Such doctrine is complicated still more because the ethnic group known as Jews tends to confuse itself with the religious tradition known as Judaism, so that people define Judaism as the religion of Jews. That definition does not serve because Jews, like other ethnic groups, exhibit diverse and contradictory convictions on matters of religion. Furthermore, even "Judaism" means diverse and conflicting things to diverse communities. Any account of a particular doctrine therefore must specify the source for the normative rule—whether theological or legal—and its context in the particular encompassing and larger system to which reference is made.

Because our problem with regard to altruism focuses on issues of definition and systemic coherence, we represent the doctrine of Judaism in its classical context, provided by the Hebrew Scriptures of ancient Israel as mediated by the Rabbinic authorities of the first six centuries of the Common Era. Their writings of legal exposition and scriptural interpretation form a coherent system of law and theology, and they have defined the norm for Judaism from antiquity to modern times. Diverse Judaic religious systems from the nineteenth century forward have evaluated the classical writings in diverse ways, and most, though not all, of the Judaisms of contemporary times continue to consult those writings and accord them normative standing—albeit in some instances allowing them only a vote but not a veto on contemporary practice and belief. The "classical Judaism" under discussion here, therefore, comprises the legal and theological system that animates the Rabbinic canon.[1] Any account of Judaic doctrine must encompass two different types of writing: legal, or Halakhic, and theological, or Aggadic. For exemplary cases of altruism, we have chosen a theological narrative and a legal exposition of the hierarchy of philanthropic conduct, respectively.

Altruism as Unselfish Behavior to the Benefit of Others

Narratives of singular acts of altruistic conduct do circulate in the formative canon of normative Judaism. We now explore a set of stories about how heavenly favor is shown to a simple man by reason of his self-sacrifice for which no reward was anticipated. Important in these stories is that no articulated religious obligation—*mitzvah*, or commandment—thereby is carried out. The conduct is supererogatory. Through deeds that the law of the Torah cannot require but must favor, one commits an act of altruism—beyond the measure of the law. This altruism encompasses what one does on one's own volition, beyond a commandment of the Torah that embodies God's volition:

Yerushalmi Taanit 1:4.I.

L. A certain ass driver appeared before the rabbis the context requires: in a dream and prayed, and rain came. The rabbis sent and brought him and said to him, "What is your trade?"

M. He said to them, "I am an ass driver."

N. They said to him, "And how do you conduct your business?"

O. He said to them, "One time I rented my ass to a certain woman, and she was weeping on the way, and I said to her, 'What's with you?' and she said to me, 'The husband of that woman [me] is in prison for debt, and I wanted to see what I can do to free him.' So I sold my ass and I gave her the proceeds, and I said to her, 'Here is your money, free your husband, but do not sin by becoming a prostitute to raise the necessary funds.'"

P. They said to him, "You are worthy of praying and having your prayers answered."

The ass driver is represented as having a powerful lien on Heaven, so that his prayers are answered, even while those of others are not. What did he do to get that entitlement? He did what no law could demand: impoverished himself to save the woman from a "fate worse than death." He had no expectation of reward. He did not ask the Rabbinic sages about his power to pray for rain; rather, they asked him. His act of altruism was to give up his means of making a living.

Yerushalmi Taanit 1:4.I.

Q. In a dream of R. Abbahu, Mr. Pentakaka ["Five Sins"] appeared, who prayed that rain would come, and it rained. R. Abbahu sent and summoned him. He said to him, "What is your trade?"

R. He said to him, "Five Sins does that man [I] do every day, for I am a pimp: hiring whores, cleaning up the theater, bringing home their garments for washing, dancing, and performing before them."

S. He said to him, "And what sort of decent thing have you ever done?"

T. He said to him, "One day that man [I] was cleaning the theater, and a woman came and stood behind a pillar and cried. I said to her, 'What's with you?' And she said to me, 'That woman's [my] husband is in prison, and I wanted to see what I can do to free him,' so I sold my bed and cover, and I gave the proceeds to her. I said to her, 'Here is your money, free your husband, but do not sin.'"

U. He said to him, "You are worthy of praying and having your prayers answered."

This second story moves us still further because the named man, a reprobate, has done everything sinful that one can do; more to the point, he has done and does wicked deeds every day. We are shown the singularity of the act of altruism, which suffices to outweigh a life of sin even if done only one time. Here too the man sold the necessities of life to spare the woman a life of sin.

These narratives meet the requirements of our preliminary definition of altruism: action that is unselfish and gratuitous, carried out without anticipated reward, to the actor's disadvantage. Whether the set of stories qualifies by a more rigorous definition remains to be seen. The set occurs in an authoritative document, and it is clearly intended to encourage self-sacrifice in behalf of another.

The issue of context and proportion, however, presents itself. May we characterize the system that values these stories as altruistic? In the context of Rabbinic Judaism, with its emphasis on the priority of learning in the Torah as a means of acquiring merit, the two players—the unlettered man, the woman in each story—represent outsiders. The system's norms—mastery of the Torah, consistent conformity to the law, maleness—are not met. Neither player is represented as a master of Torah learning. In Rabbinic Judaism, with its emphasis on the long-term disciplines of the law, leading to a life of piety lived out in consistent daily discipline, the stories make a further point. A single action accomplishes what an entire life of piety and Torah learning accomplishes.

In both cases—the unlettered man and the woman excluded by definition, with the single action outweighing a life of sin—we therefore deal with a systemic reversal: outsiders who do not keep the law acting beyond the outer requirements of the law. The transvaluation of values accomplished by the narratives indicates that we have located the very heart of the system: provision for the spontaneous in the midst of the routine. That singular act, which outweighs all else, embodies what God cannot command but what man can freely give: uncompensated self-sacrifice. In the setting of the creed, "You will love the Lord your God with all your heart, soul, and might," altruism conforms to the paradigm of the relationship for which God yearns but only human beings can realize of their own free will—love, which God cannot command and coerce, only respond to.

Of equal probity, however, in our judging of the larger place of altruism within classical Judaism is the fact that our assessment of the story to this point, which recounts the incident only from Mr. Five-Sins' point of view, essentially camouflages the tale's contextual meaning. The deepest purpose of the story as the Talmud tells it is not principally to highlight Mr. Five-Sins' altruistic act. It is for the reader to know that, in the end, whatever Mr. Five-Sins' own expectations, he receives divine compensation for his action. In other words, rather than simply promoting selfless, altruistic behavior, in context the story advances a foundational conception of the system of Rabbinic Judaism as a whole: Acts of kindness toward others bring divine reward. On one hand, then, the story of Mr. Five-Sins offers a model for how the rabbis expect their adherents to behave. On the other hand, people's imitation of Mr. Five-Sins' righteousness is not, within the system of Rabbinic Judaism, valorized as a simple act of altruism. Such behavior is encouraged and justified by the claim that such actions bring divine benefit. Even if Mr. Five-Sins' behavior went beyond the technical requirements of the law and therefore was altruistic, the rabbis do not encourage such behavior because it is selfless. From the perspective of the Rabbinic system, these acts, which are depicted as leading to certain divine reward, do not fall under a strict definition of altruism at all.

So much for an Aggadic representation of matters, in which altruism hardly emerges as the norm. What about a Halakhic formulation? The system makes its normative statements in law, not in narrative, so we must turn to a legal document for an authoritative picture of the way our rough-and-ready definition of altruism guides us to a view of Judaism on that matter. We turn to part of the definition of proper philanthropy—the Hebrew word is *tzedakah*, or righteousness—that is set forth by Moses Maimonides (1135–1204), who codified the law of the Talmuds, commentaries, and existing codes in a highly systematic and rational statement.

Maimonides sets forth "the eight stages of *tzedakah*." What we wish to identify is a place for altruism in the transactions of philanthropy:

There are eight degrees of *tzedakah*, each one superior to the next.

1. Than which there is none higher is the one who upholds the hand of an Israelite reduced to poverty by handing that person a gift or loan, or by entering into a partnership with him or her, or by finding that Israelite work, in order to strengthen that person's hand, so that she or he will have no need to beg from others. Concerning such a person it is stated, "You shall uphold that one, as a stranger and a settler shall that person live with you"—meaning, uphold that person, so that she or he will not lapse into want.

2. Below this is one who gives alms to the poor in such a way that the giver knows not to whom the alms are given, nor does the poor person know from whom the alms are received. This constitutes the fulfilling of a religious duty for its own sake, and for such there was a chamber of secrets in the Temple, where the righteous would contribute sums secretly, and where the poor of good families would draw their sustenance in equal secrecy. Close to such a person is the one who contributes directly to the charity fund.

3. Below this is the person who knows the one receiving, while the poor person knows not from whom the gift comes. Such a donor is like the great among the sages who would set forth secretly, throwing money before the doors of the poor. This is an appropriate procedure, to be preferred if those administering charity funds are not behaving honorably.

4. Below this is the instance in which the poor knows the identity of the donor, but remains unknown to the donor. The giver is thus like the great among the sages who would place money in the folded corner of a linen sheet, throw the sheet over their shoulders, and allow the poor to come up from behind them and remove the money without being subject to humiliation.

5. Below this is the one who hands charity directly to the poor before being asked for it.

6. Below this is the one who hands charity to the poor after the poor has requested it.

7. Below this is the one who gives to the poor less than what is appropriate, but gives it in a friendly manner.

8. Below this is the one who gives charity with a scowl.

At what point does an act of philanthropy qualify as altruistic? It enters only in Maimonides' highest forms—specifically, at the second stage, when the donor is anonymous and gets no public credit for his action and the donor also does not know to whom the funds have gone. In this case the self-sacrificial act—the surrender to the other of scarce resources—is done "for its own sake," not for the sake of a reward. Yet even in this circumstance, the donor pleases Heaven and furthermore gains satisfaction from knowing that he or she has helped some poor person, if not a particular individual. The donor has carried out an obligation to Heaven, such as philanthropy embodies. It is difficult to represent the transaction as true altruism, unrewarded self-sacrifice. The systemic representation of virtuous actions in response to God's commandments leaves little space indeed for truly altruistic conduct in normative Judaism.

The highest level of charity has no bearing on our problem but embodies a social philosophy for philanthropy beyond altruistic limits. The highest form of philanthropy is attained by rendering philanthropy itself altogether unnecessary: giving a fish hook, not a fish. That matter has no bearing on our problem, so we stop at the second-highest level. On the surface, therefore, we may say that classical Judaism does set forth a doctrine of altruistic behavior: acts of love for another that not only are not done for the sake of a reward but also exact a cost in the resources or circumstances of the altruistic actor.

How does Judaism represent the act of self-sacrifice for the good of the community at large? Does such an act qualify as unselfish self-sacrifice for the public welfare? Can Judaism say that no greater merit attaches to any deed than to give up one's life for one's fellow, for the public good? The scripture describes such a case in the setting of Joshua's exchange with Achan. In the description of how the death penalty was inflicted, the law of the Mishnah invokes the case of Achan in connection with the confession. Specifically, Joshua 7 tells the story of how the Israelites lost a skirmish in conquering the Land and blamed it on a sin committed in their midst. Joshua located Achan, who had violated the divine instruction on the disposition of the spoils of war, and the Mishnah represents the transaction as follows:

Mishnah Sanhedrin 6:2

A. When he was ten cubits from the place of stoning, they say to him, "Confess," for it is usual for those about to be put to death to confess.

B. For whoever confesses has a share in the world to come.

C. For so we find concerning Achan, to whom Joshua said, "My son, I pray you, give glory to the Lord, the God of Israel, and confess to him, and tell me now what you have done; hide it not from me." And Achan answered Joshua and said, "Truly have I sinned against the Lord, the God of Israel, and thus and thus I have done" (Josh. 7:19). And how do we know that his confession achieved atonement for him? For it is said, "And Joshua said, 'Why have you troubled us? The Lord will trouble you this day'" (Josh. 7:25): This day you will be troubled, but you will not be troubled in the world to come.

D. And if he does not know how to confess, they say to him, "Say as follows: 'Let my death be atonement for all of my transgressions.'"

At issue is the welfare of the community. Achan sacrifices himself for the community's future relationship with God. His confession also is to his own advantage, however. He enjoys a very concrete reward: atonement and reconciliation with God, leading to eternal life. Within the very center of the Halakhic exposition is the theological principle that the death penalty opens the way for life eternal. Achan pays the supreme penalty but secures his place in the world to come. This confession is not an act of altruism at all but an act of repentance committed to Achan's own advantage.

The Major Categories of Behavior for the Welfare of Others

When we turn to the agenda of issues of altruism addressed to the principal religious traditions of humanity, we place into systemic context the episodic lessons set forth above. We can find narratives that value altruistic behavior, conventionally defined, but do these narratives represent a systemic component of critical consequence? In context, does altruistic behavior define a norm of everyday conduct or an exception to what is expected in ordinary circumstances? We answer the question by asking how the system that tells these stories provides for the welfare of others in a workaday world of common folk, not in a world of transvaluation and exceptional conduct. We begin with classifications for the welfare of others. Judaism does not leave systematic maintenance of people who are poor, needy, and disempowered to the vagaries of human initiative and volition. It provides obligatory support—and does so as a matter of routine. Supporting the poor is a religious duty, and this duty occurs in concrete and detailed patterns. Altruism does not enter into action for the welfare of others, conventionally construed, which is commanded and not self-initiated.

To ask the Halakhic system of Judaism how it makes provision for the welfare of others is to demand a comprehensive survey of the system viewed whole. The Halakhic system portrays a comprehensive account of the social order—all things in proper place, all transactions yielding a proportionate outcome. What the individual component of the social order, the private person, does must take account of the rights of others in that same society. The law covering economic transactions—the disposition of scarce resources—rests on a theory of distributive economics that prohibits one party to an exchange from emerging with more value than he or she brought to the transaction, another with less. Moreover, the system understands by welfare relationships of not only a social but a supernatural character. The conduct of Temple offerings yields atonement for the collective sin of all Israel, the holy people, and forms a critical component of the public welfare.

The conventional category of "welfare of others" addresses support of the poor, the landless, the unempowered. In the Halakhic system, that category encompasses the priests and Levites, who are landless, as well as the poor. What is important is that the same procedures apply. God and the householder are deemed partners in the ownership of the Land of Israel; when the householder lays claim to his or her share of the crop, God's interest in the crop is provoked, and the householder's share is to be set aside. Then the householder must set aside God's share of the crop to be given to the priesthood for their rations and to the poor for their support. Roger Brooks states the matter definitively:

> Tractate Peah asserts that needy Israelites are entitled to a portion of each crop that grows on the Land of Israel. The householder must designate some of his produce to meet this entitlement, while other gifts become the property of the poor entirely through processes of accident. What these various types of food have in common is the fact that they are reserved for the poor alone—no one else may eat them. So the fundamental claim of this tractate is that the poor should receive some bit of the Land's yield for their exclusive use. This notion of poor-relief emerges through Mishnah's discussion of the procedures for designating and distributing the several poor-offerings mentioned in Scripture. Tractate Peah deals with each offering specified in the Mosaic Codes in the order in which they are separated during the harvesting process: that which grows in the rear corner of the field (Peah; Lev. 19:9; 23:22), gleanings (Lev. 19:9; 23:22), forgotten sheaves (Deut. 24:19), separated grapes (Lev. 19:10), defective clusters (Lev. 19:10; Deut. 24:21), and poorman's tithe (Deut. 26:12). In sum, the tractate takes as its topic the entire repertoire of Scriptural references to poor-offerings.
>
> What conception stands behind this analogy between the poor and the priests? It is their common claim on God for protective

support. Because neither group possesses a portion of the Land of Israel, neither can produce the food it needs. The priests, for their part, are forbidden by Scriptural law to own land (see Deut. 18:1–5). Instead, they act as God's servants in the Temple and are accorded food on that account. Similarly, the poor have lost whatever portion of the Land they may have possessed, and so are entitled to receive some of its yield. God supports both the priests and the poor because they neither own land nor attain the economic prosperity promised to all Israelites who live in the Land (see Deut. 8:7–10).

These claims on God are satisfied through the action of the ordinary Israelite householder. As a tenant farmer, he works God's Land and enjoys its yield, with the result that a portion of all that he produces belongs to God. In order to pay this obligation, Israelites render to the priests grain as heave offering, tithes, and other priestly rations. Similarly, a specific portion of the Land's yield is set aside, by chance alone, for the poor. So underlying the designation of both priestly rations and poor-offerings is a single theory: God owns the entire Land of Israel, and, because of this ownership, a portion of each crop must be paid to him as a sort of sacred tax (see Lev. 27:30–33). According to Mishnah's framers, God claims that which is owed him and then gives it to those under his special care, the poor and the priests.[2]

Support for the poor and the priesthood cannot be classified as altruistic. It is routine, not spontaneous; it is exacted as an obligation and does not fall beyond the measure of the law; above all, it yields a benefit to the donor, who thereby acquires access to the portion of the crop that God, as landowner, assigns the householder, as tenant farmer, for his share. The absence of intentionality is striking: The selection of the portion of the crop for the priests' rations and the poor is done by chance.

We have now eliminated from the realm of altruistic conduct three classifications of activity for the welfare of others: donations to sacrificial service in the Temple; exchanges of scarce resources in commercial transactions, broadly construed; and donations in support of scheduled castes—the priesthood and the poor. All of these activities represent areas in which the criteria of altruistic conduct do not pertain. On the contrary, the good that is done for others produces a commensurate advantage for the one who does the deed.

Does nothing correspond? A saying in the collection of wise sayings, *The Sentences of the Fathers* (tractate Pirqé Abot), captures the matter:

Tractate Abot 5:10
A. There are four sorts of people.
B. (1) He who says, "What's mine is mine and what's yours is yours"—this is the average sort.
C. (And some say, "This is the sort of Sodom.")
D. (2) "What's mine is yours and what's yours is mine"—this is a boor.
E. (3) "What's mine is yours and what's yours is yours"—this is a truly pious man.
F. (4) "What's mine is mine and what's yours is mine"—this is a truly wicked man.

Here we find ourselves near the conception of altruistic conduct: unrewarded, unselfish sacrifice for another. It comes with the truly pious man, who does not take but only gives. The conduct of Mr. Five-Sins would qualify—if he knew that Heaven would ignore his behavior and if he acted deliberately on condition that he not be compensated. The story does not suggest whether, from Mr. Five-Sins' perspective, those conditions were met; from the perspective of the editor, whose focus is on the divine reward Mr. Five-Sins received, they certainly are not met.

Behavior for the Welfare of Others: What Is Meant by "Others"?

What does the religion mean by "others," both doctrinally and historically? For example, in the classical texts, do "others" include people outside the religious community?

Who is the "other" who is the object of altruistic conduct? Our opening narratives assume that we deal with Israelites in an interior transaction. The support for the poor outlined in tractate Peah and described by Brooks sustains Israel's scheduled castes. The systematization of levels of philanthropy outlined by Maimonides explicitly refers at the highest level to making it possible for an Israelite to support himself or herself. The four types of people in tractate Abot recapitulate the same assumption— that we speak of transactions within the community of Israel. The Judaic theology of gentiles, which regards them as an undifferentiated phalanx of enemies of God who worship idols, deliberately ignoring the truth, leaves little basis for affirming altruistic conduct toward "others." On the contrary, even ordinary transactions that express simple compassion are subjected to doubt:

Mishnah Abodah Zarah 2:1
A. They do not leave cattle in gentiles' inns,
B. because they are suspect in regard to bestiality.
C. And a woman should not be alone with them,
D. because they are suspect in regard to fornication.
E. And a man should not be alone with them,
F. because they are suspect in regard to bloodshed.
G. An Israelite girl should not serve as a midwife to a gentile woman,
H. because she serves to bring forth a child for the service of idolatry.
I. But a gentile woman may serve as a midwife to an Israelite girl.
J. An Israelite girl should not give suck to the child of a gentile woman.
K. But a gentile woman may give suck to the child of an Israelite girl,
L. when it is by permission.
Mishnah Abodah Zarah 2:2
A. They accept from them healing for property,
B. but not healing for a person.
C. "And they do not allow them to cut hair under any circumstances," the words of R. Meir.
D. And sages say, "In the public domain it is permitted,
E. "but not if they are alone."

The prevailing attitude of suspicion of gentiles derives from the definition of gentiles: They are idolaters, enemies of God. One should not anticipate a rich repertoire of rulings on how one must sacrifice for the welfare of the gentile-other. We cannot point to narratives that suggest one must, let alone laws that obligate it. There is one motivation to sacrifice for the outsider, however; one supports the poor of the gentiles "for the sake of peace":

Mishnah Gittin 5:8
L. They do not prevent poor gentiles from collecting produce under the laws of Gleanings, the Forgotten Sheaf, and the Corner of the field, in the interests of peace.
Mishnah Gittin 5:9
I. And they inquire after their [gentiles'] welfare,
J. in the interests of peace.

This behavior is not unrewarded, carried out gratuitously. It is a matter of sound public policy, leading to communal peace and amity. "They do not prevent . . . they inquire after their welfare"—minimal gestures of common courtesy prevent needless enmity. They accommodate the gentile-other, but they do not accord selfless love to him. Altruism within Judaism is embodied in stories that presuppose the Israelite identification of actors and beneficiaries. Judaism sets forth a social system that distinguishes, in humanity, those that know and love God from those who serve idols and hate God.

Assessing the Meaning of Behavior for the Welfare of Others

For instance, does Judaism assess behavior for the welfare of others in terms of its impact on the recipient, in terms of the action itself, in terms of the motivation or intention of the actor, or some combination of the above? If the actor's intention or motivation is a factor in determining the action's meaning, how is intention or motivation known and assessed? Does the actor determine what motivated the action, or is there some other source that makes such a determination?

To answer these questions, we turn back to the narratives of extraordinary, altruistic conduct we set forth at the outset of this chapter. We begin with a reprise of one of the two stories; the other follows the same pattern.

Yerushalmi Taanit 1:4.I.

Q. In a dream of R. Abbahu, Mr. Pentakaka ["Five Sins"] appeared, who prayed that rain would come, and it rained. R. Abbahu sent and summoned him. He said to him, "What is your trade?"

R. He said to him, "Five Sins does that man [I] do every day, for I am a pimp: hiring whores, cleaning up the theater, bringing home their garments for washing, dancing, and performing before them."

S. He said to him, "And what sort of decent thing have you ever done?"

T. He said to him, "One day that man [I] was cleaning the theater, and a woman came and stood behind a pillar and cried. I said to her, 'What's with you?' And she said to me, 'That woman's [my] husband is in prison, and I wanted to see what I can do to free him,' so I sold my bed and cover, and I gave the proceeds to her. I said to her, 'Here is your money, free your husband, but do not sin.'"

U. He said to him, "You are worthy of praying and having your prayers answered."

JACOB NEUSNER AND ALAN J. AVERY-PECK

We take up each of the aforementioned questions in turn. How does Judaism assess the meaning of behavior for the welfare of others? The foregoing story values conduct for the welfare of others. This valuation is attributed to heaven. When Mr. Five-Sins prayed for rain, rain would follow. The context of the capacity to pray for rain and elicit a response from Heaven is the public liturgy for communal prayers, as follows:

Mishnah Taanit 2:6

A. (1) For the first [ending] he says, "He who answered Abraham on Mount Moriah will answer you and hear the sound of your cry this day. Blessed are you, O Lord, redeemer of Israel."

B. (2) For the second he says, "He who answered our fathers at the Red Sea will answer you and hear the sound of your cry this day. Blessed are you, O Lord, who remembers forgotten things."

C. (3) For the third he says, "He who answered Joshua at Gilgal will answer you and hear the sound of your cry this day. Blessed are you, O Lord, who hears the sound of the shofar."

D. (4) For the fourth he says, "He who answered Samuel at Mispeh will answer you and hear the sound of your cry this day. Blessed are you, O Lord, who hears a cry."

E. (5) For the fifth he says, "He who answered Elijah at Mount Carmel will answer you and hear the sound of your cry this day. Blessed are you, O Lord, who hears prayer."

F. (6) For the sixth he says, "He who answered Jonah in the belly of the fish will answer you and hear the sound of your cry this day. Blessed are you, O Lord, who answers prayer in a time of trouble."

G. For the seventh he says, "He who answered David and Solomon, his son, in Jerusalem, will answer you and hear the sound of your cry this day. Blessed are you, O Lord, who has mercy on the Land."

Able to pray for rain and evoke a response from Heaven, Mr. Five-Sins now finds his classification among the great saints of Israel's history—saints acknowledged by Heaven's favor in precisely the same way in which Mr. Five-Sins' virtue is acknowledged.

Does the law of Judaism assess such behavior in terms of its impact on the recipient, in terms of the action itself, in terms of the motivation or intention of the actor, or some combination of the above? We find here a matter of judgment. Mr. Five-Sins' act is valued for its impact on the woman. The narrator also admires, however, the self-sacrifice that leads Mr. Five-Sins to give up his livelihood in favor of the woman. Hence the selfless action, joined to pure intention ("for its own sake") and its desired result—the saving of the woman from a fate worse than death—join together.

If the actor's intention or motivation is a factor in determining the action's meaning, how is intention or motivation known and assessed? The narrative appears to take for granted the intention and motivator of the actor: the capacity to make the trouble facing the other into one's own concern—the power to turn sympathy into empathy.

Does the actor determine what motivated the action, or is there some other source that makes such a determination? The narrator creates the entire transaction. The act is—and must be, to qualify as altruistic—self-motivated, not in response to a religious duty or divine commandment because no religious commandment in Judaism imposes the obligation to sacrifice in behalf of the other. The important participant is the divine witness, God, who values that love that cannot be coerced or commanded but only elicited by one's own capacity for empathy and empathetic response. God knows what motivated the action. That is because God's record—in the context of responding to the prayers of Abraham at Moriah, Israel at the sea, Joshua at Gilgal, Samuel at Mispeh, Elijah at Carmel, Jonah in the fish, and David and Solomon at Jerusalem—is replicated by Mr. Five-Sins. He has acted like God in responding to pathos, and his selfless service is what a human being can do to act like God.

Consequences

Does Judaism create a context in which it is possible that intentional action for the welfare of others can have only a neutral or negative consequence on the actor? Is it possible for action on behalf of others to have no beneficial consequence for the actor?

Nothing in the foregoing rapid review of some high points of the Judaic law and narrative of service to others suggests that action on behalf of others can have no beneficial consequence for the actor. On the contrary, the one who intentionally commits an act of altruism—selfless, unrewarded service to others at considerable cost to oneself—by definition cannot produce neutral, let alone negative, results for the actor. Self-sacrifice for others elicits God's empathy. That is why it is not possible for an action for others to produce no consequence for the actor; such a possibility lies beyond the imaginative power of the system.

Once God craves but cannot coerce one's love, God's own record intervenes. What one gives freely, to one's own cost, is bound to win God's recognition and appreciation. The only difference between a good deed for others that is commanded by God, such as support for the poor, and a good deed that cannot be commanded by God, such as support for the poor that is beyond the measure of the law, is the greater response, in proportion, provoked in Heaven by authentic altruism on earth. With such a reward in prospect, however—as the narrative at hand underscores—self-sacrifice is not an act of altruism. Heaven itself, by its very nature, renders null the very category of selfless action for another's benefit without beneficial consequence for the actor. God is always present to assure appropriate response: "Pray and one's prayers for rain are answered," for example. Altruistic conduct is difficult to locate in classical statements of the law and theology of Judaism because the category-formations of Judaism—with their emphasis on human obligation to carry out the divine will, with reward or punishment the consequence of obedience or rebellion—make no provision for a critical role of unselfish, unrewarded behavior that benefits others at a cost to oneself. Altruism so defined is asystemic and antisystemic because it turns virtuous conduct into supererogatory action, while the commandments govern: Greater is the action of one who is commanded and acts than the one who is not commanded but acts, in context, to carry out a virtuous deed.

No Altruism? The Problem of a Religion's Native Categories

Our analysis to this point yields two central points regarding the absence of a doctrine of altruism within early Rabbinic Judaism. The first point emerges from the recognition that to accurately comprehend any religious tradition, we must first identify the larger system that comprises that faith: the beliefs, practices, and theologies that fit together to form an encompassing and internally logical worldview supported by a commensurate way of life. Insofar as the classical Judaic system legislates almost all aspects of proper behavior between one individual and another, it has little room for the category of altruism—behaviors that, by definition, go beyond what any law can require. Even if we do, therefore, find apparent examples of altruism within the Rabbinic literature, we cannot say that the system as a whole supports altruism as a doctrine.

The second point has been fully to evaluate apparent examples of altruism that appear within the Rabbinic corpus to better understand why Rabbinic Judaism does not highlight this category of behavior. The result of this analysis is that even cases that appear to valorize altruistic behavior either do not fall into that category at all or, if they do, do not promote altruism as a general value. The story of Mr. Five-Sins, the closest the tradition comes to depicting a truly altruistic act, has been instructive: Mr. Five-Sins acts contrary to his own character traits and self-interests to benefit a person he does not even know; he neither expects nor can foresee any compensation or reward for giving to the woman what is of value to himself. Thus, at least from his own perspective, he acts altruistically. As we have seen, however, this assessment misses the story's contextual meaning within the literature of Rabbinic Judaism. Within that context, the point is for the reader to know that ultimately, whatever Mr. Five-Sins' own expectations, he was rewarded. Rather than promoting altruistic behavior, the story advances a foundational conception of the system of classical Judaism: Acts of kindness toward others bring divine reward. Thus, even as Mr. Five-Sins offers a model for how Rabbinic Judaism expects its adherents to behave, people's imitation of his righteousness is not valorized as an act of simple altruism. Leading to certain divine reward, such acts do not fall under a strict definition of altruism at all.

We have seen that, overall, the absence of altruism from classical Judaism results from the religious system's foundational doctrine that God has told people how to behave and is active in the world to assure appropriate rewards for correct behavior. In the context of such an ideology, because deeds of charity or loving kindness are demanded and always rewarded, altruism per se is impossible. A doctrine of altruism is necessary to explain why people behave in selfless ways when they have no apparent reason to do so. Rabbinic Judaism has a simple and consistent explanation, however, for why people should—and therefore do—behave in ways that, at least in the short run, are contrary to their own apparent best interests. This explanation is the absolute justice of God, which assures that all good deeds are rewarded even as sinful ones are punished. Thus, the rabbis set out a detailed system of right behaviors covering all aspects of the relationships among people and treating as matters of law even behaviors we generally subsume under the category of discretion. On one hand, we have the example of poor-gifts: charity that within the Rabbinic system is legislated much as a tax would be. On the other hand, it should be clear that the Rabbinic system recognizes in all righteous deeds—even in those that cannot be strictly set out by the law—the opportunity for divine reward. Thus, the well-known passage at M. Peah 1:1 states:

C.   These are things the benefit of which a person enjoys in this world, while the principal remains for him in the world to come:
D.   (1) [deeds in] honor of father and mother, (2) [performance of] righteous deeds, (3) and [acts that] bring peace between a man and his fellow.

Honoring parents, righteous deeds, bringing peace to the world—behaviors that no law can adequately define and require—bring divine compensation. A similar point, it bears noting, appears at the heart of the liturgy of Yom Kippur, the Day of Atonement, in the declaration that "repentance, prayer, and acts of righteousness avert God's severe decree" against sinners. In the Rabbinic system, all righteous deeds have a benefit to the one who performs them and thus are not selfless. Mr. Five-Sins may have been oblivious to the divine reward his act would earn; he therefore may be deemed personally to have acted altruistically. Practitioners of Rabbinic Judaism are not meant to be so uninformed, however. Behaviors that benefit others at a cost to the one who performs them are to be carried out not simply because they are the right thing to do. Thus, we find repeatedly that Rabbinic Judaism has no place for—indeed, cannot make use of—a doctrine of altruism because in that Judaism, even though righteous behavior may be of highest value, altruism per se does not come into play.

What remains is more thoroughly to explore the significance of the fact that Judaism contains no doctrine of altruism. This issue is worth addressing for two reasons. The first is that the absence of altruism seems contrary to what contemporary Jews or others might expect—indeed, hope—to find. Modern expectations of Judaism and other religions are shaped not by any understanding of the reality of ancient religious tradition; they emerge from the contemporary sensibility that values altruistic action and finds selflessness to be the primary human behavior that religions should promote. It is important, therefore, to advance our discussion by more completely detailing the theological setting within which classical Judaism emerged absent this doctrine.

This discussion also leads to a more important point: whether the question, "Does classical Judaism yield a doctrine of altruism?" is the right question to ask of classical Judaism in the first place. Does this approach to analyzing Judaism represent a potentially fruitful path of inquiry that will allow us to comprehend Judaism in comparison to other religions? The very concept of altruism was essentially impossible within the worldview of the ancient rabbis. Hence, the question, "Does classical Judaism yield a doctrine altruism?" attempts to evaluate Judaism through a category of thought that is entirely foreign to it. As a result, our determination that classical Judaism does not evidence this doctrine must be recognized as telling us more about our modern expectations of religion than it does about the thought-world of the ancient rabbis. The point becomes clear when we examine the place—or absence—of the idea of altruism within ancient theories of humanity in general.

The problem is that altruism as a category for assessing the nature of human behavior is an invention only of the modern world. It is an explanatory category that was created to address questions about the human psyche and about human behavior that the authorities of Rabbinic Judaism could not themselves have either framed or understood. Alasdair

MacIntyre phrases the issue that lies behind the invention of the category altruism as follows:

> Why do we sometimes prefer to consult the interests of others rather than our own interests? What is the relationship between selfishness and benevolence? Is altruism merely a mask for self-interest? At first sight these may appear to be empirical, psychological questions, but it is obviously the case that even if they are construed as such, the answers will depend on the meaning assigned to such key expressions as "self-interest," "benevolence," "sympathy," and the like. It is in connection with elucidating the meaning of such expressions that philosophical problems arise—problems which are of particular interest because we cannot understand such expressions without committing ourselves, in some degree, to some particular conceptual schematism by means of which we can set out the empirical facts about human nature. That there are alternative and rival conceptual possibilities is a fact to which the history of philosophy testifies. The problems with which we are concerned do not appear fully-fledged until the seventeenth and eighteenth centuries. That they do not is a consequence of the specific moral and psychological concepts of the Greek and of the medieval world. In neither Plato nor Aristotle does altruistic benevolence appear in the list of the virtues, and consequently the problem of how human nature, constituted as it is, can possibly exhibit this virtue cannot arise.[3]

We emphasize the last sentence, concerning the absence of altruism from Plato and Aristotle's lists of virtues. This fact suggests the extent to which the Rabbinic failure to exhibit a doctrine of altruism is not unexpected at all. Like others in antiquity and through early modern times, the rabbis saw no need to explain human benevolence and therefore did not imagine, let alone explore, the idea we call altruism.

MacIntyre goes on to explain how, in the *Republic*, Plato never probes the concept of altruism because of his understanding that the pursuit of the good in general and the pursuit of one's own good in particular always necessarily coincide. Even in the medieval world, although the approach is different, the result is similar. As MacIntyre puts it, "The underlying assumption is that man's self-fulfillment is discovered in the love of God and of the rest of the divine creation. So although Aquinas envisages the first precept of the natural law as an injunction to self-preservation, his view of what the self is and of what preserving it consists in leads to no special problems about the relation between what I owe to myself and what I owe to others."[4]

Although Rabbinic Judaism has its own distinctive response to the problem of the relationship between what I owe myself and what I owe others, it shares with these other systems the fact that it never gets to— cannot get to—the question of altruism. The reason is that, as in the philosophical response of Plato and the theological understanding of Aquinas, the question of the nature of the relationship between the self and the other finds in the rabbis a ready definition: The relationship is determined by the divine desire that people show responsibility toward each other, and it is controlled by the divine reward and punishment that polices that desire and creates a human reality in which actions I take on behalf of another always benefit myself as well. For the rabbis—as for Plato, Aristotle, and Aquinas—there is, therefore, no special problem created by the question of the relationship between what I owe to myself and what I owe others. These obligations are essentially identical.

The question of the relationship between what I owe myself and others emerges as a theoretical issue only in the beginning of modern times, when Thomas Hobbes (1588–1679) depicts human nature (again quoting MacIntyre) "as essentially individual, nonsocial, competitive and aggressive." Only in light of such a characterization does the apparent contradiction between human nature and human benevolence need to be explained at all. Hobbes' solution is to suggest that what appears on the surface to be altruistic behavior in fact always emerges from selfish self-interest. Only in response to that view do religious thinkers rush in to stand up for believing humanity. They do so by defining the human being who accepts the divine will as essentially good. The very idea of altruism, and the conception that religions promote altruistic behavior, accordingly become central products of, responses to, modern and secular ways of looking at the world and at human beings. The rabbis of Rabbinic Judaism did not simply fail to include within their religious worldview a doctrine of altruism. Their worldview could not even conceive of such an idea because their central belief in the nature of God's creation of humanity and God's absolute justice and control of the world made explaining humanity's ability for goodness unnecessary.

Hobbes, for his part, denied the existence of altruistic behavior by arguing that even one who voluntarily gives alms to a beggar does so not just to relieve the beggar's distress but also to relieve his or her own distress at seeing the beggar's distress. Later theologians disagreed, arguing that people give alms to beggars because, cognizant of divine trait of justice, they wish simply to do what is right—hence, altruism. The Rabbinic system required no such twists of logic in either direction, however. Certainly the rabbis held that one gives alms to a beggar because to relieve the beggar's distress is to make the world more like God intends it to be, because to feed the hungry or to clothe the naked is indeed to behave like

God. The rabbis who depicted matters in these terms were not struggling with the theoretical question of the goodness of humanity, however. They believed that, in the nature of things, such behaviors, on one hand, are required by divine law and, on the other, bring concrete rewards—in the words of Tractate Peah, the benefit that a person enjoys in this world and the principal that remains in the world to come. Thus, in this system, people have plenty of good reasons to act on behalf of others, and the argument that they do so, or could do so, for altruistic reasons could not even enter the picture.

The point, then, is that we must be careful to answer the question, "Does Classical Judaism yield a doctrine of altruism?" with somewhat more than a simple, "No." The answer is that within the framework of early Judaism, this question could not be even a question. We do not deal with a matter of the rabbis' theological choice or their theoretical reflection on the nature of human goodness. The concept of altruism can have made no sense to the authorities whose texts are before us because they understood at base that God's justice, rather than intrinsic traits of humanity, in all cases shapes human action. Their Judaism demanded that individuals act on behalf of others, that they act at times and in certain circumstances in ways that are costly to their own immediate self-interests.

Because the rabbis did not and could not explain human actions within the framework of the theoretical issues that surround the question of altruism, we must be clear that by asking about their theory of selfless behavior we reveal more about ourselves and our own expectations than about them and their world. There is no doctrine of altruism in classical Judaism. More important for our comprehension of that system is to be clear that outside the much later philosophical context in which human goodness required an explanation, the classical rabbis could not imagine, let alone explore, the concept of altruistic benevolence.

Notes

1. The normative canon comprises the Mishnah, a philosophical law code of the late second century CE, and its documents of amplification and exegesis; the Tosefta, a collection of supplements to the Mishnah, of ca. 300 CE; the Talmud of the Land of Israel, a commentary to thirty-nine of the Mishnah's sixty-three topical expositions or tractates, of ca. 400 CE; and the Talmud of Babylonia, a comparable commentary to thirty-seven of the Mishnah's tractates, of ca. 600 CE; as well as about a dozen large compilations of exegeses of law and theology of scripture called "Midrashim," which originate from the third to the seventh centuries CE. This canon is carried forward in later times by a continuous tradition of exegesis of law and scripture.

2. Roger Brooks, *The Law of Agriculture in the Mishnah and the Tosefta: Translation, Commentary, Theology,* vol. 2, *Peah* (Leiden, The Netherlands: Brill, 2004–2006), 4.
3. Alasdair MacIntyre, "Egoism and Altruism," in *Encyclopedia of Philosophy* (New York and London: Macmillan, 1972), 462.
4. Ibid.

Chapter 3

Altruism in Christianity

Bruce Chilton

The Gospels and the other writings of the New Testament were produced a generation after Jesus' death for people who were about to be baptized (as adults) or had already been baptized. The communities involved were Greek speaking, predominantly non-Jewish, urban, and culturally different from the people living in the Galilee of Jesus' time.

The communities that produced the Gospels developed ethics appropriate to their own environments.[1] The Gospel according to John—written after Matthew, Mark, and Luke, around 100 CE—provides a good example of that process. The last meal of Jesus with his disciples in John 13 is a gathering for a Hellenistic symposium, complete with a discourse that continues for several chapters in a philosophical idiom that is foreign to the earlier Gospels and consumes the bulk of John's attention.

In the introduction (John 13:1–12b) Jesus performs the menial task of washing his disciples' feet, to exemplify the sort of mutual service he demands from his followers. The Gospel according to John has Jesus drive the point home directly and categorically (13:12c–17):

> He said to them, Do you know what I have done for you? You call me teacher and lord, and you say well; I am. If, then, I—lord and teacher—washed your feet, you also ought to wash one another's feet. For I have given you an example, so that just as I have done to you, so you also might do. Truly, truly I say to you, A servant is not greater than his lord, nor an apostle greater than the one who sent him. If you know these things, you are blessed if you do them.

John's placement of the scene—as the formal equivalent of the "Last Supper" in the Synoptics—indicates the importance of the model Jesus is held to convey. By means of this presentation, John's Gospel makes serving others the functional equivalent of Jesus' ministry, the performance of his purpose.

The relative privilege of menial poverty within early Christianity also is reflected in pivotal sections of the earlier Gospels (Matthew 19:16–30, ca. 80 CE; Mark 10:17–31, ca. 73 CE; Luke 18:18–30, ca. 90 CE). These passages concern a would-be disciple with property and Peter (Jesus' premier disciple, whose name literally means "Rock," as in this translation):

Look: Someone came forward to him and said, What good should I do so that I might have perpetual life? But he said to him, Why do you question me about the good? One is good! But if you want to enter into life, keep the decrees. He says to him, Which? But Jesus declared, Do not murder, Do not commit adultery, Do not steal, Do not witness falsely, Honor your father and mother, and, Love your neighbor as yourself. The young man says to him, All these things I have kept; what do I still lack? But Jesus told him, If you want to be perfect: depart, sell your belongings, and give to the poor, and you will have a store in heavens. And come on, follow me. The young man heard this word and went away grieving, because he had many possessions. Yet Jesus said to his students, Amen, I say to you that a rich person with labor will enter the kingdom of the heavens! Yet again I say to you: It is easier for a camel to enter through a needle's hole than for a rich person to enter into the kingdom

(continued on next page col. 1)

He was proceeding out on a way and one ran up to him, and kneeling to him, interrogated him, Good teacher, what should I do so that I might inherit perpetual life? But Jesus said to him, Why do you say I am good? No one is good, except one: God! You know the decrees, do not murder, do not commit adultery, do not steal, do not witness falsely, do not deprive, honor your father and mother. But he told him, Teacher, I have kept all these things from my youth. Yet Jesus looked at him, loved him, and said to him, One thing is lacking you: depart, sell as much as you have and give to poor people, and you will have a store in heaven. And come on, follow me. But he was appalled at the word and went away grieving, because he had many effects. Jesus looked around and says to his students, With what labor will those who have effects enter the kingdom of God! But his students were astonished at his words; but Jesus replying again, says to them, Children, what labor it is to enter

(continued on next page col. 2)

And some ruler interrogated him, saying, Good teacher, by doing what shall I inherit perpetual life? But Jesus said to him, Why do you call me good? No one is good, except one: God! You know the decrees: Do not commit adultery, do not murder, do not steal, do not witness falsely, honor your father and mother. But he said, I have kept all these things from youth. Jesus heard and said to him, One thing escapes for you: everything, as much as you have, sell and distribute to the poor, and you will have a store in heavens. And come on, follow me. He heard and was saddened, because he was exceedingly rich. Jesus saw him and said, With what labor will those who have effects proceed into the kingdom of God! Because it is easier for a camel to enter through an instrument's hole than for a rich person to enter into the kingdom of God. But those who heard said, And who can be saved? Yet he said, What is impossible with people is possible with God. But Rock said, Look: we have left our

(continued on next page col. 3)

of God! The students heard and were exceedingly overwhelmed, saying, Therefore: who can be saved? Jesus looked at—and said to—them, This is impossible with people, but everything is possible with God. Then Rock replied, said to him, Look: we left everything, and followed you. What, then, is for us? But Jesus said to them, Amen, I say to you, that you who followed me, in the regeneration, when the one like the person sits upon the throne of his glory, you will also sit yourselves upon twelve thrones, judging the twelve clans of Israel. And everyone who has left homes or brothers or sisters or father or mother or children or lands for my name's sake will receive many times over, and inherit perpetual life. But many first shall be last, and last first.

the kingdom of God! It is easier for a camel to pass through a needle's hole than for a rich person to enter into the kingdom of God. But they were completely overwhelmed, saying to one another, So who can be saved? Jesus looked at them and says, Impossible with people, but not with God: because everything is possible with God. Rock began to say to him, Look: we left everything, and followed you. Jesus stated, Amen, I say to you, there is no one who has left home or brothers or sisters or mother or father or children or lands for my sake and the sake of the message, except that shall receive a hundred times over—now in this time—homes and brothers and sisters and mothers and children and fields—with persecutions—and in the age that is coming perpetual life. But many first shall be last, and the last first.

own to follow you. Yet he said to them, Amen I say to you, that there is no one who has left home or wife, brothers or relatives or children for the sake of the kingdom of God, who shall not receive a many times in this time and in the age which is coming perpetual life.

The enthusiastic catechumen is told, much to his dismay, to sell up and give to the poor, in order to have treasure in heaven (Matthew 19:16–22; Mark 10:17–22; Luke 18:18–23). The normative value of the cautionary story is reinforced by Jesus' statement about rich people and the kingdom of God: A camel would have an easier time wriggling through the eye of a needle than the rich would have getting into the kingdom. Only God's capacity to overcome what is humanly impossible gives them any hope (Matthew 19:23–26; Mark 10:23–27; Luke 18:24–27). Peter, speaking for the body of Jesus' peripatetic followers, calls attention to their voluntary poverty and is promised rewards as a consequence (Matthew 19:27–30; Mark 10:28–31; Luke 18:28–30).

The message of these passages is trenchant: People who are poor, simply because they belong to underclasses, enjoy relative proximity to the kingdom, and the rich may enter only by means of the exceptional grace of God. Peter and his companions, however, by means of their voluntary poverty for the sake of the movement, are assured of life everlasting. The pericope reflects the stringent practice of Christianity in the circle of Jesus' followers that looked to Peter for leadership.

The story of Ananias and Sapphira in the book of Acts also derives from that circle. Ananias and Sapphira claimed to have sold up their property for the benefit of the apostles, but in fact they retained some of the profit. Under Peter's interrogation (Acts 5:1–11), each died separately for deceiving the Spirit of God. Within the Petrine group, there seems to be little question that voluntary poverty was a principal means of following Jesus—that is, of enacting Jesus' ethos. The only evident alternative was death, the obvious alternative to eternal life.

Yet even the Petrine presentation of Jesus' teaching allowed for the possibility of rich people wriggling through the needle's eye. The analogy between Jesus' ministry and voluntary acceptance of conditions typical of underclasses, however much it was recommended, was not taken by itself to be a fulfillment of the imperative to follow Jesus. That analogy was preferred, and even standard; yet the analogy was no identity, such that simply accepting poverty made one like Jesus and worthy of eternal life. There was an awareness within the Petrine circle, and within other communities of the New Testament, that the needle's eye was open for those with property, because voluntary poverty was at the service of a more basic means of enacting the ethos of the Christ, a principle which might be realized by programs other than voluntary poverty.

The purest form of the Petrine statement of the larger principle appears in Matthew and Mark (Matthew 22:34–40; Mark 12:28–34):

The Pharisees heard that he had shut the Zadokites up, and were gathered together in the same place. And one from them, a lawyer, interrogated him, pressing him to the limit: Teacher, which decree is great in the law? But he told him, You shall love the Lord your God with all your heart and with all your life and with all your mind: the great and first decree	One of the scribes came forward— hearing them arguing (seeing that he answered them well)—and interrogated him, Which is the first decree of all? Jesus answered that: first is, Hear, Israel, our God is the Lord; he is one Lord. And you shall love the Lord your God from all your heart and from all your life and from all your mind and from all your strength. This is second:

(continued on next page col. 1)   *(continued on next page col. 2)*

is this. A second is like this: You shall love your neighbor as yourself. On these two decrees all the law is suspended—and the prophets!

You shall love your neighbor as yourself. There is not another decree greater than these. And the scribe said to him, fine, teacher: in truth you have said that he is one and there is not another beside him, and to love him from all heart and from all the understanding and from all the strength and to love the neighbor as oneself is overflowing all burnt offerings and sacrifices. Jesus saw he answered sensibly and answered, said to him, You are not far from the kingdom of God. And no one any longer dared to interrogate him.

In both passages, Jesus is asked by someone outside his group (a Pharisee in Matthew, a scribe in Mark) what is the greatest (so Matthew) or first (so Mark) commandment. He replies by citing two commandments from the Torah: to love God (drawing from Deuteronomy 6:4, 5) and to love one's neighbor (drawing from Leviticus 19:18). Jesus concludes in Matthew that all the law and the prophets hang from those two commandments and in Mark that there is no other commandment greater than these two.

Matthew and Mark construe the sense of the teaching distinctively. In Matthew, the organic connection among the commandments assures that they all hang together (with the teaching of the prophets) on the principle of love toward God and neighbor (Matthew 22:40). Mark, on the other hand, has the scribe who initiated the scene conclude that to love God is more than all burnt offerings and sacrifices (Mark 12:32–33). The construal in Matthew is in the direction of claiming that Jesus represents the fulfillment of the law and the prophets—a thematic concern of the Gospel generally. The construal in Mark takes the tack that Jesus' principle establishes a noncultic means of approval by God.

Both Matthew and Mark find their center of gravity, however, in the conviction that the commandment to love God and to love one's neighbor is the action that unites one with Jesus in an approach to God. The emblem of that approach is fulfillment of the law and the prophets in Matthew (22:40), nearness to the kingdom of God in Mark (12:34). The differences between those construals are not to be minimized: They represent the substantive independence of the Gospels as catechetical instruments. Nevertheless, the systemic agreement between Matthew and Mark that love is the means of access to God after the pattern of Jesus is an equally striking attribute.

Scholars of the New Testament commonly observe that the Jewish teacher Hillel—in a dictum comparable to Jesus'—is said to have taught that the Torah is a commentary on the injunction not to do what is hateful to one's neighbor (Bavli, Shabbath 31a). The centrality of the commandment to love one's neighbor also is asserted by Aqiba, the famous rabbi of the second century (Sifra, Leviticus 19:18). Although differences of emphasis are detectable and important, the fact remains that Jesus does not appear to have been exceptional in locating love at the center of the divine commandments. Any rabbi—a teacher in a city or a local village—might have come up with some such principle, although the expressions of the principle attributed to Jesus are especially apt. The principle itself is little more than proverbial: Love, after all, is not easily dismissed as a bad idea or beside the point.

Precisely because Jesus' teaching has precedents in the Judaism of his day, it is clear that the tradition presented in aggregate by Matthew and Mark aim to put that teaching in a new light. For those two Gospels, Jesus' citation of the two biblical passages that demand and define love is no longer simply a matter of locating a coherent principle within the Torah—the stated terms of reference in the question of the Pharisee or scribe. Instead, the twin commandment of love is now held to be a transcendent principle, which fulfills (according to Matthew) or supersedes (according to Mark) the Torah. Christ himself, by citing and enacting that principle, is held to offer the ethical key to communion with God.

The Lukan version of the teaching concerning love is very different from what we find in Matthew and Mark and makes especially apparent that the significance of Jesus' message lies at least as much in who is speaking as in what he says (Luke 10:25–37):

> And look, there arose some lawyer, pressing him to the limit, saying, Teacher, having done what shall I inherit perpetual life? But he said to him, In the law what is written—how do you read? He answered and said, You shall love the Lord your God from all your heart and with all your life and with all your strength and with all your mind, and your neighbor as yourself. Yet he said to him, You answered rightly: do this, and you will live. He wanted to justify himself and said to Jesus, And who is my neighbor? Jesus took up, and said, Some person went down from Jerusalem to Jericho, and thugs fell upon him, who stripped him and inflicted lesions. They went away, leaving him half dead. But by coincidence some priest went down that way; he saw him and passed by opposite. Likewise also a Levite came by the place, but he saw and passed by opposite. Some Samaritan made a way and came by him, saw and felt for him. He came forward and, pouring on oil and wine, wrapped his wounds. He mounted him up on his own animal and led him to a hostel and took care of him. On the next day he put out two denarii and gave

them to the hosteller and said, Take care of him, and that: Should you spend over, I will repay you when I come back again. Of these three, who seems to you to have become neighbor to the one who fell among the thugs? Yet he said, The one who did mercy with him. But Jesus said to him, Proceed: and you do likewise.

Here an unidentified "lawyer," rather than the Pharisee of Matthew or the scribe of Mark, asks what to do to inherit eternal life. In Luke the lawyer himself, not Jesus, cites the twin principle of love (10:27). At first Jesus merely confirms what the lawyer already knows (10:28); Jesus' peculiar contribution comes in the response to the lawyer's further question, "Who is my neighbor?" (10:29). The question and the response appear in uniquely Lukan material (10:29–37)—the presentation of Jesus' teaching concerning love that was characteristic of the church in Antioch where the Gospel according to Luke seems to have been composed.

The Antiochene transformation of the principle, in distinction from the Petrine transformation, explicitly makes Jesus' application of the commandment, not its formulation, his systemic innovation. The innovation is effected in the parable of the good Samaritan (Luke 10:29–37). Whether Jesus himself told the parable is beside the present point. What concerns us is that the parable informs the commandment to love with a new gist, and that the new gist is the systemic center of Lukan ethics, as distinct from Matthean and/or Markan ethics.

Formally, the parable is designed to answer the question, "Who is my neighbor?" That formal issue also is addressed at the close of the parable, when Jesus tells his questioner to go and do what the Samaritan did—that is, show himself a neighbor to one in obvious need (10:36, 37). The formal issue here is distinct, however, from the systemic issue.

The systemic challenge is not the goodness of the Samaritan but the fact that he is a Samaritan. The victim of the mugging is in no position to complain, but—especially as a recent pilgrim to Jerusalem—he might well have objected to contact with a Samaritan, in that Samaritan sacrifice on Mount Gerizim was regarded as antagonistic to Judaic sacrifice on Mount Zion. A priest and a Levite have already passed by, motivated by the Torah's teaching that limited their contact with corpses (Leviticus 21:1–4). In the parable, then, a victim who seemed impure is aided by a Samaritan who was actually impure, yet that action nonetheless fulfills the commandment to love one's neighbor as oneself.

The parable of the good Samaritan is a story that formally conveys how to be a neighbor and how to identify a neighbor. It is shaped systemically to insist that a person who is regarded as "impure" may be a neighbor to one who is "pure." The commandment to love is such that in its application it creates a new sphere of purity that transcends any other notion of what is clean and what is unclean. The issue of purity was crucial to the church in Antioch. In Galatians 2:11–13, Paul describes factional fighting among three groups, classed according to their leaders. On one extreme, Paul himself taught that Gentiles and Jews might freely eat with one another; on the other, James insisted on the separation of those who were circumcised. Peter and Barnabas were caught somewhere between these two extremes. Much later, around 90 CE, Luke's Gospel represents how the issue was resolved within Antiochene Christianity: The question of the boundaries established by purity was settled in terms of ethical engagement, rather than dietary practice. It is no accident, then, that it is precisely Luke that conveys its unique parable and its peculiar perspective on how Jesus' teaching regarding love was distinctive.

Jesus provides a paradigm of loving service throughout the literature of the New Testament; the foregoing examples easily can be multiplied. The link with catechumens' social situation is so strong that their lives are mirrored in Jesus' as much as his is in theirs, even when one might expect the texts to be straightforwardly historical. In both Jesus' case and believers', the ethos that goes by the name of love is transformed by distinctive conditions, so that love might be, for example, the integral principle of the Torah (Matthew), a principle beyond cultic Judaism (Mark), or the single term of reference that determines the purity of one person for another (Luke).

The "Other" and the Throne of God

The argument that love is the systemic center of Christian ethics is easily established; no recent study of New Testament ethics would find much to quarrel with in the first part of this chapter, exegetical details aside. This second section is another matter. Here I argue that the attempt to discover a unity in Christian ethics in the general principle of love has obscured its distinctive character.

Finding an objection to the principle of love is difficult from most religious perspectives. The *target* of one's love does differ radically, however, as one moves from Jesus, through Paul, and on to John's Gospel.[2] If we do not consider the target Jesus identifies, we have missed the point of his teaching, however much we might honor his principles.

Jesus commanded his followers to love their enemies (Matthew 5: 38–48; Luke 6: 27–36)[3]:

You heard that it was said, Eye for eye and tooth for tooth. Yet I say to you, Not to resist the evil one, but whoever cuffs you on your right	But I say to you who hear, Love your enemies, act well with those who hate you, bless those who accurse you, pray concerning those who revile

(continued on next page col. 1) *(continued on next page col. 2)*

cheek, turn to him the other as well. And to the one who wishes to litigate with you, even to take your tunic, leave him the cloak as well! And whoever requisitions you to journey one mile, depart with him two! Give to the one who asks you, and do not withhold from the one who wishes to borrow from you. You have heard that it was said, You shall love your neighbor and you shall hate your enemy. Yet I say to you, Love your enemies, and pray for those who persecute you, so you might become descendants of your father in heavens. Because he makes his sun dawn upon evil people and good people, and makes rain upon just and unjust. For if you love those who love you, what reward have you? Do not even the customs-agents do the same? And if you greet only your fellows, what do you do that goes beyond? Do not even the Gentiles do the same? You, then, shall be perfect, as your heavenly father is perfect.

you. To the one who hits you on the cheek, furnish the other also. And from the one who takes your garment, do not forbid the tunic! Give to the one who asks you, and do not demand from the one who takes what is yours. And just as you want humanity to do to you, do to them similarly. And if you love those who love you, what sort of grace is that for you? Because even the sinners love those who love them. And if you do good to those who do you good, what sort of grace is that to you? Even the sinners do the same. And if you lend to those from whom you hope to receive, what sort of grace is that to you? Even sinners lend so that they receive the equivalent back. Except: love your enemies and do good and lend—anticipating nothing—and your reward will be great, and you will be descendants of most high, because he is fine to the ungrateful and evil. Become compassionate, just as your father is also compassionate.

Christian theologians from Paul to the present day have resisted the simple letter of his directive.

To say, with John (as we saw above), that followers of Jesus should love one another establishes a bond of affection and mutual obligation within the community that defines them. What, however, of those outside the community, or those who are overtly hostile? John's Gospel consigns that group to "the world." In the same discourse that begins in chapter 13, Jesus says, "Fear not, for I have overcome the world" (John 16:33). Although that statement establishes an attitude of nonaggressive (if not benign) neglect toward outsiders, it is not the same as loving enemies.

On the other hand, John at least represents a distinct improvement on Paul's teaching. Writing to the Romans around 57 CE, Paul clearly refers to Jesus' summary of the Torah (Romans 13:8), but he also manages to turn the imperative to love into a stratagem of working divine vengeance against one's neighbor (Romans 12:18–21)[4]:

If it is possible for you make peace with all people, without avenging yourselves, beloved, but give place to wrath. Because it is

written, Vengeance is mine, I shall repay, says the Lord. But if your
enemy hungers, feed him; if he thirsts, give him drink—for by
doing this you will heap coals of fire upon his head. Don't be
conquered by evil, but conquer evil with good.

By this point, Paul makes clear that he sees love as a forensic principle,
whose power resides in its vindication by divine judgment.

Jesus' view is less abstract, in that it calls for love of one's enemies
without expectation of reward. Yet that pragmatic character is precisely
what makes his teaching all the more paradoxical. What is the source of
his demand that enemies should be loved?

Jesus' teaching in this regard came into focus during his last months
in Jerusalem. By uncovering those circumstances, we can appreciate the
distinctiveness of his ethics.[5] Despite Jesus' naiveté concerning the politics of Rome and therefore the growing threat of execution at the hands
of Pontius Pilate, Jesus knew that he courted danger during this period.
The constant danger took a toll on his followers, as Jesus well knew. They
actually had to be ready to give up wealth and family (as we have seen:
Mark 10:13–31; Matthew 19:13–30; Luke 18:15–30), to ruin their lives if necessary. The message that God's Kingdom was to be all-consuming, dis-
solving even Caesar's power, made it tolerable to bear the Romans' cross
if necessary. Jesus speaks of doing that when he refers to his followers as
a whole (Mark 8:34–38; Matthew 16:24–27; Luke 9:23–26), not only his
own fate.

Such travails were a small price to pay for being part of the triumph
of God's rule over human destructiveness. Jesus' demands were not—as
later teaching made them—quasi-Stoic commendations of austerity or
materialistic promises of reward later for suffering now. Jesus framed his
teaching to make hardship the gateway to the vision of seeing God within
the world. The practice of vision was basic to his own experience from
the time of his baptism (Matthew 3:13–17; Mark 1:9–11; Luke 3:21–22):

Then there came Jesus from Galilee to the Jordan to John to be immersed by him. Yet he prevented him, saying, I have need to be immersed by you, and do you come to me? Jesus replied, and said to him, Permit it now, for so it is proper for us to fulfill all righteousness.
(continued on next page col. 1)

And it happened in those days there came Jesus from Nazareth of Galilee and he was immersed in the Jordan by John. At once he ascends from the water and saw the heavens split and the Spirit as dove descending into him. And a voice came from the heavens: You
(continued on next page col. 2)

But it happened when all the people were immersed, and Jesus was immersed and praying, the heaven opened and the Holy Spirit de-scended upon him in body, in form as dove, and a voice came from heaven, You are my son, the beloved; in you I take pleasure.

Then he permitted him. Yet when Jesus had been immersed, at once he ascended from the water, and look: the heavens were opened, and he saw God's Spirit descending as dove, coming upon him. And look: a voice from the heavens, saying: This is my son, the beloved, in whom I take pleasure.

are my son, the beloved; in you I take pleasure.

Jesus' particular gift as a teacher involved the capacity to convey that visionary experience to his followers, as is attested preeminently in the story of his Transfiguration (Matthew 17:1–5; Mark 9:2–7; Luke 9:28–35):

And after six days Jesus takes Rock and James and John his brother and brings them up to a high mountain privately. And he was transmuted before them and his face shone as the sun, and his clothing became white as the light. And look: there appeared to them Moses and Elijah, speaking together with him. Rock responded and said to Jesus, Lord, it is good for us to be here; if you wish, I shall build here three lodges: one for you and one for Moses and one for Elijah. While he was still speaking, look: a glowing cloud overshadowed them, and look: a voice from the cloud, saying, This is my son, the beloved: in whom I take pleasure. Hear him.

And after six days Jesus takes Rock and James and John and brings them up to a high mountain privately: alone. And he was transmuted before them and his clothing became gleaming, very white, as a washer on the earth is not able to whiten. And Elijah appeared to them with Moses, and they were speaking together with Jesus. Rock responded and says to Jesus, Rabbi, it is good for us to be here, and we shall build three lodges: one for you and one for Moses and one for Elijah. For he did not know how he should respond, because they were terrified. And a cloud came overshadowing them, and there came a voice from the

Yet it happened after these words (about eight days), taking Rock and John and James he ascended into the mountain to pray. And it happened while he prayed the appearance of his face was different and his garments flashed out white. And look: two men were speaking together with him, such as were Moses and Elijah, who were seen in glory speaking of his exodus which he was about to fulfill in Jerusalem. Yet Rock and those with him were weighed down with sleep. But becoming alert, they saw his glory and the two men standing with him. And it happened as they were being separated from him, Rock said to Jesus,

(continued on next page col. 2) (continued on next page col. 3)

63

cloud, This is my son, the beloved: hear him.

Master, it is good for us to be here, and we shall build three lodges: one yours and one Moses' and one Elijah's (not knowing what he was saying). But while he was saying this there came a cloud and overshadowed them, and they were afraid when they entered into the cloud. And there came a voice from the cloud, saying, This is my son, the chosen: him hear.

Relative tranquility and leisure gave Jesus occasion to develop his own visionary experience and that of his followers. In the midst of chaotic circumstances of opposition, however, he also reported (Luke 10:18) that he saw Satan fall like lightning.

The scriptures of Israel provide ample precedent for visionary practice—in particular, for the conviction that God supports faithful Israelites in the midst of persecution. The classic text of that faith is the book of Daniel, in which an angel called "one like a person" appears in the presence of God, before his Throne (Daniel 7:13)—symbolizing the triumph of God's people. Jesus often spoke of Daniel's "one like a person" (or "son of man," in the traditional rendering) representing the people of Israel before God's Throne.

Near the end of his life Jesus pursued this insight further: Every person possessed the angelic likeness of the "one like a person" and mirrored some of the truth of the divine Throne or Chariot (as it was also called, because it could appear anywhere).[6] God's Throne is there, shining through the eyes of a neighbor, even if that neighbor hates you (Matthew 5:43–48; Luke 6:27–36, cited above). While Jesus was arguing with other teachers in Jerusalem, he had come to the realization that the love one owed the Throne is exactly what one owes one's neighbor (Mark 12:28–34; Matthew 22:34–40; Luke 10:25–28). Love of God (Deuteronomy 6:5) and love of neighbor (Leviticus 19:18) are basic principles embedded in the Torah, as we have seen. Jesus' innovation lay in the claim that the two are indivisible: Love of God *is* love of neighbor, and vice versa.

Every neighbor belongs within God's presence. That assertion is the basis of Jesus' distinctive and challenging ethics of love in the midst of persecution. He links his ethics to the transformed society the prophets had predicted. His words promise that individual suffering can achieve transcendence if the "other" is seen not as threat or stranger[7] but as mirroring the presence of God in the world.

Jesus did not innovate by commending a principle of love as the central command of the Torah. Rather, his spirituality of the "other" (or alter-spirituality) invested one's neighbor with the attribute of God's presence in the world, so that loving that person is tantamount to worship of God.

Conclusion

Jesus' distinctive perspective presses us to see altruism in a fresh light, perceiving that care for the other is crucial to the care of oneself. For that reason, the possibility of "action on behalf of others" with "no beneficial consequence for the actor" at all, as in William Scott Green's definition (see introduction to this volume), does not arise. Yet this "beneficial consequence" is not in the terms of this world but a function of the presence of God.

The Gospel according to Matthew articulates precisely this qualification. That articulation comes, in all probability, from a period well after Jesus' death, but it invaluably reflects how earliest Christianity addressed questions of interpretation and conduct such as those Green poses. In this Gospel, a thematic distinction is made between the public benefit that might come from public prayer and ostentatious worship and the benefit that comes "in secret" from private devotion, including almsgiving (Matthew 6:1–21). That is, concern for the other carries with it a reward from God that cannot be enhanced, and is only undermined, by anticipation of benefit in this world.

That emphasis on how the other determines the value of one's actions is brought home in another Matthean parable: the famous analogy of sheep and goats (Matthew 25:31–46). In this case, Green's second question is cast in new terms. Instead of assessing "the meaning of behavior for the welfare of others," the parable presents the welfare of others as the meaning of behavior: "As much as you did to one of the least of these, my brothers, you did to me" (Matthew 25:40).

That insight into Jesus' position brings us to Green's first question, but in the last place (to make it answerable in the terms Jesus taught): "What are the major categories of behavior for the welfare of others?" Jesus imagined that "you always have the poor with yourselves, and whenever you want, you can do them good" (Mark 14:7). He understood that the problem of altruism never has to do with lack of opportunity. Yet in this passage Jesus also refuses to make categorical assertions of what, precisely, his disciples should do for others, and that refusal feeds the impression of Jesus' insouciance in this case. Jesus' attitude proceeds, however, from the fact that the other person is the primordial fact, not a preconception of how God should be honored in that person. What endures is Jesus' insight that once action is undertaken on behalf of any person who is in God's image, that action demands—as Ananias and Sapphira discovered—the same commitment one owes God.

Notes

1. See Richard B. Hays, *The Moral Vision of the New Testament: Community, Cross, New Creation. A Contemporary Introduction to New Testament Ethics* (San Francisco: HarperSanFrancisco, 1996), and Bruce Chilton and J. I. H. McDonald, *Jesus and the Ethics of the Kingdom,* Biblical Foundations in Theology (London: SPCK, 1987); the latter also has been published outside the series in the United States (Grand Rapids, Mich.: Eerdmans, 1988).
2. I take these differences to be exemplary because they have been traced in other documents within the New Testament and early Christian literature. See Robin Gill, ed., *The Cambridge Companion to Christian Ethics* (Cambridge: Cambridge University Press, 2001).
3. For a consideration of the social conditions in Jesus' experience that this teaching reflects, see Bruce Chilton, *Rabbi Jesus: An Intimate Biography* (New York: Doubleday, 2000), 46.
4. Paul works out his position by splicing together passages from the Scriptures of Israel: Deuteronomy 32:35 and Proverbs 25:21–22. See Joseph A. Fitzmyer, *Romans. A New Translation with Introduction and Commentary,* The Anchor Bible 33 (New York: Doubleday, 1993), 656–59. For Paul's characteristic combination of Judaism and philosophical thought, see Chilton, *Rabbi Paul: An Intellectual Biography* (New York: Doubleday, 2004).
5. A more detailed analysis of the historical circumstances appears in Chilton, *Rabbi Jesus,* 197–289. Here my concern is the impact of those circumstances in shaping Jesus' distinctive ethics.
6. Chilton, *Rabbi Jesus,* provides a full discussion of the relevant texts, interwoven with narrative together with bibliography.
7. See Christopher D. Marshall, *Beyond Retribution. A New Testament Vision for Justice, Crime, and Punishment* (Grand Rapids, Mich.: Eerdmans, 2001); Robin W. Lovin, *Christian Ethics: An Essential Guide* (Nashville, Tenn.: Abingdon, 2001).

Chapter 4

Altruism in Islam

Th. Emil Homerin

n the introduction to this volume, William Scott Green defines altruism as "intentional action ultimately for the welfare of others that entails at least the possibility of either no benefit or a loss to the actor."
Moreover, Green notes that August Comte coined the term *altruisme* in
the nineteenth century, from the Latin *alter*, "other," meaning to care for
others. Muslims today speak nearly every language in the world—though
Arabic, the language of the Qur'an, holds a special place. In Arabic, altruism is translated literally as *al-ghayrîyah*, from the word *ghayr*, "other."
Like *altruisme*, however, *al-ghayrîyah* is a relatively recent term, and as
such rarely occurs in Muslim religious literature. This is not to say that
Islam lacks altruism but that over the centuries, Muslims have referred to
altruistic behaviors with several different words, which appear in the
Qur'an; the prophetic traditions (*hadîth*); and in legal, theological, and
mystical literature—each term bearing its own particular nuances.

Altruism and the Qur'an

Like so much else in the Qur'an, discussion of helping others occurs in the
context of Arabian society in the sixth and seventh centuries CE. As in other
ancient cultures, pre-Islamic Arabs held hospitality and generosity as
foundational virtues. Thus, the great poet Labîd (fl. 6th c.) ends his famous ode the *al-Muʿallaqah* with a hymn to the noble leaders of the tribe,
who sacrifice a camel to feed those in need:

> How many times have I called
> for the *mâysir* slaughter
> and the gaming lots
> of notched arrow shafts
>
> Calling the throw
> for the calfless or nursing mare,
> the portions parceled out
> to all the clans,

Distant clients and guests
as if they'd come down
to Tabâla
where the valleys are green,

Seeking refuge among the tent ropes,
weary as a stumbling camel,
weary as a ghost mare,
white-humped, left to die.

They show up when the winds wail,
the weak of kin,
the broken kin, the orphaned,
to be given an equal's share.

There is yet among us
when the council meets,
one who seizes the moment,
who takes on the burden,

Who divides and assigns,
who raises the rights of some,
others,
driving into the ground,

As he deems fit, magnanimous,
munificent,
gracious,
seeking plunder and gaining it.

[He's] from a clan whose fathers
have shown the way.
For every warrior band
there is a guide and a way.

Their honor untarnished,
their action never fallow,
their judgment does not lean
with the winds of desire.

When trust was portioned out
among the tribe,
the divider bestowed on us
the greater share.

Be content with what the sire
has given.
He who portioned merit out among us
is most knowing.

He built for us a house
with lofty roof.
Boys and full-aged men
ascend to it.

They are the protectors
when the tribe is pressed,
they are the riders,
they are the rulers.

They are life-spring
to dependents among them,
to those without provider,
when the year grows long.[1]

Here Labîd lauds the *karîm*, the noble hero celebrated for his manly character and, above all, for his munificence (*karam*)—underscored by his slaughtering his she-camel for the benefit of others. Significantly, this riding mare often symbolizes the poet himself, so her sacrifice becomes emblematic of the poet's willingness to sacrifice himself for the good of the tribe.[2] In other poems and Arab legends, Arab heroes boast of their liberality, especially when drinking:

When drinking, all I own
I spend away,
though what I am
is undiminished.

When sobered,
I don't stop giving,
true to nature
As you have come to know me.[3]

Such extravagant behavior, however, was more an assertion of honor than an act of altruism, and this is certainly the Qur'an's position in what it regards as wastefulness: "Do not be wasteful; God does not love the profligates!" (6:141; *cf.* 25:67). Nevertheless, hospitality, albeit in moderation, remains a prominent feature of Islam—based, in large part, on traditions of the prophet Muhammad:

A man asked the Prophet, may God bless him and give him peace: "What aspect of Islam is a benefit (*khayr*) [to others]?" He replied: "To offer food and greetings of peace to those whom you know and to those you don't."[4]

Likewise, in many passages, the Qur'an exhorts Muslims to feed the hungry and spend (*nafaqa*) on those in need.

They ask you [Muhammad] what they should spend [on others]. Say: "They should give what charity (*khayr*) they can to benefit parents, relatives, orphans, the destitute, and wayfarers. For, indeed, God is aware of the good deeds that you do" (2:215).

Believe in God and His messenger, and spend [on others] of the wealth that He has entrusted to you. For those of you who believe and spend [on others] will have a great reward! (57:7; *cf.* 2:270, 273–74; 13:22; 22:35; 35:29).

How will you understand what is the steep road [to righteousness]? To free a slave; to feed in time of famine, the orphan and relative or the destitute in misery, and to be among those who believe and counsel each other to be patient and kind (90:12–18).

As the Qur'an declares in these and many other verses, helping others is a cardinal virtue, and those who willingly neglect this obligation will suffer the consequences.

When it was said to them: "Spend [on others] from what God has given you as sustenance." The unbelievers said to the believers: "We should feed those whom, if God had wished, He could have fed? You are clearly wrong!" (36:47).

Have you seen him who denies religion, who pushes away the orphan and does not advocate feeding the destitute? Woe to those who are distracted from their prayers, who are hypocrites, and forbid the basic necessities to others! (107:1–7).

[On the judgment day] the evildoers will be asked: "What brought you to Hell?" They will reply: "We did not pray or feed the destitute, as we were engrossed with others, instead" (74:44; *cf.* 69: 25–37; 89:15–24).

Helping others, particularly fellow Muslims, is so important within Islam that the Qur'an includes almsgiving in a list of essential religious beliefs and actions:

> The pious person is one who believes in God and the last day, in the angels, the scriptures and the prophets, and gives of his wealth out of love of Him, to his kin, orphans, the destitute, wayfarers, supplicants, and slaves. He undertakes his prayers, gives alms (zakât), and keeps his promises, remaining patient when facing distress, adversity, or injury. These are those who are truthful and mindful [of God] (2:177).

The Qur'an often employs the terms zakâh/zakât and sadaqah (pl. sadaqât) for alms and almsgiving.[5] However, as Azim Nanji has insightfully observed:

> While the term almsgiving may suggest a simple and unfocused act of charity directed to the poor and needy, the Qur'an articulates through a variety of terms, especially sadaqa and zakât, a very textured and multivalent conception of giving which draws upon the ideals of compassion, social justice, sharing and strengthening the community. As this act aims at being both a social corrective and a spiritual benefit, it reflects the ethical and spiritual values which are associated with wealth, property, resources and voluntary effort in personal as well as communal contexts.[6]

The Qur'an places clear emphasis on these spiritual and social concerns with the frequent command to "undertake prayers and pay alms" (aqîmû as-salâta wa-âtû az-zakâta) (e.g., 2:43; 22:78; 24:56; 70:4). Traditionally, Muslim exegetes and scholars have interpreted this pairing of performing prayer and almsgiving as a concise expression of Muslim faith and action. One prays in submission and devotion to God, bearing witness that there is no deity but Him and that Muhammad is His messenger. This is the vertical dimension of faith in relation to God. Then, by giving alms, the believer fulfills God's command to help those in need, as Muslims strive to create a just society. This is the horizontal dimension of faith in action in the world.[7] Giving alms does more than help others, however; it can purify the giver as well:

> There are others who acknowledge their misdeeds and their mixing of good deeds with bad. Perhaps God will forgive them, for God is forgiving and merciful. Accept from their wealth, alms (sadaqah) with which you may purify them and make them prosper (9:102–3).

The term *sadaqah*, which is used in the foregoing passage, is related to the Arabic root *s-d-q*, with its connotations of "sincerity and truthfulness." Similarly, the word *zakât* carries the sense of "to increase" and "to purify," which may be derived from the Arabic root *z-k-â*, with its meanings of "to grow, thrive" and "to purify, improve." Both terms, with their multiple meanings, occur in the Qur'an's longest discourse on almsgiving (2:261–77)[8]:

261: Those who spend their wealth in the way of God are like a grain that germinates into seven spikes, each with a hundred grains. Indeed, God will increase in abundance whomsoever He will, and God is bounteous, all-knowing.

262: Those who spend (*yunfiqûn*) their wealth in the way of God, and do not follow up their giving with reproach or insult, they will have their reward from their Lord. They have nothing to fear, nor will they grieve.

263: A kind and forgiving word is better than alms (*sadaqah*) followed by insult. And God is self-sufficient, forbearing.

264: Oh you who believe, do not spoil your alms (*sadaqah*) with reproach and insult, like one who spends his wealth to show off to people, while he does not believe in God and the Last Day. He is like a rock covered with dirt such that when heavy rains pour down on it, they leave it bare. [Such people] gain nothing from what they had earned, and God does not guide the ungrateful folk.

265: But those who spend their wealth seeking God's satisfaction and their own fortitude are like a garden on a hill. Heavy rains pour down on it and, if not heavy rains then dew, and it brings forth twice as much fruit! God sees what you do.

266: Would any of you wish to have a garden of date palms and grape vines with all kinds of fruit there, and beneath which flowed streams, only to have old age pour down on you and weak offspring? Then a whirlwind would strike the garden and a fire, and the garden would burn up! Just so, God makes clear to you His signs; perhaps you will reflect.

267: Oh you who believe give of the good things that you have earned and what you have harvested from the earth. Do not turn to some disgusting thing, giving it, when you would not take it, save with loathing. Know that God is self-sufficient, worthy of praise.

268: Satan threatens you with poverty and commands you to commit shameless acts. But God promises you His forgiveness and bounty, for God is bounteous, all-knowing.

269: He bestows wisdom on whomsoever He wills, and one upon whom wisdom is bestowed has been given a great good. But no one thinks of that save those with insight.

270: Whatever you give as a donation (*nafaqah*), and whatever vow you make, God knows it, and the unjust have no allies.

271: If you give alms in public, they are beneficial. But if you conceal them while giving them to the poor, that is better for you, for they will atone for some of your bad deeds. God is well informed of what you do.

272: It is not for you [Muhammad] to guide them. Rather, God guides whomsoever He wills. Whatever charity (*khayr*) you give is to your benefit when you spend only for the sake of God. Whatever charity you give will be repaid to you in full, and you will not be treated unjustly.

273: [Spend] on the poor who are beleaguered in the way of God, unable to move about the land [to earn a living], though the ignorant thinks them rich because [of their] restraint. You will recognize them by their mark: they do not beg from people demanding things. Whatever charity you give, God is aware of it.

274: Those who spend of their wealth [on others] night and day, in secret and in public, they will have their reward with their Lord; they have nothing to fear, nor will they grieve.

275: Those who live by usury will not arise [on the Last Day] save as those whom have been struck down by Satan's attack. Because they say: "Usury is just a form of trade." But God has permitted trade and forbidden usury. He who receives a warning from his Lord and stops, he may keep what is past; his affair is with God. As to those who return [to usury], they will be residents of Hell, there forever!

276: God causes usury to perish, but makes alms (*sadaqât*) grow. God does not love any guilty ingrate.

277: Truly, those who believe and do good works, who undertake their prayers and give alms (*zakât*) will have their reward with their Lord. They will have nothing to fear, nor will they grieve.

This long and detailed passage highlights the social function of alms for the public good. In contrast to usury, with its ruinous rates of interest that devour the poor, alms nurture the community and help it to grow. In addition to functioning as a public charity, however, almsgiving yields spiritual benefits; it may atone for past misdeeds and lead to heavenly reward. In fact, in several instances the Qur'an likens almsgiving to giving God a loan:

Whatever charity you give will be repaid to you in full, and you will not be treated unjustly (2:272).

Whatever you give of alms (*zakât*) for God's sake, will be doubled! (33:39).

In this context, almsgiving as outlined by the Qur'an may not fall within Green's definition of altruism, which "entails at least the possibility of either no benefit or a loss to the actor"—because the giver clearly will gain religious reward from his or her action. Ambiguity remains, however, because an individual might still willingly give alms to help others without thought of obligation or reward—which seems to be the case in at least two passages in the Qur'an.

Those who fulfill their vows in full and fear a day whose ill effects will spread afar, who feed, for His sake, the destitute, orphan, and captive, [they declare]: We feed you only for God's sake; we do not desire recompense or thanks from you (76:7–9).

According to a tradition, the following verse addressed the plight of many Muslims who had immigrated to Medina from Mecca in 622 CE. These immigrants had been forced to leave behind in Mecca their homes and much of their property, and many of them lived in poverty. In Medina they were given assistance by resident Muslims; on at least one occasion, the Medinan Muslims gave up their share of booty and more to help their poor brethren. The Qur'an praises the Medinan Muslims' generosity:

Those who resided in [Medina] and came to the faith before [the Meccan Muslims arrived there], love those who immigrate to them. The [Medinan Muslims] have no need for what has been given the [Meccan Muslims]. They prefer [the Meccan Muslims] to themselves, even if that leads them to poverty. Those who are saved from their own selfishness, they are the successful! (59:9).

The verb used in this verse, *âthâra* (with its verbal noun *îthâr*), is translated here as "to prefer." Some exegetes have glossed it as "to put the other before the self" (*taqdîr al-ghayr ʿalâ al-nafs*).[9]

Alms and Almsgiving in Islam

The Qur'an often praises almsgiving and its benefits. In one verse it lists those who should receive alms:

Alms (*sadaqât*) are only for the poor, the destitute, alms collectors, for softening the hearts of others [to convert to Islam], for [freeing] slaves, and those in debt, for [those who strive] in the way of God, and for wayfarers. [Almsgiving] is a required duty (*farîdah*) from God, all-knowing, wise (9:60).

Clearly the Qur'an gives great importance to almsgiving, to the extent of declaring it a religious obligation. Yet the Qur'an never states precisely who should give alms, the amount of alms one should give, or how alms should be collected, if at all. The prophet Muhammad may have been considering these issues before his death in 632 CE because several sayings on these subjects are ascribed to him.[10] These hadîth generally reinforce and augment the Qur'an's statements on almsgiving, which were developed and codified into a system of rules and regulations by Muslim legal scholars in the eighth and ninth centuries.[11] As a result, *zakât* became a mandatory tithe of between 2.5 and 25 percent on certain types of property and wealth, collected annually by the caliphs for the state treasury—more of a tax than alms. Nevertheless, *sadaqah* remained as voluntary alms, and, perhaps as early as the eleventh century, the giving of most *zakât*, though still obligatory, was left to the donor's conscience, as well.[12]

Over the centuries, Muslims have regarded almsgiving as essential to the strength of their communities, both economically and morally. Hence, the motivation for giving has been nearly as important as the act of almsgiving itself. The Qur'an warns against selfishness and hypocrisy when giving alms, and medieval legal scholars and theologians focused on the proper intentions for almsgiving and other religious acts. Representative of this trend is the *Kitâb Asrâr al-Zakâh*, "The Mysteries of Almsgiving," a section in the famous *Ihyâ' 'Ulûm al-Dîn (The Revivification of the Religious Sciences)* by the twelfth-century theologian Abû Hâmid al-Ghazzâlî (d.1111).[13] Al-Ghazzâlî begins his discussion of almsgiving by citing several Qur'anic verses and hadîth on the subject; he then differentiates the types of obligatory *zakât* and the various laws involved. He notes that although *zakât* was made obligatory to help Muslims in need, it also was made obligatory as a test of believers' faith and servitude to God:

> The degree of a person's love is tested when he parts with his beloved. Property and wealth are much loved by all people because they are the means to enjoy the pleasures of the world, and because of them they love life and hate death, although through [death] they will meet [God] the beloved. As proof of the truthfulness of their claim that they love God they have renounced property and wealth, the objects of their [earthly] attention and devotion.[14]

Furthermore, *zakât* is essential for believers because it "purifies the person who fulfils it from the destructive impurities of niggardliness" and demonstrates their gratitude for God's blessing them with sufficient wealth for them and their families.[15] To avoid ostentation and hypocrisy, however, donors should give alms in secret to the extent that they do not know who receives them and the recipient does not know who gave them, if possible. Moreover, the donor should not be proud of his or her almsgiving or think himself or herself superior to the poor because the donor is only serving as the trustee of God, to whom all things belong. In fact, says al-Ghazzâlî, the donor should thank the recipient:

Actually, the giver should deem himself a beneficiary and the poverty-stricken, by virtue of accepting his gifts which are due to God, his benefactor. For in this lie man's justification and his salvation from Hell-fire. Had the poverty-stricken declined to accept his gifts, man would have remained under the obligation to give. It is his duty, therefore, to acknowledge that he is under an obligation to the poverty-stricken who has made his hand a substitute for that of God in receiving the dues [which man owes to] God. The Apostle of God said, "Verily, alms fall into the hand of God before they fall into the hand of the beggar who receives them."[16]

Al-Ghazzâlî turns next to those who are eligible to receive alms. He strongly urges donors to distribute alms in their own locality and to seek out the pious poor who devote themselves to God. Next in importance are recipients who are dedicated to scholarship and learning. When one Muslim was asked why he gave his alms exclusively to scholars, he replied:

I know of no rank, next to that of prophecy, which is better or superior to the rank of the learned men. If one of them were to bother himself about his needs he would not be able to devote his time to knowledge or concentrate on study. Therefore, it is better to give them all the leisure and help them to apply themselves exclusively to knowledge and learning.[17]

Regardless of the recipient, however, one who gives *zakât* should always regard himself or herself as an instrument of God, the true almsgiver. With such a humble attitude and proper intention, one who pays *zakât* will receive two rewards, says al-Ghazzâlî:

[First is] the immediate purification of himself from the quality of niggardliness and the establishment of the love of God in his heart.

. . . The second reward is the benefits which he reaps from the prayers and aspirations of the recipient, for the hearts of the righteous exert an immediate and ultimate influence.[18]

Like zakât, sadaqah, or voluntary alms, should be given in secret, if possible, to avoid spiritual pride and to save the recipient from embarrassment. Al-Ghazzâlî quotes several hadîth regarding the value of almsgiving for a healthy religious life. The prophet Muhammad, may God bless him and give him peace, said, "A single sadaqah closes seventy gates of evil." And again: "Alms given in secret turn away the wrath of God."[19] Voluntary alms can be given to atone for a variety of sins, and al-Ghazzâlî and other writers emphasized the power of voluntary alms to ward off earthly disasters and death, as well as to multiply rewards for their benefactor in the next life.[20]

This power of protection rendered by alms was important because medieval Muslims, like their Christian counterparts, believed in a purgatorial underworld in which each person must pay for past sins. The duration and severity of this purgation could be drastically reduced, however, through prayers and especially almsgiving, even given on behalf of the deceased. As a result, many wealthy Muslims, particularly those from the ruling class, established a waqf, or religious foundation, endowed—theoretically—in perpetuity. These endowments were to provide charity, often in the forms of food, water, or medical attention to those in need. Moreover, the waqfs were essential for establishing and supporting mosques, shrines, schools, and residences for the aged and homeless, travelers, ascetics, and mystics. One institution in particular, the khânqâh, was developed in the fourteenth century by the sultans of Mamluk Egypt to ensure their personal immortality. The royal khânqâhs were composed of a mosque and living quarters for as many as 400 Sufis who said daily prayers on behalf of the donor, whose tomb usually was included on the premises. The Mamluk khânqâhs, then, served as chantries, where the work of the pious and the needs of the poor were supported by the donor's philanthropy, while the donor's needs in the next world were met, at least in part, by the prayers of the living.[21]

Generally, such endowments consciously sought spiritual and, often, material gain for their benefactors, so they probably do not meet the criteria for altruism as "intentional action ultimately for the welfare of others." This situation is not as clearly the case, however, for other types of giving. For centuries Muslims have generously supported mosques, schools, hospitals, orphanages, and other charitable institutions represented today by a wide array of nongovernmental organizations, from the Red Crescent to the Young Men's Muslim Association. Though at times these organizations have enjoyed state sponsorship, most of these benevolent societies now are funded entirely by private contributions of time and money.[22] These many foundations and organizations usually have been founded to help and promote Muslim causes, although outside the Muslim world—in the United States, for example—Muslims are involved in and actively support non-Muslim social service programs as well.[23] Going even further is Farid Esack and the nascent movement for Muslim liberation theology, which asserts that the Qur'an's command to help the *al-mustadʿafûn fî al-ard*, "the oppressed of the earth," (e.g., 28:5) is a call to help all of the world's marginalized people, regardless of their faith:

> A theology of liberation, for me, is one that works toward freeing religion from social, political and religious structures and ideas based on uncritical obedience and the freedom of all people from the forms of injustice and exploitation including those of race, gender, class, and religion. Liberation theology tries to achieve its objective through a process that is participatory and liberatory.[24]

The extent to which such movements and organizations can be described as altruistic depends a great deal on the intentions of those who serve them and, of course, on interpretations of their behavior. Muslims who believe that they are giving alms to help the poor of Iraq or to relieve the poverty of Palestinians in support of their national cause may find themselves, in the United States and elsewhere, accused of sponsoring terrorism.[25] Clearly, what constitutes "intentional action ultimately for the welfare of others" may depend on who "the others" are, as well as what type of "intentional action" is being offered.

One action that I would not categorize as altruism in Islam is martyrdom. The Qur'an consistently speaks of martyrdom as a praiseworthy act that is sometimes necessary to defend Islam. The Qur'an frames this sacrifice of human life in economic terms, however: The martyr loans God his earthly life for one of immortality.

> Fight in the way of God and know that God hears and knows all. Who will give God a good loan, which He will double many times over? (2:244–45).

> So let them fight in the way of God, those who sell their life in this world below for the next [world]. Those who fight in the way of God, whether they are killed or victorious, We will give an awesome reward! (4:74).

Truly, God has bought from believers their lives and property in exchange for the garden [of paradise]. They fight in the way of God and kill and are killed. This is a promise incumbent upon Him (9:111).

Although an act of martyrdom might protect the Muslim community from its enemies, the Qur'an regards it essentially as a business transaction between the believer and God, who amply rewards the martyr for giving up his or her life.[26] In the same economic spirit, the Iranian Shîʿî thinker and theologian ʿAlî Sharîʿatî (d. 1977) discusses the "value" of martyrdom, which he compares to leaving a legacy behind for a sacred cause. Similarly, the Egyptian Hasan al-Bannâ' (d. 1949), founder of the Muslim Brotherhood and ideological ancestor to Usâmah bin Ladin, spoke of getting the most out of one's death:

[K]now, then, that death is inevitable, and that it can happen only once. If you suffer in the way of God, it will profit you in this world and bring you reward in the next.[27]

Altruism and the Sufi Tradition

If getting oneself killed is not a source of altruism in Islam, killing selfishness is. As in other religions, Islam has distinctive ascetic and mystical traditions in which individuals, and sometimes groups, have undertaken fasting, seclusion, and other forms of self-denial to discipline their body and mind as a way to deepen their religious life. Many Muslim ascetics and mystics have believed that it is essential to give up worldly rank, privilege, and possessions to concentrate solely on God. It is important to note here that this material and spiritual poverty is a religious ideal and form of piety and, as such, is not regarded by Muslims as a social disability.[28]

Nevertheless, giving away one's possessions to others may not always be altruistic, depending on one's motives. The great philosopher Ibn Sînâ (Avicenna, d. 1037) took a dim view of ascetics who were motivated by heavenly reward:

Asceticism without mystical insight is a kind of business transaction in which one sells the pleasure of this world below for the pleasure in the world to come. . . . The mystic, [on the other hand], desires only the first Truth for no reason other than Him, and he prefers nothing more than mystical insight and worship of Him.[29]

A similar view is ascribed to the woman mystic Râbi‘ah al-‘Adawîyah (d. 801):

> O my God, whatever share of this world You have given me, give it to Your enemies, and whatever share of the next world You have given me, give it to Your friends. You are enough for us.
>
> O Lord, if I worship You out of fear of hell, burn me in hell. If I worship You for hope of paradise, forbid it to me. And if I worship You for your own sake, do not deprive me of Your eternal beauty.[30]

To worship God sincerely and with undivided attention, one must give up love of all else—including the things of this world, future heavenly rewards, and, most of all, love of oneself. Muslim mystics have long known that there is a slippery slope between legitimate self-interest for one's health and welfare and selfishness, which may become a form of polytheism as one puts one's own desires before those of God. Thus, almsgiving and other religious acts may serve as the means for moral discipline and purification:

> One should be mindful of those whom God has entrusted to you and cease self-regard. It is related about ‘Abd Allâh ibn ‘Umar, may God have mercy upon him, that he would feed his slaves, but go hungry, that he would cloth them, but go without himself. He preferred them in their needs to his own, saying: "This is the easiest way for me to be vigilant against the evil of selfishness."[31]

Subduing selfishness and concupiscence (nafs) was requisite among Muslims who followed the traditions of al-futuwwah (chivalry) and al-tasawwuf (mysticism). Al-tasawwuf means following the Sufi way—the term sûfî being a probable derivative of sûf, or "wool," from which ascetic frocks were originally made.[32] Al-futuwwah is related to the Arabic word fatâ, which in pre-Islamic Arabic poetry meant a young hero or brave; hence its association with chivalry.[33] Discussing al-futuwwah with reference to the Qur'an, the respected Sufi authority al-Qushayrî (d. 1074) wrote:

> "The companions of the cave (18:13) are called fitya because they believed in their Lord without any intermediary." It is said, "The chivalrous man is he who smashes idols, for God Most High says, 'We heard a youth [fatan] denounce the idols. He is called Abraham' (21:60), and 'He smashed the idols to pieces' (21:58). The idol of every man is his own self [nafs]. So one who opposes his passions is truly chivalrous."[34]

The true hero, then, must rein in his selfish desires by putting the needs of others before his own:

[The Sufi] Maʿrûf al-Karkhî [d. 815], may God have mercy upon him, said: "One who claims to be chivalrous must have three qualities: fidelity without fear, generosity without thought of praise, the ability to give without being asked."[35]

Chivalry is when one does not hold himself or his actions in high regard, nor expects a return for his effort.[36]

One of the wise men has said: "He who possess these six traits has complete chivalry: he is thankful for the little he has, patient with great adversity, treating the ignorant with his kindness, educating the miser with his munificence; he does not do good for people's praise, nor does he stop doing good due to their blame."[37]

Chivalry is that one does not discriminate in service and giving.[38]

Chivalry is to show compassion to all of creation all of the time.[39]

Significantly, *îthâr*, "preferring others to oneself," became an important religious ideal and a central tenet of Muslim chivalry and mysticism, based in part on the Qur'anic verse praising the Medinan Muslims for assisting the Muslims from Mecca. This verse begins the following detailed analysis of *îthâr* by the noted Persian Sufi al-Hujwîrî (d. 1071):

God said: "And they prefer them to themselves, although they are indigent" (59:9). This verse was revealed concerning the poor men among the Companions in particular. The true nature of preference consists in maintaining the rights of the person with whom one associates, and in subordinating one's own interest to the interest of one's friend, and in taking trouble upon one's self for the sake of promoting his happiness, because preference is the rendering of help to others, and the putting into practice of that which God commanded to His Apostle: "Use indulgence and command what is just and turn away from the ignorant" (7:198).

Now, preference is of two kinds: first, in companionship, as has been mentioned; and second, in love. In preferring the claim of one's companion there is a sort of trouble and effort, but in preferring the claim of one's beloved there is nothing but pleasure and delight. It is well known that when Ghulâm al-Khalîl [d. 888] persecuted the Sufis, Nûrî [d. 907] and Raqqâm and Abû Hamza were

81

arrested and conveyed to the Caliph's palace. Ghulâm al-Khalîl urged the caliph to put them to death, saying that they were heretics (*zanâdiqa*), and the Caliph immediately gave orders for their execution. When the executioner approached Raqqâm, Nûrî rose and offered himself in Raqqâm's place with the utmost cheerfulness and submission. All the spectators were astounded. The executioner said: "O young man, the sword is not a thing that people desire to meet so eagerly as you have welcomed it; and your turn has not yet arrived." Nûrî answered: "Yes; my doctrine is founded on preference. Life is the most precious thing in the world; I wish to sacrifice for my brethren's sake the few moments that remain. In my opinion, one moment of this world is better than a thousand years of the next world, because this is the place of service (*khidmat*) and that is the place of proximity (*qurbat*), and proximity is gained by service."[40]

Nûrî's reference here to *qurbat* most likely refers to the advanced mystical station of "drawing near" or "proximity" to God.[41] In a popular Sufi tradition, God says:

One drawing near Me does so by carrying out what I have made obligatory for him, and the worshipper continues to draw near Me by willing acts of devotion until I love him. Then, when I love him, I am his hearing and sight, his tongue and hand, so by Me, he hears; by Me, he sees; by Me, he speaks; and by Me, he grasps.[42]

Thus, by willingly performing additional acts of devotion above and beyond religious obligations, the Muslim mystic not only helps others, he prepares himself for a mystical union with God. Then the mystic's will is subsumed in the will of God, who acts through His worshipper. This proximity to God is said to be the station of the great Muslim mystics and saints, who nevertheless continue to act selflessly on God's behalf in the world. Not surprisingly, then, one of their noteworthy characteristics is caring for others, and Muslim hagiographies are filled with stories of saintly generosity toward all of God's creation, especially the poor. [43] One story regarding the pious Egyptian scholar Abû ʿAbd Allâh Muhammad (d. 1130) should suffice:

Shaykh Abû ʿAbd Allâh Muhammad, who was actually quite wealthy, once decided to eat a good meal to help him recover from an illness. An expensive chicken worth two dînârs was accordingly prepared for him. Just as the feast was placed before Shaykh Abû ʿAbd Allâh there suddenly came a knock at his door. The shaykh ordered his servant to see who it was and what they wanted. The servant found a poor widow at the door seeking charity. Without hesitating, Shaykh Abû ᶜAbd Allâh gave his chicken dinner to the poor woman. She gratefully accepted the shaykh's gift and took the chicken home to her children. Just as her family was sitting down to eat the feast, however, there was a knock at the door. An agent of the owner of the house had come to collect their rent. The poor woman told the rent collector she had nothing to offer him except the wonderful chicken meal they were just about to eat. The chicken was so impressive that the rent collector was sure that his employer would be pleased by it, so he agreed to take the chicken in place of the rent. As it turned out, the rent collector worked for Shaykh Abû ᶜAbd Allâh, who owned the poor widow's house without knowing it. When the shaykh saw the chicken return to his table once again, he was surprised. He asked how his agent obtained it, and the man told the story of the poor widow who could not afford to pay her rent but offered this wonderful chicken in its place. Abû ᶜAbd Allâh promptly instructed the man to return immediately to the woman and inform her that the house she lived in henceforth belonged to her. The shaykh also made arrangements that each year the woman would receive what she and her children needed to live on.

The shaykh prepared once more to eat his chicken meal. Before he could begin, however, there came yet another knock at the door. This time it was a poor neighbor seeking assistance. Once again Abû ᶜAbd Allâh told his servant to take the chicken meal from the table and offer it to the needy man. The neighbor gratefully accepted the fine chicken, but on his way home he decided that he was not fit for such a great feast. Just then he passed by someone on the road, and the poor man asked if the passer-by would like to purchase the chicken. The stranger was pleased by the sight of the splendid chicken, and bought it for two dînârs. He then exclaimed to himself: "This is a meal fit for my father!" and he took the chicken home to Abû ᶜAbd Allâh. When the shaykh saw the chicken returning yet another time, he asked his son where it had come from. The son told him how he had bought the chicken from someone he passed on the way to his father's house. Abû ᶜAbd Allâh asked his son how much he had paid in exchange for the chicken and his son said two dînârs. The shaykh then instructed his son to go to their unfortunate neighbor and offer him another fifty dînârs.

Shaykh Abû ᶜAbd Allâh sat down to eat his meal a third time, but once again there came a knock at his door. Abû ᶜAbd Allâh instructed his servant to answer the door, but vowed that if it was another poor person seeking help, the shaykh would manumit his servant on the spot. She returned and confirmed that there was indeed another needy person at the door seeking the shaykh's help. Shaykh Abû ʿAbd Allâh, true to his word, asked his servant to take the chicken once again to the person at the door and afterwards she herself was free.[44]

Motives and Meaning

In evaluating the actions of Muslims, declaring an act to be one of altruism is no easy matter. As the Qur'an makes clear, the actor's intentions are critical in judging an action's moral quality and religious value, and al-Ghazzâlî and other Muslim scholars have carefully considered the ramifications and ambiguities involved in seemingly selfless good deeds toward others. The Sufi term *îthâr*, "preferring the other to the self," probably is the closet medieval Muslim equivalent to altruism—but how close an equivalent it is will depend, again, on definitions. The *îthâr* of Muslim chivalry and mysticism may fit Green's definition of altruism as "intentional action ultimately for the welfare of others that entails at least the possibility of either no benefit or a loss to the actor." This will be the case, however, only if we conceive of "benefit" and "loss" in material and social, not spiritual, terms. By contrast, *îthâr* would not meet the criteria of Jacob Neusner and Alan Avery-Peck's definition of altruism as "unselfish, unrewarded behavior that benefits others at a cost to oneself" (see chapter 2 in this volume). In fact, given such a restrictive definition, there can be no altruism whatsoever in Islam because God has promised in the Qur'an to reward every good deed done by any person:

> On [the Judgment] Day, people will come forward separately to be shown their deeds, and, so, whoever did an atom's weight of good will see it (99:6–7).

> [On the Judgment Day,] God will not wrong anyone by even an atom's weight. As for good deeds, God will double them, and He will give an awesome reward (4:40).

If the possibility of heavenly and/or spiritual reward for an action disallows it from being considered altruistic, it is difficult to see how altruism could be "a useful and appropriate category for the academic study of religion" (see Introduction to this volume). In this case, altruism would appear to be a secular, not religious, category.

84

A second and equally thorny problem is the interpretation of actions. A Muslim woman in England gives a donation to Hamas aimed ultimately for the welfare of the Palestinians. Her donation entails a loss to her bank account, with no direct benefit to her. The money is then used to finance an act of violence. Was the woman's act altruistic? Some Muslims will think so, but other Muslims and non-Muslims will disagree. Here I return to the incisive observation by David Konstan that "altruism is not, in the first instance, a question about behavior but about the interpretation of behavior"[45]—and, one might add, politics. Nevertheless, it is hard to question the good intentions of the pious shaykh Abû ʿAbd Allâh Muhammad and his help to those in need. We can only hope that the sumptuous meal found its way back one last time to the generous old man—who, by the end of the story, must have been famished even for cold chicken.

Notes

1. Labîd, *Dîwân Labîd* (Beirut: Dār Sādir, n.d.), 178–80. Translated by Michael Sell in *Desert Tracings* (Middletown, Conn.: Wesleyan University Press, 1989), 43–44.
2. For example, Sells, *Desert Tracings*, 21.
3. ʿAntarah, *Sharh Dîwân ʿAntarah* (Beirut: Dār al-Kutub al-ʿIlmīyah, 1985), 122–23; translation by Sells, *Desert Tracings*, 52.
4. Al-Bukhârî, *Sahîh al-Bukhârî* (Medina: Dār al-Fikr, n.d.), 1:19 (Bk 2, chap. 6, #11). Also see Valerie J. Hoffman, "Hospitality and Courtesy," in *Encyclopaedia of the Qur'ân* (hereafter *EQ*) (Leiden, The Netherlands: E. J. Brill, 2001), vol. 2, 449–54.
5. Concerning both terms, including their possible relation to Hebrew equivalents, see T. H. Weir and A. Zysow, "sadaqah," in *Encyclopaedia of Islam*, 2nd ed. (hereafter *EI2*) (Leiden, The Netherlands: E. J. Brill, 1960–), vol. 8, 708–16, and A. Zysow, "zakât," in *EI2*, vol. 11, 406–22.
6. Azim Nanji, "Almsgiving," in *EQ*, vol. 1, 64.
7. See Tariq Ramadan, *Western Muslims and the Future of Islam* (Oxford: Oxford University Press, 2004), 88–89.
8. All translations of the Qur'an are my own, unless noted otherwise.
9. *Cf.* al-Baydâwî, *Anwâr al-Tanzîl* (Beirut: Dār al-Jīl, 1992), 726, and *Mashaf al-Sharûq* (Cairo: Dār al-Sharūq, 1987), 627.
10. E.g., al-Bukhârî, *Sahîh al-Bukhârî*, book 24: *Zakât*.
11. E.g., Mâlik ibn Anas, *Al-Muwatta*, trans A. A. Bewley (London: Kegan Paul International, 1989), 93–110, 419–21.
12. *EI2*, vol. 11, 408–18.
13. Al-Ghazzâlî, *The Mysteries of Almsgiving*, trans. Nabih Amin Faris (Beirut: American University of Beirut, 1966).
14. Ibid., 25.
15. Ibid., 28–29.
16. Ibid., 36.

17. Ibid., 47. No doubt most college and university professors would agree with this enlightened argument.
18. Ibid., 52.
19. Ibid., 72.
20. Ibid., 71–89, and *EI2*, vol. 8, 710–12.
21. Th. Emil Homerin, "Saving Muslim Souls: The Khânqâh and the Sufi Duty in Mamluk Lands," *Mamlûk Studies Review* 3 (1999): 59–83. Also see Adam Sabra, *Poverty and Charity in Medieval Islam: Mamluk Egypt, 1250–1517* (Cambridge: Cambridge University Press, 2000).
22. See Jonathan Benthall, "Financial Worship: The Quranic Injunction to Almsgiving," *Journal of the Royal Anthropological Institute* 5, no. 1 (March 1999): 27–42; idem, "Organized Charity in the Arab-Islamic World: A View from the NGOs," in *Interpreting Islam*, ed. Hastings Donnan (London: Sage, 2002), 150–66; and Morroe Berger, *Islam in Egypt Today* (Cambridge: Cambridge University Press, 1970).
23. Zogby International, *American Muslim Poll November/December 2001*, available at http://www.projectmaps.com/PMReport.htm, table 4 and discussion.
24. Farid Esack, *Qur'ân, Liberation and Pluralism* (Oxford: Oneworld, 1997), 83, 98–103.
25. E.g., "U.S. Indicts Muslim Charity," *Rochester Democrat and Chronicle*, 28 July 2004, 3A.
26. See E. Kohlberg, "shahîd," in *EI2*, vol. 9, 203–7.
27. See Daniel Brown, "Martyrdom in Sunni Revivalist Thought," in *Sacrificing the Self: Perspectives on Martyrdom and Religion*, ed. Margaret Cormack (Oxford: Oxford University Press, 2002), 107–17, and M. Abedi and G. Legenhausen, eds., *Jihâd and Shahâdat: Struggle and Martyrdom in Islam* (Houston: Institute for Research and Islamic Studies, 1986).
28. Sabra, *Poverty and Charity in Medieval Islam*, 8–35.
29. Ibn Sînâ, *al-Ishârât wa-l-Tanbîhât* (Leiden, The Netherlands: E. J. Brill, 1891), 11, 13.
30. Translated by Paul Losensky in *Early Islamic Mysticism*, ed. Michael Sells (New York: Paulist Press, 1996), 169.
31. Al-Sulamî, *al-Futuwwah*, ed. Ihsân Dhunûn Thâmirî and Muhammad ʿAbd Allâh al-Qadhât (ʿAmmân: Dār al-Rāzī, 2002), 73; my translation. For a complete translation see Tosun Bayrak al-Jerrahi, *The Way of Chivalry* (Rochester, Vt.: Inner Traditions International, 1991).
32. For Sufism, see Annemarie Schimmel, *Mystical Dimensions of Islam* (Chapel Hill: University of North Carolina Press, 1975).
33. See Cl. Cahen, "Futuwwa," in *EI2*, vol. 2, 961–65, and Michael Chodkiewicz and al-Jerrahi, "Introduction," in al-Jerrahi, *The Way of Chivalry*, 6–28.
34. Al-Qushayrî, *The Principles of Sufism*, translated by B. R. Von Schlegell (Berkeley, Calif.: Mizan Press, 1992), 215.
35. Al-Sulamî, *al-Futuwwah*, 88.
36. Ibid., 17.

37. Ibid., 70.

38. Ibid., 86.

39. Ibid., 42.

40. Al-Hujwîrî, *Kashf al-Mahjûb*, translated by R. A. Nicholson (Karachi, Pakistan: Darul-Ishaat, 1990), 190–95, esp. 190–91. Also see al-Sulamî, *al-Futuwwah*, 50, and ʿUmar al-Suhrawardî, *ʿAwârif al-Maʿârif* (Cairo: Maktabat al-Qāhirah, 1973), 226–31.

41. Al-Hujwîrî, *Kashf al-Mahjûb*, 249.

42. For this *al-hadîth al-qudsî*, or "Divine Saying," see William A. Graham, *Divine Word and Prophetic Word in Islam* (The Hague: Mouton, 1977), 173–74.

43. See Christopher Taylor, *In the Vicinity of the Righteous* (Leiden, The Netherlands: E. J. Brill, 1999), esp. 99–106, and Josef W. Meri, *The Cult of the Saints Among the Muslims and Jews in Medieval Syria* (Oxford: Oxford University Press, 2002).

44. Ibn al-Zayyât, *al-Kawâkib al-Sayyârah* (Baghdad: Maktabat al-Muthannā, n.d.), 164–65, as recounted in Taylor, *In the Vicinity of the Righteous*, 104–6 (with minor variations).

45. David Konstan, "Altruism," *Transactions of the American Philological Association* 130 (2000): 1–17, esp. 2; also cited in Green, "Altruism and the Study of Religion" (introduction to this volume), n. 4.

Chapter 5

Altruism in Classical Buddhism

Todd Lewis

> O monks, wander! We will go forward for the benefit of many
> people . . . out of compassion for the world, for the good, wel-
> fare, and happiness of gods and humans.
>
> —*Catusparishad Sūtra*[1]

> Someone may build a precious reliquary, as high as the world;
> It is said that training others to generate
> The altruistic intention is more excellent.
>
> —Aryadeva[2]

In considering the case of Buddhism and the phenomenon of altruism, it is noteworthy that the sentiments expressed in the first quotation above were spoken just as the Buddha Shākyamuni began his
teaching, establishing the world's initial missionary faith. This recurring
trope from the earliest canonical accounts expresses the Buddha's ethos
for his religious movement and his intentions for sharing his Dharma
("teachings") with the world. He often instructs his converts to spread
his teachings with this same altruistic exhortation; later scholars, such as
the monk Aryadeva (170–260 CE), also quoted above, have echoed the
singular importance of compassion in this religion. Such prominent expressions of social engagement at the starting point of this great tradition may surprise a contemporary reader, having perhaps encountered
modern treatments of Buddhism that focus on elite philosophy and individualistic soteriological practices.

"Altruism" in Cross-Cultural Definition

From the outset, we must define the concept of altruism in the textual
tradition. There is a rich vocabulary for expressing modes of human caring for others in Buddhism: *karunā*, "compassion"; *maitrī* (Pali: *mettā*),[3]
"loving kindness"; *dāna*, "charity." In this context, we find occasional use
of the canonical Sanskrit term *arthacaryā* (P. *attha-cariya*), which closely
matches the English term "altruism." As used in Buddhist texts composed
in early India, *arthacaryā* refers to conduct beneficial to others, almost
always with a religious motivation.[4] Donors, ritual sponsors, and reli-

gious teachers act in ways that are *arthacaryā*. In later Buddhist documents, *arthacaryā* actions are listed as one of four means of drawing people into the religious life. In trying to work on comparisons between traditions, having an approximate emic or indigenous term in the canonical language religions is a promising discovery.[5]

So defined, living altruistically—benefiting religious persons, institutions, and other beings in basic needs—has been a central characteristic of Buddhism from the earliest records: in the history of the monastics, as recorded in ancient inscriptions across India by donors, in the records of the expansion of monasticism across Asia and into countries such as Burma, where today householders put out on their home porches pitchers of clean drinking water for passersby. Far from being a residual category, altruism is integral and foundational to all Buddhist traditions.

In this chapter I explore the origins of Buddhist altruism through an examination of its metaphysical foundations, surveying texts and historical precedent from the Theravāda and Mahāyāna traditions; I also contextualize its role in the classical development of Buddhism and trace its evolution in East Asia.

Historical Background

The sixth century BCE in northern India was a time of spiritual seeking unparalleled in the history of religions. Among the many individual teachers then regarded as having achieved *nirvāna*—an exalted state of salvation—was one who called himself a "Buddha": one "awakened" by having seen reality clearly and transformatively. Feeling compassion for beings who suffered on the wheel of life and death, he founded the world's first missionary religion, created a community of renunciate monks and nuns (the *sangha*), and shared his teachings with everyone who was interested in hearing them.

Born a prince, Gautama renounced his own line to a royal throne; his early disciples, almost all ascetics, were taught to cultivate detachment from the householder's lifestyle and so entanglements in worldly matters. For the student interested in altruism, therefore, a discussion of the Buddhist understanding of this phenomenon might seem to be a forced or barren pursuit. Such an interpretation, however, would lack a fundamental sociohistorical understanding and ignore important canonical and popular texts. As Buddhism gained ever-wider popularity beyond the ascetics and spread out of its region of origin, it developed in breadth and scope: soon after the Buddha's death, most Buddhist disciples were householders (more than 95 percent in most societies), and few—even among the monastics—were aloof from social concerns.

Although Buddhism's successful trans-Asian pilgrimage originates with an inspiring vision of conquering human suffering and bondage in the cosmos, its 2,500 years of popular support also was a result of the fact that it helped householders secure worldly prosperity and participate in a moral civilization. Buddhism was so successful in this arena that it found acceptance in almost every type of human society: from nomadic communities to urbanized polities, from the tropics to the vast grasslands of northern Asia, from the Arabian Sea to the Pacific Ocean. Buddhism's distinctive doctrinal and institutional flexibility contributed to its success. This flexibility is based in part on the core Buddhist belief that individuals and societies are different by virtue of their different backgrounds—that is, persons have different past lives and hence inherit the past *karma* of unique and widely varying personalities, moral natures, and habits. Buddhism's characteristic acceptance of pluralism in social life is also a result of the tradition's vast collection of religious literature with no single text, canon, or institution holding universal authority. In constructing a "Buddhist view of altruism," then, it is important to note that expressions of Buddhist ethical thought and practices have varied regionally and that the treatment in this chapter necessarily entails broad generalizations. My exploration begins with the universally held doctrine of *karma*.

Metaphysical Reality:
The Doctrine of Karma and Its Implications

Unlike the western monotheisms, for which life and destiny is contained within a "one time around" reality, the Hindu-Buddhist worldview understands life as an ongoing succession of incarnations—a "wheel of life" (*samsāra*) where individual beings undergo rebirth and redeath, relentlessly suffering according to their deeds. This notion of *samsāra* includes the view that what a human does—in Buddhist reckoning, by one's body, speech, and mind—creates a causal force in the universe, karma, through which every action elicits a just moral retributive reaction in the future. Doing a good deed leads inevitably to reward; doing evil begets inevitable proportionate punishment. All living beings on earth therefore reside in a *karmabhūmi* ("realm of karma")—an interactive, interrelated universe that is subject to this natural moral law.

Several ideas about karma are pivotal to understanding Buddhist altruism. First, this doctrine is not fatalistic because one is continually, every moment, creating new *punya* ("merit") or *pāp* ("demerit") to change the ongoing calculus of karmic destiny. Indeed, Buddhist philosophy emphasizes that certain acts engender strong karma effects, setting off mechanistic causal connections between past and future; the totality of a person's karma, like all phenomena, changes every instant.

Furthermore, the Buddhist understanding of causality is that not all contingencies in life are karma-dependent. In fact, events that affect individuals are more likely than not to have been caused by forces other than karma. For the future, however, the logic of the karma doctrine has motivated Buddhists everywhere to manage their fate: avoiding doing evil and making good karma. Here is the foundation for and, indeed, the necessity for individuals to do altruistic deeds.

Buddhist doctrine never held that poverty was a noble state for householders.[6] Even monks and nuns benefited from having enough wealth to make meritorious donations. The texts emphasize that accumulating wealth is the fruition of good past karma, and giving away one's wealth (in altruistic practices) to earn merit is the best expenditure. Every Buddhist householder knows that one's material possessions cannot be taken beyond this life—but merit as good karma can be. As one early text states:

> The beings, O Brahmin, have their karma as their own, they have their heritage from the karma, the karma determines their birth, the karma is their friend and ultimate refuge, and it is the karma that divides them, relegating them either to an inferior or to a superior state of existence.[7]

This principle was incorporated into early canonical definitions of the good Buddhist life for householders. On several occasions the Buddha instructed householders to seek the "Four Conditions" and do the "Four Good Deeds":[8]

Four Conditions (to seek):	Four Good Deeds (to use wealth for):
Wealth achieved by lawful means	Make family, friends happy
Good renown in society	Ensure security against worldly dangers
Long life	Make offerings to family, friends, gods, ghosts
Birth in heaven	Support worthy religious people

These doctrinal guidelines have been as influential for the laity as the "Four Noble Truths" were for philosophers. They allow the historian to imagine early householders being "good Buddhists" by fully engaging in their social milieu: fostering family ties; cultivating the ethos of "energetic striving" for economic success; encouraging altruistic feeding of hungry ghosts and local gods; applauding rightful seeking after worldly happiness and security; supporting family, friends, and religious seekers. (I examine the record of actual Buddhist practices in a subsequent section of this chapter.)

Doctrines of Self, Impermanence,
Process, and Interdependency

Later philosopher-monks argued that altruism was a logical extension of the Buddha's metaphysical teachings. A core and universal Buddhist doctrine asserts that reality has three basic characteristics: impermanence, no-soul, and suffering. The first insists that reality is a process of ceaseless change and is not reducible to permanent things. The second concept, *anātman* ("no-*ātman*" or "non-self"), expresses the Buddha's rejection of any notion of an essential, unchanging interior entity at "the center" of a person. As a result, these philosopher-monks analyzed the human "being" as the continuously changing, interdependent relationship among five components (*skandhas*).[9] The spiritual purpose of breaking down any expectation of changeless phenomena around us or of an unchanging locus of personal individuality is to demonstrate that there is never "any thing" to be attached to or around which to organize one's primordial existential desires or attachments.[10]

Highlighting the universality of suffering, the third characteristic of reality, provides Buddhists with an ethical focus: Compassion is the proper human response to moral living—an ethos that underlies all Buddhist practices of altruism. The early texts often cite suffering from "illness, old age, death, and rebirth" as the baseline human reality. The benefits to the practitioner of altruistic service also are highlighted, as in an early biography of the Buddha, the *Buddhacarita*:

> Those who in charity renounce their wealth
> Cleanse away avarice and attachment.
> Giving in compassion and respect,
> They drive away envy, hatred, and pride.[11]

The teachings of impermanence and suffering point to two additional basic facts of life in the Buddhist worldview: The universe is a vast web of connections (conditioned by karma and other causalities), and beings are linked and sustain their lives through multiple interdependencies. For millennia Buddhist teachers have instructed humans to regard all beings in their midst as having once been, in former lives, their own beloved kin: mothers, fathers, children. Accordingly, one sees that one's present life has been shaped by the past, that current actions inevitably affect one's destiny, and that all others—both now and in the future—are linked inescapably by the contingencies of karmic fruition.

Doctrinal Voices from Monastic Libraries:
Altruism in Buddhist Texts

Like all world religions, Buddhism is multivocalic and has generated vast written discourse, with shelvesful of texts regarded as authoritative. Buddhist texts also speak with different voices[12] as they range over common spiritual issues; given the naturally assumed range of human spiritual capacities resulting from different karma, these texts must always be read according to the intended audience. Indeed, the most common mistake in using Buddhist texts, from Max Weber until the present, has been to attempt to apply ideas, practices, and behavioral norms composed for the monastic elite (renunciants who constitute at most 5 percent of the Buddhist community) to a society centered on the householder majority. The monastic elite recorded, redacted, composed, and copied all Buddhist texts, so their male, ascetic voice is overwhelmingly that of the virtuosi renunciants. As a result, the texts provide relatively few spaces where the Buddhist householder's life circumstances or worldview are even discussed. Because altruism is construed as a social virtue and therefore is largely in this domain, treatments of it, not unexpectedly, are scattered.

As a result, caution is required in examining the selection of texts I cite in this essay. We know that ideas on altruism definitely were articulated by the Buddha and from the time of the early Buddhist writers onward; what we cannot specify well, however, is how many of these teachings made it "out of the stacks" and into Buddhist cultures and societies at different places and times over the past two millennia. Despite the fact that we know little about the culture and contexts of texts in the history of Buddhism, it is worthwhile to sample ideas on altruism from the earliest textual sources onward. Finally, there are many historical problems in dividing textual sources according to Theravāda and Mahāyāna traditions as I do here; for the purposes of this essay, however, painting with a broad brush can render an apt portrait of the diversities within Buddhism.

Altruism in Theravāda Sources and Tradition[13]

I have cited textual expressions drawn from the Theravādin school's Pali Canon to frame the overall formative Buddhist understanding of altruism. In texts, inscriptions, and meditation practices, altruism constitutes a common theme.

At monasteries and shrines across ancient India, Theravādin adherents left a record of their patronage gifts by having donor inscriptions made on cut stone and metal plates. The majority of these inscriptions by monks, nuns, and householders contain a common ending phrase that records an altruistic motivation for their gift. To cite one example from fourth-century Mathura:

> On this date an image of the Blessed One Shākyamuni was set up by the monk Buddhavarman for the worship of all Buddhas. Through this religious gift may his preceptor attain nirvāna, (may it also be) for the cessation of all suffering of his parents . . . (and) for the welfare and happiness of all beings.[14]

Early Pali texts argue that compassion for all beings should be as central to humanity's moral compass as the organic ties to one's own kin. As stated in the *Samyutta Nikāya*:[15]

> Thus as a mother with her life
> Will guard her son, her only child,
> Let him extend unboundedly
> His heart to every living being.
> And so with loving-kindness for all the world
> Let him extend unboundedly
> His heart, above, below, around,
> Unchecked, with no ill will or hate.

The later Buddhist poet Ksemendra goes so far as to argue that compassion is natural and innate in all creatures.[16]

Among the many early meditative traditions inherited by all Buddhist schools was cultivation of the *Catur Brahmavihāras* ("Abiding in the Four Sublime States"): benevolence, compassion, joy, and equanimity. In the Theravāda practice, meditators begin by developing the sublime state mentally and then extending it outward, in succession, to a neutral person, a friend, an enemy, and finally toward all sentient beings. The first two *brahmavihāras* are clearly designed to train the individual to foster an altruistic mindset.

Many Theravāda texts argue strongly that compassion should be expressed by improving the world. This compassion is not left to be a general exhortation, however, but can be directed toward special recipients for the best results. (I return to the early merit hierarchy below.) The most-praised altruistic donation is best directed to aiding religious seekers and doing so, most emphatically, for the maximum merit it earns. As another Pali passage urges:

> Let givers pleasant hermitages make,
> Therein let them for scholars find a home;
> And make in arid jungle water-tanks,

And where 'tis rough to go, clear passages.
Let them with candid trusting heart bestow
Food and water and dried meats and gear
And lodging on the men of upright mind. . .
Yea, wise, he scatters gladly what he hath
And bidding: Give ye! Give ye! Doth he cry.
And thus he thunders, raining like the god,
His generous gifts upon the giver's self
As rich and copious showers of merit fall.[17]

Thus, the Theravādin texts hold that the "good life" for a householder should be balanced between the inner life and social action. The Buddhist lay disciple should deepen his or her religious faith and spiritual understanding but balance this spiritual practice by the practices of moral living and altruistic giving. This idea is clearly expressed in the *Vyagghapajja Sutta*,[18] again emphasizing the personal benefits derived from charity:

The four conduce to a householder's weal and happiness in his future life. Which four? The accomplishment of faith, the accomplishment of virtue, the accomplishment of charity, and the accomplishment of insight. . . . What is the accomplishment of charity? Herein a householder feels at peace with heart free from the stain of avarice, devoted to charity, open-handed, delighting in generosity, attending to the needy, delighting in the distribution of alms.
Energetic and heedful in tasks
Wisely administering wealth
One lives a balanced life,
Protecting what has been amassed.

Altruism in Mahāyāna Sources and Tradition

On the popular level, there are strong and important continuities between the two great streams of Buddhist history in terms of karma and other core doctrines, merit-making, and monastic tradition. Until the last centuries of Indian Buddhism Mahāyāna exponents were a small minority expounding an alternative doctrinal system, but this tradition completely dominated the central Asian, east Asian, and Himalayan diasporas of the faith. These historical facts, along with the new contexts to which the tradition had to adapt in East Asia (Confucianism, imperial states, a faith originating among foreigners and first expounded by "barbarian" missionaries), explain why common early doctrines and practices developed as they did. Focusing on altruism also highlights how the bodhisattva doctrine of Mahāyāna philosophers was an innovative interpretation of the ideal Buddhist life.

The Mahāyāna tradition shows strong continuities with the early canons in seeing that aiding others also entails spiritual benefit to the donor. This boon is visible not only in the inevitable karmic benefit but also in the strengthening of the individual's habit of detachment. This perspective is concisely stated in the only Indic Buddhist play, *Lokānandanātaka* ("Joy for the World") by Chandragomin (c. 440 CE)[19]:

> May you by your virtues fulfill
> The most cherished desires
> Of all sentient beings!
> May you in the desert of suffering
> Become the sea of sustenance;
> A ladder on which to ascend
> The mountain of salvation.

Because altruism is a "ladder to nirvāna," what is striking in the Mahāyāna texts is how they go into very exacting detail to specify its applications. Mindful of how an individual's wealth and personal capacities could vary and hence condition altruistic work, several texts depict the Buddha discussing how the good Buddhist should bestow charity. The *Upāsakashīla-Sūtra*[20] is a good example, discussing how an individual can set out to disseminate the greatest benefit when trying to help others:

> Good Son, there are three fundamentals to all kinds of giving: (1) giving compassionately to the poor, (2) giving to foes without seeking rewards, and (3) giving joyfully and respectfully to the virtuous. . . . If one can teach others before giving them material things, one is called a great giver. . . . if a wise person is wealthy, he should give like that. If he is not wealthy, he should teach other wealthy people to practice giving. . . . If he is poor and has no nothing to give, he should recite curative mantras, give inexpensive medicines to the needy, sincerely take care of the ill for recuperation, and exhort the rich to provide medicines; if he knows medical remedies . . . he should provide treatment according to the diagnosis. . . .
> Good son, when a wise person seeks enlightenment, if he is wealthy, he should learn medicine. He should build hospitals and provide needed food and medicine for the sick. If there are holes in the road he should repair them and broaden it to clean thorns,

dung, and other filth from it. At dangerous places, he provides needed boards, ladders, or ropes. In the wilderness, he builds wells, plants fruit trees, and builds water channels. In places where there are no trees, he erects posts and builds animal sheds. He builds guest houses and supplies necessities such as wash basins, lamps, beds, and bedding. . . . He builds bridges over rivers and provides rafts. . . . He personally helps the old, the young, and the weak to cross. . . . He does all these things himself and teaches others to do likewise.

The most striking doctrinal difference represented by the Mahāyāna exponents is their claim that all humans should aspire to become Buddhas and so live as bodhisattvas, "future Buddhas," vowing to undergo many lifetimes to perfect themselves. This ideal was worked out in greater specificity over the centuries. Exact steps in developing the bodhisattva's eventual enlightenment were regarded as balancing the person's interior spiritual understanding, *prajñā* (P. *paññā*, "insight, gnosis"), with the practice of acting selflessly with *upāya* ("skillful means") to serve all creation compassionately.

Mahāyāna exponents systematized their bodhisattva doctrine by specifying the seven (or ten) qualities necessary for reaching buddhahood, the *pāramitās*, and stages one reaches on that many-lifetime path, *bhūmis*.[21] What is notable for this comparative consideration of altruism is that in the latter formulations of bodhisattva doctrine, very advanced bodhisattvas who could enter *nirvāna* can choose to take further rebirths in *samsāra* for no other goal than assisting others. They do so because they have infinite merit to share and great powers to use in rescuing others. Spiritually perfected and beyond merit accumulation, such bodhisattvas are like a Buddha in performing fully selfless altruistic actions.[22]

Mahāyāna understanding of the full career of the bodhisattva is most fully and eloquently expressed in the *Bodhicaryāvatāra*, the classic treatise by the monk Shāntideva (685–763 CE)—one of the tradition's greatest scholars. The most popular treatise on the Mahāyāna path to enlightenment, this text is centered on an analysis of the human condition and the twin themes of serving the world while cultivating spiritual clarity and ultimately release from *samsāra*. Shāntideva shows in compelling language how these dual focal points are not artificially tied but that through compassionate altruism the dualism of self and world is seen as an empty set, an illusion. This text famously declares[23]:

May I allay the suffering of every living being.
I am medicine for the sick.

May I be both doctor and their nurse, until the sickness does not
  recur,
May I avert the pain of hunger and thirst with showers of food and
  drink...
May I be an inexhaustible treasure for impoverished beings.
May I wait upon them with various forms of offerings...
May I be a light for those in need of light.
May I be a bed for those in need of rest.
May I be a servant for those in need of service, for all embodied
  beings.

Other Mahāyāna texts show a striking missionary voice, regarding
altruism as a skillful tool in spreading the faith. The *Mahāvyupatti Sūtra*
lists four chief means at the disposal of a bodhisattva to that end: charity
(*dāna*); persuasiveness (*priyavāditā*); altruism (*arthacaryā*); and recep-
tivity toward all beings (*samānārthatā*).[24]
Even the various "pure land" sects that arose in the Mahāyāna fold
lauded altruistic acts as those that could win the grace of celestial
bodhisattvas and Buddhas. This perspective is stated especially emphatically in the *Mahānirvāna Sūtra:*[25]

Cause no affliction to living beings
Let your thoughts always be of compassion...
Dig good wells beside roads in the desert,
Plant and cultivate orchards of fruit trees,
Always give nourishment to beggars...
If you can give charity to the sick,
Even if it is just a piece of fruit
And giving them a pleasant, cheering glance,
Then you will be reborn in Akshobhya's Pure Land.

Another voice in later Mahāyāna discourse exalts the ideal of compassion and altruistic service. Perhaps because of the belief in the Buddha's
predictions that humanity would suffer inevitable decline in its spiritual
capacity,[26] these later treatises highlight the value of the singular pursuit of
altruism. Whatever else one can do successfully in one's own "interior"
religious practice, at the very least one can serve and be transformed by
dedication to altruism. This view is expressed clearly in the widely circulated treatise *Klong-chen rab-'byams-pa* by the gifted Tibetan monk
Longchenpa (1308–1354 CE):

Even if the ethical impulse is not distinctly operative,
Compassion's wholesome stream is rising ever higher...

98

All you do by way of body and speech will be meaningful
And you become a veritable shrine in all the worlds with all their
　gods . . .
The root or seed of all and everything is compassion.
Even in this world of fictitious being it yields many fruits of
　happiness . . .
Fearless in the world and acting for the sake of living beings,
By always being sympathetic and concerned with their welfare
only, man's world has become meaningful.[27]

Another, more contemporary, monk, the Tibetan Patrul Rimpoche
(1808–1887), also argues for the priority of compassion in his treatise *Words
of My Perfect Teacher*:

In everything you do, simply work at developing love and compassion until they become a fundamental part of you. That will serve
the purpose, even if you do not practice the more outward and
conspicuous forms of Dharma such as prayers, virtuous activities
and altruistic works. As the *Sūtra that Perfectly Encapsulates the
Dharma* states, "Let those who desire Buddhahood not train in
many Teachings but only one. Which one? Great Compassion.
Those with great compassion possess all the Buddha's teaching as
if it were in the palm of the hand."[28]

The Mahāyāna tradition's enculturation of altruism also is evident
in its distinctive meditation traditions. Especially in fasting and visualization practices, the individual "takes refuge" in the Buddha/Dharma/
Sangha as well as in the bodhisattvas, then vows to seek their perfections
(*pāramitās*). Many of these meditation practices conclude with dedica-
tory pronouncements that highlight the Mahāyāna doctrine that seeking
personal enlightenment entails serving others and that altruistic actions
are central to the final realization of the advanced spiritual seeker. As one
ritual dedicated to Avalokiteshvara concludes, the meditator repeats:

Through this virtue may I quickly become
A greatly compassionate one
And lead each and every being,
None excepted, to his pure land.[29]

Finally, it also is common for the celestial bodhisattvas in Mahāyāna
meditations to be regarded as the "embodiments of compassion."[30] This
practice entails concentrated effort that involves visualizing the celestial
bodhisattvas in the mind's eye, repeating their *mantras*, and seeking

total existential identification with them; the effect on the practitioner is regarded as transformative. This practice yields a compassion-filled mindset, worldly assistance, and merit—all fostering the quest for enlightenment.[31] Although it is unclear how far beyond the monastic preaching halls the sophisticated doctrines of Mahāyāna Buddhism reached, what is certain is that everywhere this school was established, householders were drawn to the deity called Avalokiteshvara,[32] who embodies compassion—the celestial bodhisattva universally revered for acting on his altruistic vow to aid all who call upon him for worldly needs or spiritual aid.

The Classical Buddhist Ideal: Civilization as Altruistic Endeavor

Built on and nurtured by these doctrinal ideas, a conception of Buddhist civilization developed from the circumstances of its Indic genesis. The tradition was sustained by exchanges between householders and renunciants—the monks and nuns whose advanced ascetic lifestyle entailed abandonment of most worldly comforts. Buddhist monasticism arose to provide refuge and support for renunciants seeking enlightenment, but the tradition survived by building multifaceted relationships with lay followers who provided for the monks' and nuns' subsistence (see diagram).

↗ progeny ↘

↗ material support ↘

HOUSEHOLDERS   *SANGHA*

↖ merit ↙

↖ dharma ↙

Buddhists articulated the foundations for the ideal society, one with spiritual and moral dimensions. Monks and nuns served the world through their example of renunciation and meditation, by performing rituals, and by providing other services. They become a "field of merit" that allows people who make donations to them to earn the good karma required for a better life both in the present and in future incarnations. In this way, Buddhist seekers and saints fulfilled the Buddha's injunction to "wander forth for the welfare and the weal of the many, out of compassion for the world."

Thus, Buddhism developed a broad vision for an integrated spiritual community and a clear sense of proper social practice. The texts speak of the devout layman's and monks' duty to help others grow in faith, morality, knowledge, and charity. This "imagined community" enabling spiritual pursuits has depended on a constant altruistic effort by householders: By giving up a portion of their household's material wealth to sustain Buddhist monastics and their institutions, they support exemplary individuals in their midst seeking refuge to realize *nirvāna*. Powered by altruistic giving, the agency of merit can benefit all individuals in society by positively affecting their path through *samsāra*.

The Early Buddhist Hierarchy of Altruism

The conceptions of karma and merit-making shaped a distinctly Buddhist disposition toward altruism. Spiritually advanced beings were thought to possess greater increments of good karma, with humans recognized as the sole beings in the universe capable of reaching *nirvāna*. Based on this conception, the early tradition held that the higher the spiritual status of the recipient of a gift (food, clothing, shelter), the greater the return in merit to the giver. One influential listing of the resulting hierarchy from the Theravāda tradition summarizes this doctrine:

Hierarchy of Merit Recipients
Buddha
Pacceka Buddha
Arhat
One on the way to Arahatship
One Never to be reborn
A Once-returner on earth
One who has Entered the Stream
Refuge Taker on the way to the Stream-enterer
An outsider aloof from sensuality
Ordinary but virtuous man
Ordinary nonvirtuous man
Animals

Buddhists across Asia acted on the basis of the logic of this scheme. Householders have sought out individuals regarded as enlightened—or nearly so—both to experience the presence of a spiritual person as well as to make the most rewarded meritorious material gifts to them. Furthermore, one can see that there is no inherent reason—for merit-making purposes—why Buddhists would feel compelled to prioritize the eradication of poverty. Nonetheless, humans were still thought to be deserving of altruism, as the record of Buddhist charities established over the millennia makes clear.

Finally, it is noteworthy that animals and spirits have standing in the merit hierarchy. The record of Buddhists incorporating offerings to hungry ghosts in daily life is clear from the earliest days until the present. Small food items are taken from the plates and set out by monks near the monastic walls and by householders outside the front door. Buddhists also regard their rituals for departed spirits as an important altruistic practice. In the Buddhist cosmos of *samsāra*, among the six spheres of rebirth many beings are reincarnated as *pretas*—ghosts who are "stuck" in various unpleasant statuses, potentially for long time periods because they have no kin or their kin fail to perform rituals to ease their pain or send them to their next existence. Twice a year for millennia, Buddhist monasteries in east Asia performed rituals designed to feed the *pretas* and transfer merit to them, seeking to alleviate their pain and allow them to move on to another rebirth state.

The Issue of Collective Karma

It is commonly thought that the karma doctrine of Buddhism embraces a strict nexus of individualistic retribution: What a person sows by intended action, one reaps oneself, in the present lifetime or in a future rebirth. In fact, however, there are texts that point to special circumstances in which there is collective action and collective karmic retribution. Altruistic acts by leaders can lift the whole, whereas evil plotted and done by them can lead to collective punishment.

Famous examples of both are found in the *jātaka*s—stories told by the Buddha about his previous lives. Several dozen such tales clearly portray how a person's worldly and spiritual destiny also can be profoundly affected by simple proximity to significant others, especially spouses, shipmates, monks, and kings.[33] The negative example is found in a narrative that recounts the collective massacre of the Buddha's native Shākya clan and their republic late in his life—a karmic event even he could not forestall. In their previous lifetimes, the Buddha states, the Shākyas united to poison a river to punish people living in their adversary city-state; in retribution, the entire Shākya population was reborn and killed together because of this previous collective evil action.[34]

The positive collective example often appears in tales of kingship, such as that in Pali Jātaka 276 when the deity Indra seeks to discover why his heaven[35] is suddenly becoming so overcrowded. He investigates and discovers that the spiritual rule of a virtuous king is the reason: Not only does the king's altruism lead citizens to reach the heavens, it also leads to the land's prosperity:[36]

Then their king practiced the Kuru precepts and the five Virtues. And then in the realm . . . the rain fell; the three fears were allayed; the land became prosperous and fertile . . . and then with his subjects went to fill the heavens.[37]

I return to the role of kings in Buddhist altruistic traditions below.

Buddhist Monasteries as Altruistic Centers

The community of monks, nuns, and devout lay followers established monasteries and shrines that rooted the faith in many localities. When Buddhist monasticism spread across Asia, it introduced independent, corporate institutions that engaged local societies and regional polities. Although monastics constituted only a small percentage of the population in Buddhist societies, they performed crucial roles in perpetuating the faith.

The typical Buddhist community had its center in a monastery (*vihāra*), where monks (or nuns) would take their communal vows, recite an affirmation of conformity to monastic rules fortnightly, and undertake meditation and/or textual study. As the faith grew, some monks specialized in performing rituals, establishing schools, preaching from popular texts, or managing the institution.

It also is clear that the early Buddhist monks were free to be innovative figures in the history of Asian medicine. Given the emphasis the Buddha put on suffering as a prime reality and compassion as the crucial human orientation to life, it is understandable that some monks would specialize in alleviating suffering by practicing the healing arts. In one incident in the monastic chronicles, the Buddha confronted monks who were allowing an elderly monk in failing health to lie in his own filth; after cleaning up the infirmed one himself, the Buddha sternly tells the assembly that caring for the sick is as meritorious as attending to him.[38] As a result, one of the few personal possessions allowed monks was the medicine of cow urine. Subsequent texts make clear a tradition of collecting, classifying, and case testing a great variety of medicines. As Kenneth Zysk has shown, "Buddhism played a key role in the advancement of Indian medicine through its institutionalization of medicine in the Buddhist monastery. The medical doctrines codified in the monastic rules probably provided the literary model for subsequent enchiridions of medical practice, and gave rise to monk-healers and to the establishment of monastic hospices and infirmaries, and proved to be beneficial assets in the diffusion of Buddhism throughout the subcontinent."[39]

In sum, then, in a development that has been common in the history of religions when institutions develop in ways not fully imaginable to their founders, Buddhist monasteries by 800 CE across Asia had become centers of education, charity, and medical practice—that is, institutions of altruism.

The Buddhist Tradition of Missionary Altruism

Successful monasteries expanded; the pattern was to send out monks to establish satellite institutions of that lineage. Underlying this expansion, by the time Buddhism entered China (125 CE), was a clear sense of purpose and order in spreading the faith. According to one text in the Chinese canon, Buddhists should missionize by engaging in the follow services for local communities:

- Build monastic halls and temples
- Plant fruit trees and shade trees and then excavate bathing pools
- Freely supply medicines to heal the sick
- Construct sturdy boats
- Safe placement of bridges suitable for the weak or ill
- Dig wells near roads for the thirsty and weary
- Enclose sanitary toilets.[40]

In many places where Buddhism thrived from India to China, some monasteries in cities and towns evolved to become complex institutions that were much more than refuges for ascetics. The Buddhist monastery often was the only local school, and members of the sangha served their societies by spreading literacy. Monks and nuns thereby accumulated practical knowledge (sanitation, horticulture, road building) to serve the surrounding community.

Many *vihāras* also organized endowed charities that fed the poor and dispensed free medical care. Allied with monasteries was a common institution that unified monks and householders for religious pursuits: the lay committees (Skt. *gosthis*). These committees would stage periodic festivals (image processions, chariot festivals), arrange for regular public recitations of popular narratives, and organize other rituals designed to cultivate both devotion to the Buddha-Dharma-Sangha and material blessings for the local community. In my own research in Nepal, I have documented the survival of these institutions among Newar Buddhists who work to ensure proper cremations for everyone, regular textual chanting, and festivals of rice distribution.[41]

Kingship and Altruism: The Ashokan Paradigm

The world in which the Buddha lived and early Buddhism flourished was a world in which kingship was the norm. Buddhist sources predominantly assume the reality of kingship. They also proclaim that karmically gifted persons who command wealth and power must perform the most significant altruistic activity. Buddhist texts provide religious support for the understanding of kingship as a special presence in society. Following the example of the Buddha in his last lifetime (and many births before that)—who was born as a crown prince—Buddhist doctrine considers that an individual who becomes king does so as the result of extremely good karma, a reward for almost immeasurable spiritual development in past lifetimes. Like the future Buddha in many incarnations, just kings can do great spiritual good; kingship's power also can be the cause of rapid descent into hells or lower births if wealth and power over the multitudes are used selfishly or for evil.

The texts counsel rulers to respect prisoners and appoint their punishments with compassion; invest in schools, rest houses, water systems, and medicines; be sensitive to the plight of farmers in exacting taxes; and make certain that the police truly protect the citizens. The towering figure of beneficent kingship in Buddhist reckoning is Ashoka.

When the world conquest campaign of Alexander the Great (355–323 BCE) faltered in northwest India, the small states on the Indus River that were weakened by his incursions were subdued and integrated into India's first great empire—that of the Chandragupta Maurya. When his grandson Ashoka (274–236 BCE) assumed the throne, he followed Hindu norms of rulership and consolidated his frontier regions with brute force. Most prominently, he directed an assault at Kalinga, a coastal region encompassing modern Orissa. The widespread destruction and bloodshed that his army caused in securing the victory, however, greatly dismayed Ashoka. At just this time, the emperor encountered a charismatic Buddhist monk and became a staunch devotee. Having extended the Mauryan empire across most of the Indian subcontinent, Ashoka sent ambassadors and scribes throughout his realm to explain "the Dharma" that the emperor embraced; these emissaries reached the borders of his state and beyond.

Ashoka's edicts—inscribed on rocks and tall, stone-carved pillars—were both general and specific in their explanation of "Dharma," a principle he held as key to creating a good society. In Pillar Edict I he writes, "Dharma is good. But what does Dharma consist of? It consists of few sins and many good deeds, of kindness, liberality, truthfulness, and purity."[42] Although several inscriptions allude to the value of meditation, Ashoka's chief concern was for Buddhism to be a moral force in society:

"One should obey one's father and mother. One should respect the supreme value and sacredness of life. One should speak the truth. One should practice these virtues of Dharma."[43]

Having stated these principles and had them placed in prominent public places, Ashoka also sought to have his bureaucracy administer the empire with reference to them: "My officials of all ranks—high, low, and intermediate—act in accordance with the precepts of my instruction. . . . For these are the rules: to govern according to Dharma, to administer justice according to Dharma, to advance the people's happiness according to Dharma, and to protect them according to Dharma."[44] In the capital, Ashoka had trees and wells planted to aid travelers, declared certain days when animal slaughter was prohibited, and worked to limit religious conflict.

Although Buddhists in India eventually lost awareness of Ashoka's inscriptions, they preserved memories of Ashoka's actions (with many embellishments) in extracanonical narratives.[45] Buddhist exponents in subsequent centuries invoked Ashoka as a model householder and ruler, whose example challenged later Buddhist kings to regard their vocation as spiritual.

The tradition's memory of Ashoka, then, established that charity, justice, concern with the common good, and generosity toward the *sangha* became the norms by which a "good Buddhist ruler" was measured. The recurring message is that political power should be wielded as a means of creating a society in which compassion flourishes. In many of the popular *jātaka* narratives, a good king's duty is likened to that of a parent caring for children or a son caring for an aged parent.[46] Holding political power is not just an end, the coronation of one's past good karma, but the means to an end: shaping the world with justice and kindness. As B. G. Gokhale has observed, "The state was not merely a punitive instrument but primarily an agency for the moral transformation of man as a political animal. [The Buddhists] . . . found in morality of a higher order the solution to the dilemma of power."[47]

Thus, like the Buddha, a just ruler in Ashoka's example should understand that in a world marked by suffering, attention to collective welfare is needed; moreover, by virtue of being in a position of wielding power, one must bear the burden of moral cultivation and detachment to dispatch one's political responsibilities fully. As the great Buddhist monk Buddhaghosa observes in his *Visuddhimagga* (IX, 124):

> For the Great Beings' minds retain their balance by giving preference to beings' welfare, by dislike of beings suffering, by the desire for the various successes achieved by beings to last, and by imparting impartiality toward all beings. And to all beings they give gifts,

which are a source of pleasure, without discriminating. . . . And in order to avoid doing harm to beings they undertake the precepts of virtue. . . . They constantly arouse energy, having beings' welfare and happiness at heart. When they have acquired heroic fortitude through supreme energy, they become patient with beings' many kinds of fault.[48]

Mahāyāna Buddhist Altruism: Expressions in China

Buddhism's successful domestication into China and east Asia was one of history's most significant instances of cultural diffusion, connecting India to east Asia. Over the centuries, Buddhism had to adapt to an established imperial system and the Confucian tradition that emphasized, among other things, circles of beneficent social engagement that extended from kin (including dead ancestors) to service for the wider community. What seems clear from a review of the Indic texts and the unmatched records of Chinese history is that in China the altruistic Buddhist ideals were extended and implemented as nowhere else in the world.

Chinese Buddhists defined the field of compassionate service first in the traditional Indic arena of the monastic community, or *ching-t'ien* ("field of respect"). To emphasize that its own place in society was not parasitic (a common Confucian criticism), however—and doubtless reflecting their inclination toward the Mahāyāna tradition and its greater emphasis on compassion—Chinese monastics worked hard to organize charities and therefore exhorted donors to give to the second "field," *pei-t'ien* ("field of compassion"). To shore up their service intentions, some authors even wrote an apocryphal text in which the Buddha endorses charity to both "fields":

In various sermons I have stressed the perfection of charity, for I wish that my disciples, both monks and laymen, would cultivate the compassionate heart, and give to the poor, the needy, the orphaned, and the aged, even to a famished dog. However, my disciples did not understand my idea, and only offered gifts to the *ching-t'ien* and not the *pei-t'ien*. When I speak of the field of respect, I speak of the Buddha, dharma, and Sangha. When I speak of the field of compassion, I refer to the poor and needy, the orphaned, the aged, and even the ant. Of these two categories, the field of compassion is the superior one.[49]

In Chinese monasteries, monastics and householders alike joined in setting up and funding charitable trusts called Inexhaustible Treasuries (*Wu-chin tsang yuan*). Across China, these Treasuries were set up to receive money, precious metals, and goods while serving as banks—lending funds at interest to multiply the wealth they garnered. Most divided the expenditures three ways: between monastic repairs, ritual sponsorship, and charities for medical treatments and feeding the poor. In famous instances householders competed with each other to make donations to these Treasuries; nobles and commoners joined their contributions to share in the merit earned from expenditures benefiting monasteries and the needy. Some monks devoted themselves almost exclusively to altruistic campaigns, and their biographies constitute a special section in the Chinese monastic annals. The accounts mention monks organizing vegetarian feasts available for everyone; other monks specialize as road builders, bridge builders, well diggers, tree planters, and river channel diggers. As the monk Te-mei (585–648 CE) reported, "Pious foundations thus make it possible to feed the clergy and the laity at the same time, for even though the donors presented their offerings to the monks, their kindness in fact extends to all without distinction."[50]

Lay associations aided in many of these monastic-led endeavors, following ancient Indian precedents. In the modern era, however, householders also established independent organizations for altruistic purposes. For example, in 1920 Hangzhou businessmen established the Right Faith Society, which ran schools, old-age homes, soup kitchens, and gifted coffins for the poor; in Shanghai, the contemporaneous Buddhist Pure Karma Society established an orphanage and free medical clinics. When missionaries introduced Buddhism into Japan, they consciously imitated the Chinese precedent—setting up trusts and monastery-administered almshouses, hospitals, and dispensaries. In the modern period, the same phenomenon of Buddhist householder organizations forming to do altruistic work is clear. The Sōka Gakkai and its global mission of fostering world peace is the most well-known example.[51]

William Scott Green's Three Questions about Altruism

I now respond to the three questions raised by William Scott Green in the introduction to this book.

What are the major categories of behavior for others? What does the religion mean by "others"?

Buddhist tradition defines any intentional bodily act, speech act, or thought as a means of significantly affecting the world and so earning karmic reward or punishment. Buddhist philosophers imagine the world as one of thoroughgoing interrelation. Every being has the material world "flowing through" it naturally. Likewise, the natural law of karma causes Buddhists to see an ongoing and dynamic connection between humans, animals, plants, spirits of various sorts (ghosts, demons), and the deities that populate various heavens. All of these "others" have been objects of altruistic action by Buddhist monastics and householders.

How does the religion assess the meaning of behavior for the welfare of others?

Buddhist karma belief in its doctrinal context gives the Buddhist grounds to critique any proposition that would imagine divesting any conceivable altruistic action of its benefits to the individual. The natural law of karma plants the seeds of future reward in the individual's future and does so inevitably. Because the universe as *karmabhūmi* is interconnected and interdependent, as an inextricable part of the whole every individual who performs an altruistic act that benefits the whole inevitably is a benefactor.

Does the religion create a context in which it is possible that intentional action for the welfare of others can have only a neutral or negative consequence for the actor?

Buddhists have devoted extensive thought to the mechanisms and logic of karma, especially how it adds up and leads to retribution. Given the inevitable good karma coming to the actor, unenlightened humans will always benefit from their own good deeds. The Buddha and the saints (Theravāda Arhats, Mahāyāna bodhisattvas) who have reached enlightenment can be regarded as the only Buddhist altruists under Green's definition, however. Why? Once one has reached enlightenment, all seeds of karma have been "burned up," and the causal mechanisms of additional karma generation have been forever "unplugged." Yet these Buddhist saints who help others are still embodied as humans, so they are subject to nonkarma consequences, and continuing to act can still lead an enlightened individual to suffer from natural causes and the unpleasantness of disease, old age, and death. The prime example is the life of Shākyamuni Buddha: After he is enlightened, he first is inclined to enter *nirvāna* and die to the human world because of humanity's addiction to desire and ignorance. As I note at the beginning of this chapter, however, the gods intervened and asked him to preach, out of compassion for the world. They argued that enough humans existed who would benefit from his teaching. So for the next forty-five years he took on all the natural, nonkarmic suffering that embodied life entailed. Following his example, other Buddhist saints have made the same choice.

Conclusion

Several final observations follow from the foregoing consideration of the Buddhist tradition's understanding of altruism and its history of compassionate engagement. First, far from being a side issue or marginal to the tradition, altruism occupies a central place in Buddhist thought and for Buddhists at every level of spiritual development. In many respects, understanding altruism's role in Buddhist history provides special insight into the spiritual vision underlying the living Buddhist cultures across Asia. As an expression of compassion, altruism shaped the development of Buddhist monasticism, particularly in terms of how the monasteries became centers of medical practice, education, and humanitarian services. Monastic altruism in the development of medical care certainly contributed to the success of the tradition.

A second observation about altruism is that it clarifies the intra-Buddhist comparison between Theravāda and Mahāyāna traditions and the respective cultures they formed in south/southeast Asia and east Asia. Pali texts rarely discuss the implementation of altruistic intentions in specific detail. When compassionate service is discussed, it is defined most often as an individual spiritual attitude that yields karmic benefit to the individual benefactor. Feeling compassion and lovingkindness to the depths of one's being is the focus, rather than the tireless doing of altruistic deeds. In east Asia, however—where Mahāyāna traditions dominated—adherence to the bodhisattva ideal led to more engagement with altruistic practices and extensive development of institutions to implement them.

Finally, Buddhist tradition places special emphasis on inculcating the ethos of altruism among elite nonmonastic disciples, especially affluent patrons and rulers. The early Buddhists seemed to understand clearly that given the interrelatedness of all beings, if the prosperity of a society was not sincerely and generously dedicated to serve the common good, the spiritual vitality of the community's elite inevitably would be impaired.

Notes

1. Translation by Ria Kloppenborg, *The Sūtra on the Foundation of the Buddhist Order* (Leiden, The Netherlands: E. J. Brill, 1973).
2. Translation by Ruth Sonam and Geshe Sonam Rinchen, *The Yogic Deeds of Bodhisattvas: Gyel-tsap on Aryadeva's Four Hundred* (Ithaca, N.Y.: Snow Lion, 1994).
3. The main Indic Buddhist canonical languages are Sanskrit (Skt.) and Pali (P.). I provide both spellings in this chapter; the absence of a Pali term indicates identical spelling.

4. Franklin Edgerton, *Buddhist Hybrid Sanskrit Grammar and Dictionary* (New Haven, Conn.: Yale University Press, 1953), 66. I discuss below why, in the Buddhist belief system, "altruism" cannot be defined as a phenomenon that could ever deny benefit to the donor. The term is not attested in the Hindu sources.

5. My use of the term "altruism" assumes the tradition's own definition, unless otherwise indicated.

6. For example, see the Pali Canon, *Anguttara Nikāya*. Translation in E. M. Hare, *The Book of Gradual Sayings* (Oxford: Pali Text Society, 1988), vol. 3, 249.

7. Pali Canon, *Majjhima Nikāya*. Translation in I. B. Horner, *Middle Length Sayings* (Oxford: Pali Text Society, 1976), vol. 3, 249.

8. Pali Canon, *Anguttara Nikāya*. Translation in Hare, *The Book of Gradual Sayings*, vol. 4, 61.

9. The five *skandhas*: the physical body (*rūpa*), which is made of combinations of the four elements (earth, water, fire, air); feelings (*vedanā*), which arise from sensory contact; perceptions (*samjñā*), which attach the categories good, evil, or neutral to these sensory inputs; habitual mental dispositions (*samskāras*), which connect karma-producing will to mental action; and the consciousness (*vijñāna*), which arises when mind and body come in contact with the external world.

10. The *anātman* doctrine, however, presented exponents of Buddhism with the perpetual problem of explaining moral causality: How can the doctrine of karma—with its emphasis on moral retribution—operate without the mechanism of a transmigrating soul? Early texts show that this question was clearly posed to Buddha: If there is no soul, how can the karmic "fruits" of any good or evil act pass into the future? The standard explanation is that *karma* endures in habitual mental energies (*samskāras*) that are impressed in the fifth *skandha*, consciousness (*vijñāna*). Although always evolving and hence impermanent, *vijñāna* endures in this life, exits the body, and passes over to be reincarnated in the next.

11. The first biography of the Buddha, by Ashvaghosa, usually dated to about 150 CE; translation in Richard Robinson, *Chinese Buddhist Verse* (London: John Murray, 1954), 11.

12. The historian of religion must emphasize that world religions have benefited from having such wide-ranging textual pronouncements in the service of historical adaptation. Just as the Christian Bible gives us ethnic cleansing in the Book of Deuteronomy, it also exhorts us to love one's enemy in the Gospels. Textual multivocalism may discomfit textual literalists, but it provided working proof texts for historical actors involved in adapting religious institutions to new or changing circumstances.

13. The Theravādins are the last surviving school of the Staviravādins. Using the latter term is more historically accurate for the ancient era, but given the former term's greater recognition, I use Theravāda in this chapter.

14. Translation by Gregory Schopen, "Two Problems in the History of Indian Buddhism: The Layman/Monk Distinction and the Doctrines of

the Transference of Merit," *Studien zur Indologie und Iranistik* 10 (1985): 9–48, at 31. Mahāyāna inscriptions also record this sentiment, although they consistently direct the universal good to be final enlightenment (*anuttara-jñāna*) by all beings.

15. Chapter 1:8.
16. Har Dayal, *The Bodhisattva Doctrine in Buddhist Sanskrit Literature* (London: Routledge and Kegan Paul, 1932), 181.
17. *Samyutta Nikāya.* Translation in F. L. Woodward, trans., *The Book of Kindred Sayings* (Oxford: Pali Text Society, 1992), vol. 3, 5.
18. *Anguttara Nikāya*, VII, 54, as translated in Narada Thera, trans., *Everyman's Ethics* (Kandy, Sri Lanka: Buddhist Publication Society, 1966).
19. Translated in Michael Hahn, trans., *Joy for the World: A Buddhist Play by Chandragomin* (Berkeley, Calif.: Dharma Publishing, 1987).
20. "*Sūtra*" implies that this was an account of the Buddha's teaching. The text is known only through the extant Chinese translation by Dharmaraksha around 425 CE. The translation is from Heng-ching Shih, *The Sutra on Upasaka Precepts* (Berkeley: Numata Center for Buddhist Translation and Research, 1994), chapter 19.
21. A discussion of the varying textual definitions of these terms is found in Dayal 1934. See also Paul Williams, *Mahayana Buddhism: The Doctrinal Foundations* (New York: Routledge, 1989).
22. This idea is the religious foundation for the system of more than 300 reincarnate teachers that developed in Tibet beginning in the thirteenth century—the most famous of whom is the Dalai Lama.
23. *Bodhicaryāvatāra*, III, 9–9; 18; V, 84–85, translated in Kate Crosby and Andrew Skilton, *The Bodhicaryavatara by Shantideva* (New York: Oxford University Press, 1996).
24. Text dating to about 200 CE, as cited in Jacques Gernet, *Buddhism in Chinese Society* (New York: Columbia University Press, 1995), 368.
25. An influential text attested to in 300 CE. Quote is from Robinson, *Chinese Buddhist Verse*, 62–63.
26. Jan Nattier, *Once upon a Future Time: Studies in a Buddhist Philosophy of Decline* (Berkeley, Calif.: Asian Humanities Press, 1991).
27. Translation by Herbert Guenther, *Kindly Bent to Ease Us, Part One: Mind, by Longchenpa* (Berkeley, Calif.: Dharma Publishing, 1975). The passage is in chapter 8.
28. Translation by Padmakara Translation Group, *The Words of My Perfect Teacher* by Patrul Rinpoche, 2nd ed. (Walnut Creek, Calif.: Altamira Press, 1998), 209–10.
29. Translated in Roger Jackson "A Fasting Ritual," in *Religions of Tibet in Practice*, ed. Donald S. Lopez (Princeton, N.J.: Princeton University Press, 1997), 271–92, at 291.
30. In this same ritual, the focal figure is described as "Treasure of compassion who looks down//Perpetually with a thousand compassionate eyes/ On the countless tormented and protectorless beings." Ibid., 291–92.
31. From the same ritual, the transfer between the compassionate bodhisattva and practitioner is visualized as follows: "The noble, Greatly

compassionate One, is . . . in the space before me, at the head of his retinue. A stream of nectar falls from his body parts. It bathes the outside, inside, and middle of my body and purifies without exception all the illnesses, demons, sins, obscurations." Ibid., 290–91.

32. Chinese: *Guan-Yin*; Japanese: *Kannon*; Tibetan: *Chenrizi*; in east Asia, this bodhisattva also is revered in female form.

33. I discuss stories in these areas in Todd T. Lewis, *Popular Buddhist Texts from Nepal: Narratives and Rituals of Newar Buddhism* (Albany: State University of New York Press, 2000).

34. James P. McDermott, "Is There Group Karma in Theravāda Buddhism?" *Numen* 23, no. 1 (1976): 67–80, at 78–80.

35. Heaven is a highly desirable rebirth venue, praised as a goal of householder Buddhists; it is impermanent, however, and one must eventually be reborn in other spheres. Significantly, one cannot escape the world of rebirth (*samsāra*) from heaven.

36. Despite the universally declared individual hope for *nirvāna* in a distant time, worldly prosperity and heavenly rebirth are the two primary goals that have motivated Buddhist householders from antiquity to the present. The royal stories underline that these goals were the central concerns in the imagination of typical Buddhists in Asian societies.

37. Number 276 in E. B. Cowell, trans., *The Jātaka* (London: Routledge and Kegan Paul, 1957), vol. 3, 260.

38. "[Buddha:] If you do not look after each other, who will look after you? Let him who would look after me look after one who is sick." (Pali Canon, *Vinaya, Mahavagga*, 8:26).

39. Kenneth Zysk, *Asceticism and Healing in Ancient India: Medicine in the Buddhist Monastery* (New York: Oxford University Press, 1991), 118.

40. *Chinese Tripitaka*, Taisho 16, no. 683.

41. See Lewis, *Popular Buddhist Texts from Nepal.*

42. Source: N. A. Nikam and Richard McKeon, eds. and trans., *The Edicts of Ashoka* (Chicago: University of Chicago Press, 1978), 41.

43. Ibid., 43.

44. Ibid., 42.

45. See, e.g., the Sanskrit *Ashoka-avadāna*, the *Mahāvamsa* and other chronicles of Sri Lanka (Wilhelm Geiger, ed., *The Mahavamsa* [London: Luzak and Co., 1958]), and the Thai text *Trai Phum Phra Ruang* (Frank E. Reynolds and Mani B. Reynolds, *Three Worlds According to King Ruang* [Berkeley, Calif.: Asian Humanities Press, 1982], 172–88).

46. "Just as an aged father . . . ought to be cared for by an able-bodied son, so too ought all the people be protected by the king" (Pali Jātaka no. 432; Cowell, *The Jātaka*, vol. 9, 305).

47. B. G. Gokhale, "Early Buddhist Kingship," *Journal of Asian Studies* 26 (1966): 15–22, at 20.

48. Bhikkhu Nyanamoli, trans., *The Path of Purification (Visuddhimagga) by Bhadantacariya Buddhaghosa* (Berkeley, Calif.: Shambhala, 1976), vol. 1, 353.

49. Cited in Kenneth K. S. Chen, *The Chinese Transformation of Buddhism* (Princeton, N.J.: Princeton University Press, 1973).

50. From Gernet, *Buddhism in Chinese Society*, 221.

51. These examples are mentioned in Helen Hardacre, "Laity," in *Encyclopedia of Buddhism,* ed. Robert E. Buswell (New York: Macmillan, 2004), 445–49, at 447.

Chapter 6

Altruism in Contemporary Buddhism: Thich Nhat Hanh's Socially Engaged Buddhism

Bradley S. Clough

I t is a commonplace among historians of religion that religions must adapt to changing conditions and concerns in different times and places to remain viable traditions that continue to affect people's lives. In the case of modern Buddhism, one of the things that many Buddhists in many places have desired is that their religion become more active in political, social, and economic realms. As Todd Lewis shows in chapter 5, compassion—unselfish concern for the welfare of others—is a central concern in the religion's "classical" sources. Lewis also rightly points out that for most Buddhists over the course of history, the goal of gaining merit (Sanskrit: *punya*) for good karma has been central. Moreover, the Buddhist worldview sees positive results coming from actions: Even selfless action with no concern for merit will bring about the positive result of making the actor a more liberated person. Hence, Buddhism cannot be said to be altruistic, according to William Scott Green's strict definition in the introduction to this volume.

I argue, however, that a definition of altruism that holds that an unselfish action done for the welfare of others must entail the possibility of negative or neutral consequences risks defining altruism out of existence: What type of action doesn't involve *some possibility* of positive results for the actor, even when he or she puts himself or herself at the greatest risk? Nevertheless, I think we can still apply the term *altruism* as Green defines it to the new form of Buddhism I discuss in this chapter. I follow Robert Berchman's useful suggestion that altruism can be a useful category for thinking about religion and ethics if we consider religious action that bears—to use Wittgenstein's language—a "familial resemblance" to altruism as defined by Green. Furthermore, if we follow the definition of altruism proposed by Nancy K. Morrison and Sally Severino[1]—a definition that focuses on the motivation of the actor and the nature of the action and regards the result that an action has on its actor as irrelevant—and we follow the qualities they associate with altruism (such as a sense of interconnectedness and a breakdown of a self/other dichotomy that is dismissed as delusional), there is little doubt that the Buddhist subjects I discuss in this chapter are altruistic. I revisit these issues in this chapter's conclusions, but first I turn to an investigation of the case at hand.

Many Buddhists are aware of living in a world in which large numbers of people are politically, socially, and economically oppressed in various ways and are cognizant of Buddhism's focus on elimination of suffering. Many new Buddhist movements have arisen among these adherents, especially in the past half-century, with the specific aim of relieving the pains experienced by such oppressed people. The work of these movements and the thought of the visionary leaders who have spawned them are widely referred to as "socially engaged Buddhism." Socially engaged Buddhism often has involved interpreting and extending the teachings of classical Buddhist texts in new directions. To more fully understand what Buddhism has had to say about altruism, then, it is important to devote attention to this phenomenon.

In this chapter, instead of trying to capture all the philosophies and activities of the wide range of socially engaged Buddhist individuals and groups, I focus on a single figure—Thich ("Venerable") Nhat Hanh—the causes he has led, and especially one central dimension of his thought. Nhat Hanh is a Zen Buddhist master who was raised in the traditions of Vietnamese Buddhism[2] and now, at age seventy-eight, leads his community of lay and monastic practitioners and activists from his center in southern France known as Plum Village. Ordained as a monk at age sixteen, by age thirty he had established two monasteries and a new order of monks and nuns within the Lam Te Zen school[3] to which he belonged. Originally he founded this order—the Tiep Hien, or "Order of Interbeing"—on the conviction that his fellow monastics were not working in any significant way to alleviate the immediate and great suffering that villagers throughout his war-torn country were undergoing. In 1964 he created a Buddhist university in Saigon (Van Hanh University) dedicated to training monks and nuns to perform helpful work for the people and to ethically and meditatively develop the measure of tranquility, lovingkindness, and awareness that he deemed necessary to carry out such work. That same year, Nhat Hanh also founded the School of Youth for Social Services—a grassroots relief organization that rallied and trained more than 10,000 students to enter war zones to help evacuate and then rebuild bombed villages, establish ceasefire lines outside villages, set up schools and medical centers, resettle homeless families, counsel traumatized victims of the war, house and school orphans, and organize agricultural cooperatives. Van Hanh University and the School of Youth for Social Services formed a major part of the Unified Buddhist Church of Vietnam, which was the primary vehicle for engaged Buddhism during the Vietnam War.

Surely this work alone would qualify Nhat Hanh and his followers as altruists, according to Green's definition, because they were engaged repeatedly in "intentional action ultimately for the welfare of others that entails at least the possibility of either no benefit or loss to the actor." Nhat Hanh has extended his altruistic work, however. While continuing to help lead one of the great nonviolent resistance movements of the twentieth century—a movement that had early success in bringing an end to the cruel and brutal regime of Ngo Dinh Diem in South Vietnam—he also founded an influential weekly activist magazine that advocated peaceful reconciliation between North and South Vietnam. His writings eventually caused him to be exiled by the governments of both South and North Vietnam, which regarded his words as posing a threat. This exile forced him to continue his work abroad. In the mid-1960s he traveled to the United States to make the case for peace to federal and Pentagon officials. He may have changed the course of U.S. and world history when, while on a speaking tour in the United States in 1966, he spoke so powerfully in favor of a ceasefire and negotiated settlement that he convinced Martin Luther King Jr.—who nominated Nhat Hanh for the Nobel Peace Prize the following year—to oppose the Vietnam War publicly. Nhat Hanh led the Buddhist delegation to the Paris peace talks. After the Paris Accords were signed in 1973, he was refused permission to return to Vietnam, so he settled in France, beginning a small community there and going into retreat for several years. Upon emerging from retreat, he established Plum Village, a major center for Buddhist practice and activism.

From Plum Village and throughout much of the world, Nhat Hanh has continued to give lectures on mindful living and social responsibility. He also has led retreats for many groups, including Vietnam war veterans, mental health and social workers, prison inmates, ecologists, police officers, members of Congress, and Israeli and Palestinian adversaries. He and his community of practitioner-activists—the Order of Interbeing— also continue their work to help alleviate the suffering of refugees, boat people, political prisoners, and hungry families in Vietnam and other economically poor countries around the world.

In forming and leading his Order of Interbeing for several decades, Nhat Hanh has successfully established what I regard as an altruistically revolutionary *sangha,* or community of Buddhist practitioners. Some examples drawn from the set of moral teachings that form the core of his Order of Interbeing—teachings known as the Fourteen Mindfulness trainings—evidence this altruism, in their emphasis on selfless concern for others. For example, the Fifth Training points out that the usual things we pursue self-interestedly—wealth, fame, and sensual pleasure—are wrongly assumed to be sources of joy and in fact are obstacles to true happiness, which is rooted in peace, freedom, compassion, and social solidarity. The antidote is simple living—by which Nhat Hanh means living in ways that avoid directly or indirectly supporting forms of social oppression and economic exploitation and are free from stress, depression, high blood pressure, and other "modern diseases," as he puts it.[4] The Ninth Training involves determination not only to speak words that inspire hope and confidence and avoid words that cause division or hatred but also to avoid lying for the sake of personal interest or reputation. These ways of speaking come from an awareness that words have the power to cause suffering or happiness.[5] The Twelfth Mindfulness Training reads as follows: "Aware of the great suffering caused by conflict, and war, the determination to cultivate nonviolence, compassion, and understanding on our daily lives, to promote peace education, mindful meditation, and reconciliation of families, communities, nations, and the world."[6] Moral commitments such as these, though they clearly have strong roots in classical Buddhist texts, are indicative of a charter that moves Buddhism as an enterprise of altruism in new, more socially activist, directions.

Nhat Hanh certainly is worthy of special attention for his altruistic deeds, which have been exemplary for socially engaged Buddhist movements—and for coining the term "engaged Buddhism" itself to describe the combination of mindfulness practice and compassionate activism that he has advocated publicly since the 1950s. I focus on him in this chapter, however, because his teachings—in the form of lectures, articles, and more than 100 books (more than 40 of which have been published in English, some of them bestsellers)—have arguably influenced more Buddhists who are oriented to active betterment of others' lives than any other Buddhist teachings of this generation. As such, they tell us a great deal about what Buddhists today have to say about altruism.

In this chapter, I examine how Thich Nhat Hanh has reformulated and extended an important traditional Buddhist teaching to create new expressions of what it means to be altruistic in Buddhism. The teaching I investigate is the Buddhist concept of dependent co-arising (Sanskrit: *pratitya-samutpada*), or intercausality.

Mindful Meditation as a Central Component in Thich Nhat Hanh's Socially Engaged Buddhism

Before beginning a discussion of Nhat Hanh's use of this concept, I offer a brief treatment of the practice of mindfulness—a practice that lies at the heart of Nhat Hanh's program for self-betterment and altruistic action. In an important sense, Nhat Hanh follows the long-held Buddhist tradition that holds that before one can effectively help others, one must first establish within oneself a significant degree of tranquility, lovingkindness, equanimity, and awareness of the way things truly are in the present moment. Such states of being can be achieved only through intensive ethical and meditative training. For Nhat Hanh, training in what is known as mindfulness meditation is the technique *par excellence*. In short, mindfulness practice involves undistracted, highly concentrated observation of life in process. It involves giving bare, nonjudgmental, and nonreactive attention to the flux of one's own ever-changing physical, emotional, and mental states, as well as mental objects of the outside world. There are two main goals of mindfulness practice. The first is to gain the ability to remain in the present moment at all times—or at least as much as is possible. The second is to live the experience of impermanence: to realize that everything within oneself and outside oneself is subject to change. Understanding the fleeting nature of things leads one to a spiritually liberating nonattachment to the things of this life. Also worthy of note is the Buddhist belief that the practice of mindfulness meditation leads to great calm and equability. In phenomenological terms, individuals who are advanced in this practice describe achieving a state of awareness in which, among other things, the usually rock-solid conviction of one's individuality or separate existence breaks down in the face of seeing one's existence as highly dependent on and interconnected with the existence of other things and beings.

Where Nhat Hanh makes a significant departure from much past Buddhist tradition is in his conviction that one need not—and, in fact, should not—practice meditative cultivation in isolation from the world. Active care for others must be involved. In describing the fruits of meditation, Nhat Hanh says that "mindfulness . . . will bring us a calm, and joy, and ability to see situations with clarity and even-handedness that can benefit people, animals, and plants even in difficult situations."[7] He describes how in the 1950s he and his fellow monks and nuns in his order faced a choice of whether to continue to develop mindfulness—the ability to be acutely aware of what is happening in the present moment—or leave the monastery to help people suffering from the war. They decided that they must do both: They must go out and help people, doing so in mindfulness. This venture is what Nhat Hanh termed "engaged Buddhism." The conviction he had then and continues to have to this day is that Buddhists must be aware of the real problems of the world. Once they see these problems, action is imperative.[8] Understanding implies action—as Nhat Hanh shows in his etymological analysis of the English word "comprehend," which means to pick something up and be with it.[9]

Thus, Nhat Hanh brings mindfulness into the realm of social activism.[10] The basic Buddhist instruction to be aware of suffering is extended: One must inform oneself well about situations of political, social, and economic oppression that are going on in the world today. Then, one must fully attune oneself to all that is involved in specific situations that one becomes involved in and fully consider the possible consequences of one's actions to be a truly effective agent for positive change. Nhat Hanh invokes the image of the bodhisattva Avalokiteshvara, who often is envisioned with an eye in each of his 1,000 hands—the eyes conveying the breadth and depth of attention that must be paid and the hands indicating the high degree of active involvement called for.[11] Mindfulness also involves listening to others to understand their suffering. In mindfulness practice, one must listen without reacting or making judgments. This kind of listening itself can alleviate much of a person's pain.[12] It also should be extended to everyone—especially one's enemies. If we show a capacity to listen to as well as an interest in understanding others, they will be more likely to listen to us.[13] This summary provides a foretaste of what I focus on below: How Nhat Hanh applies the Buddhist teaching of interrelatedness, here with respect to the idea that one person's demeanor and behavior can and does affect and alter another's in profound ways.

For Nhat Hanh, altruism is not possible without mindfulness training. He has often remarked that when people whose awareness is raised about other people's suffering try to change things for the better, most ultimately lack the strength to continue the intense involvement that is required. Such strength can come only from "a deep, inner peace born of meditation, of practicing mindfulness in each moment of our daily lives," free from regrets about the past and worries about the future. "With clarity, determination, and patience—the fruits of meditation—we can sustain a life of action and be real instruments of peace."[14]

Thich Nhat Hanh's Rearticulation and Reapplication of the Buddhist Teaching of Intercausality

I now turn to an examination of Nhat Hanh's interpretation and application of the Buddhist concept of dependent co-arising or intercausality.

Along with compassion, the main goal of Buddhist practice is to achieve *prajna*—liberating insight or understanding. *Prajna* is an experientially integrated knowledge of the nature of reality, according to the Buddhist worldview. It is the practical internalization of Buddhist philosophy. Nhat Hanh is a well-educated East Asian Zen Buddhist monk who taught philosophy at his Buddhist university. His understanding of the world stems from a school of thought that developed in China between the seventh and ninth centuries, with the purpose of understanding and explicating what its members saw as the highest realization of the Buddha; this teaching is found in a text known as the *Flower Garland Sermon* (Sanskrit: *Avatamsaka Sutra*; Chinese: *Huayan Jing*). The school of thought dedicated to explicating this text's teachings was known simply as the Huayan or Flower Garland School. This sermon is far more than a single discourse; it is a work of encyclopedic scope that brings together different shorter texts of Indian, central Asian, and Chinese origin. It probably was compiled around the third or fourth century.

Most compelling for adherents who accept this scripture as presenting the highest truth (it has been popular in Vietnam since the eighth century) is its vision of the universe as an infinite whole made up of interfused parts. Certain key sections of the *Flower Garland Sermon* expand on of the fundamental Buddhist teaching of the interdependent nature of all existing things; many Buddhists and scholars of Buddhism regard it as the most elegant and sophisticated presentation of this teaching.

In Huayan philosophy, as laid out by the school's seventh-century master Fazang, every existing entity—or, to put it in Buddhist Sanskrit language, every *dharma*—is identical in essence, in the sense that each *dharma* has causal efficacy. Each *dharma* has the power to create certain results, in that each *dharma* possesses a function that is different from those of any other, dissimilar, thing. No single *dharma* is completely autonomous, however, in its ability to create a result. Fazang, in his magnum opus, the *Huayan Yicheng Jiao Yi Fen Qi Zhang*, uses the analogy of a wheat seed. A wheat seed is considered to be the main cause of a new plant, but to produce a new wheat plant a seed requires sun, water, and soil. All of these elements that participate in the production of a new plant *must work together* because the seed alone lacks the natures of the other conditions and cannot produce the resulting plant alone.[15] The need for supporting conditions by each causal *dharma* results in the universal situation of pervasive intercausality, which Fazang and the Flower Garland School called the "interpenetration of all things" (Chinese: *shishi wu'ai*). By "interpenetration" Fazang meant that a *dharma* that is considered to be causal also includes within it, through a kind of borrowing or usurpation, the qualities possessed by the contributing conditions. In the seed analogy, the seed is said to borrow and include within itself the qualities or natures of water, sun, and soil, and only by embracing these qualities is it able to produce its result.[16] From this standpoint, any *dharma* possesses the qualities of all the aiding conditions within itself, and everything in existence is a condition aiding that one *dharma*. Therefore, there is an infinite interpenetration of all *dharmas*. Going beyond the analogy of the seed, the Flower Garland School teaches that in a more general area of causation—that is, the whole universe—the causal flow is multidirectional, so that what is a cause from one standpoint is a result from another, and vice versa. Therefore, the *dharma* that acts as a cause for the whole at the same time is—as part of the whole—the result of another cause. Interpenetration results from a situation in which the cause includes the conditions within itself and itself is a result of other causes, its qualities being absorbed into the other. Thus—and this is one of the major points of the philosophy—a part includes the whole, and the whole includes the part.

Thus, according to the *Flower Garland Sermon* and its major school of interpretation, what the Buddha realized upon achieving a liberating awakening to the true nature of reality was a universe that was one living organism of mutually identical (in the sense of "corresponding") and interdependent parts. The school's favorite method of exemplifying this manner in which things exist is another analogy, known as "Indra's Net." According to this analogy, the universe is a divine abode made up of a wonderful net, hung by the architect of the gods so that it stretches infinitely in all directions. The net represents the whole. In each "eye" of the net is a single glittering, multifaceted jewel. Each jewel represents one of the world's variegated parts—one of its *dharmas* or entities. Because the net is infinite in dimension, the jewels are infinite in number. If one were to closely inspect one of the jewels, one would discover that all of the other jewels are reflected on its polished surface. Furthermore, one would see that each jewel reflected in this one jewel is also reflecting all other jewels, so that a continuing reflecting process is occurring.[17]

The Flower Garland School has been fond of this image—which appears throughout its literature—because it symbolizes a cosmos in which there is an infinitely repeated interrelationship among all the individual part or existents. Each individual element in our universe is at once the cause for the whole and caused by the whole. The school puts it succinctly: The part is in the whole and the whole is in the part, or the many are in the one and the one is in the many. Existence is a vast body made up of persons and things, all sustaining and defining each other.

In such a state of affairs, when one individual changes in nature or does something, all things are affected to greater or lesser extents. One of the most important implications of this understanding is that every single thing in the world has an important place in the scheme of things. In this "Great Barn"—yet another Huayan analogy for the universe—every rafter, shingle, and nail is important: Where can we find a barn apart from these things? The apparently insignificant shingle is a necessary condition for the barn; in fact, it *is* the barn. Clearly, the barn or universe does not collapse when one shingle or thing falls away, but it is no longer *the particular* whole that it was when that part survived. At the same time, the particular shingle that is a necessary condition for the whole is not a shingle outside the context of the barn of which it is a part because "shingle" has meaning only in its proper context. True, there is no building without this little shingle, yet it is equally evident that "shingle" has neither existence nor meaning outside the barn of which it is a part.[18]

This vision of the world—in which everything interpenetrates in mutual identity and mutual interdependence, everything needs everything else, and everything plays a part—lies behind what Thich Nhat Hanh has taught and done. The complexity of this philosophy raises the following question, however: How has he sought to convey his understanding of it to as large an audience as possible (which is his desire), and how does it inform his agenda of selflessly given aid for the welfare of others in society?

As a beginning, Nhat Hanh provides a basic definition for simple understanding. For the Chinese term rendered as "dependent co-arising," Nhat Hanh prefers the rendering "interbeing." As Nhat Hanh points out, the two Chinese words used in the compound word, *tiep* and *hien*, mean "mutual" and "to be," respectively. Nhat Hanh puts in succinctly for his readers: "We and all things mutually exist. I am, therefore you are. You are, therefore I am. We interare."[19] Elsewhere he says with equal straightforwardness: "Everything co-exists with each other. To be is to 'inter-be': We cannot just *be* by ourselves alone. We have to inter-be with every other thing. One thing is because everything else is."[20]

Where does he go from this point? Perhaps the most-repeated message in Nhat Hanh's writings is the Flower Garland teaching that things in their interrelatedness are not separate and not utterly different. In his thought, no living being is truly other. Separating oneself from others is delusional because the destinies of all beings are intertwined. Thus, Nhat Hanh often emphasizes looking at things not as separate entities but as integrated parts of the whole to which all things belong. With respect to ecology and our relationship to nature, Nhat Hanh emphasizes that we humans, as animals, must see ourselves as part of, not apart from, nature. In one of his most famous writings, a poem titled "Please Call Me by My True Names," Nhat Hanh eloquently conveys the identity he feels with nature, while advising his audience to endeavor to arrive at the same feeling:

Look deeply: every second I am arriving
to be a bud on a spring branch,
to be a tiny bird, with small fragile wings,
learning to sing in my new nest,
to be a caterpillar in the heart of a flower,
to be a jewel hiding itself in a stone.

I am still arriving, in order to laugh and cry,
in order to fear and hope,
the rhythm of my heart is the birth and death
of every living creature.

I am a mayfly metamorphosing
on the surface of the river,
And I am a bird
that swoops down to swallow a mayfly.

I am a frog swimming happily
in the clear water of a pond,
and I am the grass-snake
that silently feeds itself upon the frog. . . .[21]

One may notice first in this passage the deep identity with the life of natural beings, even with inanimate natural forms such as a stone. The human author's identification with the creatures mentioned in the poem is strongly brought out by Nhat Hanh's use of the pronoun "I." If we saw things in this way, Nhat Hanh asserts, we would not exploit nature—as we so often do, for our own gain—but would deal with it as we deal with ourselves, in a nonharmful way. Because we are part of nature, to harm nature is to harm ourselves.[22]

Nhat Hanh's belief that the "other" who is the recipient of altruism includes all aspects of earthly existence is evident in the two main vows that members of the Order of Interbeing *sangha* must take: "I vow to develop my compassion in order to love and protect the life of people, animals, plants, and minerals"; and "I vow to develop understanding in order to be able to live in harmony with people, animals, plants, and minerals."[23] Because we are interrelated, the only sane course of action is harmonious coexistence.[24] One is reminded of the Flower Garland School's seed analogy, in which the seed *must work together* with the rain, the sun, and the soil to produce the positive result of the plant. People, too, must work together to produce results that are beneficial for all.

In discussing his principles for the work of bringing reconciliation to rival parties, Nhat Hanh emphasizes the importance of not taking sides. As long as people stick to an ideology and will not move from it, there is no chance of resolving conflict. The first two of the Order of Interbeing's Mindfulness Trainings instruct practitioner-activists to not be ideological, even with respect to Buddhist doctrines, because attachment to views may well lead us to harm others in the name of opinions that aren't worth killing or dying for; and to practice nonattachment to views, to be open to others' insights and experiences. One must be aware, Nhat Hanh teaches, that whatever knowledge we currently possess is subject to change, like everything else, so there are no absolute truths to cling to. Truth can be found only in the ever-changing life around us, of which one should always be mindfully aware.[25] Nhat Hanh maintains that these trainings and teachings are well supported by the experience of the Vietnam War—the context in which the Mindfulness Trainings were developed; that war clearly brought home the lesson of the enormous harm that can be done when people regard ideologies as absolute truths.[26]

Nhat Hanh takes the Buddhist instruction that one must give up attachment to views in the process of arriving at spiritual awakening, which he says is the Buddha's single most important teaching,[27] and brings it into the political realm. The teaching of mutual identity through interconnectedness is involved as well; Nhat Hanh maintains that action to bring about reconciliation is based on sympathy for and identification with all parties engaged in conflict. This kind of altruism was demonstrated when his movement involved itself in trying to make peace between North and South Vietnam, to end the people's great suffering caused by their war. Common Vietnamese villagers were suffering the most in the war, so it made sense from a Buddhist perspective to take their side. In doing so, however, Nhat Hanh's movement aligned with neither North nor South. Even the perpetrators of the war deserved compassion because all were intertwined with the painful conditions of war. Nhat Hanh advised his followers to "see that every person involved in the conflict is a victim. . . . See that the situation is possible because of clinging to ideologies and to an unjust world economic system which is upheld by every single person through ignorance and through lack of resolve to change it. See that the two sides in a conflict are not really opposing, but two aspects of the same reality. See that the most essential thing is life and that killing or oppressing one another will not solve anything."[28]

Nhat Hanh's understanding of a world of interrelated phenomena offers him and his followers a way to develop compassion even for others who cause war because they too are caught in its web of pain. Even more remarkable, his vision sees, as Flower Garland School philosophy would have it, that we all play a role in whatever happens in the world—in this case, because we either support or fail to oppose the war. Even outside forces pressing the war are not to be regarded as others or enemies unworthy of sympathy. No harm should be done to American soldiers, he said, because they also are victims of greater powers that created a confluence of events in which these troops were caused to kill and be killed. Even U.S. government and military leaders are not to be opposed because they too are products of outside forces, such as the American public's views, political constraints and the like.[29]

Nhat Hanh saw the whole situation in terms of nonseparation (no one is truly other) and, to use his term, interbeing. From this perspective, no single person can be blamed because, on one hand, the teaching of interbeing tells us that all people are involved and, on the other hand, a person's actions are inextricably connected with a vast network of conditions such as the global economy and political ideologies.

Although understanding interbeing prevents placing of blame, it does not mean that action should not be taken; the Buddhist imperative to eliminate suffering compels one to try to care for beings in all situations, especially when one is convinced that one is unavoidably involved in all situations. Moreover, one must be cognizant of one's individual responsibility.

Blaming government or society does not jibe with the vision of the world as a net of jewels constantly reflecting one another, with things at once participating as causes or conditions of certain results and being results of other causes and conditions coming together. Government is only a reflection of society, which in turn is a reflection of our own consciousness. We as individuals *are* society; we *are* government, Nhat Hanh has said. A part contains the whole. We often think that government can make any policy it wishes, but its freedom to do so depends on how we live our daily lives. We can live in a way that can have an impact on political decisions.[30]

We also must not delude ourselves, Nhat Hanh has insisted, that we are ever apart from the world, apart from society. Even when one enters into meditative retreat, what one carries in one's heart is society itself. One brings the whole world with oneself when one meditates. Thus, meditation practice is never some kind of isolated withdrawal from the world. Hence, when one meditates, it is not just for oneself but for everyone. Likewise, one seeks solutions not only for oneself but for all beings.[31] Thus, if we want real peace, we must transform ourselves. We will move those in power only if we show them love and understanding.[32]

Examining this poem further, what also stands out is Nhat Hanh's insistence that although I, as a human, am part of the joyful emerging existence and life of nature (in the opening stanza, for example, where he announces his arrival as a newborn singing bird, as well as in later stanzas where he identifies himself with a river-gliding mayfly and a happily singing frog), I am just as much the bird who eats the mayfly and the snake who consumes the frog. What is Nhat Hanh trying to convey by these associations? First, he wants to demonstrate that if we are going to live in the world from the perspective of interpenetration, we cannot connect only with birth and life; we also must acknowledge and accept the reality of death and killing—and our complicity in them. He reminds his fellow pacifist altruists that even they inevitably must destroy life to survive. It is very difficult, Nhat Hanh asserts, to say a person is violent or nonviolent; we can say only that a person is more or less nonviolent at a particular time.[33] We must realize that violence is within us and see that the dualistic division of reality into camps—violent and nonviolent—is false. To have a real impact, "we must work on ourselves and also work with those we condemn."[34]

Nhat Hanh acknowledges that nature can be cruel and disruptive at times and does need to be controlled. In speaking of cruelty and disruption in human societies, he maintains that such societies destroy the harmony of the human family and nature and that among the healing measures needed is legislation that does not do violence to ourselves and nature but helps prevent us from being cruel and disruptive. We should handle nature in the same way. We should control it when necessary, not to dominate or oppress it but to bring it into harmony and balance with us. Nhat Hanh cites overuse of pesticides, which do kill harmful insects but also poison the earth, as an example of an unwise effort to control nature. Once again, because of the interrelatedness of humanity and nature we harm ourselves in such a case because through such action we make the earth less habitable.[35]

In this same poem, interestingly, Nhat Hanh goes on to draw a parallel between the nature of the animal world and that of the human world as a way of bringing the audience into military and political situations:

I am the child of Uganda, all skin and bones,
my legs as thin as bamboo sticks.
And I am the arms merchant,
Selling deadly weapons in Uganda.

I am the twelve-year-old girl,
refugee on a small boat,
who throws herself into the ocean,
after being raped by a sea pirate.
And I am the pirate,
my heart not yet capable
of seeing and loving.

I am a member of the politburo,
with plenty of power in my hands,
and I am the man who has to pay
his "debt of blood" to my people,
dying slowly in a forced-labor camp...[36]

Once again, as he did in invoking the precarious existence of the mayfly and frog, Nhat Hanh invites people to the moral imperative of empathizing with endangered lives because without truly connecting ourselves with the suffering plight of others, we will not be moved to help them. The normal barrier we set up between self and other must be broken down (and it will be broken down, once we see that our notion of ourselves as separate individuals is delusional and hence must be dismissed). Here the main point that Nhat Hanh wants to make, it seems, is that according to the law of dependent co-arising, we all are very much the products of the conditions we live under. Just as beings who are born as frogs will swim happily in ponds, and those born as snakes are likely to consume those frogs, so a child born in Uganda probably will grow up in life-threatening poverty, and one raised among pirates is likely to be rapacious. Of course, there must be compassion for the starving Ugandan girl and Vietnamese boat-girl because they are victims of the conditions of their birth, and the main point of Buddhism is to eradicate suffering.

Nhat Hanh's apparent equation of the Ugandan and Vietnamese girls with flies and frogs may appear degrading on first inspection, but it is not for a Buddhist such as Nhat Hanh—for whom humans are not special beings different in nature from other life forms. How do animals behave? A mayfly metamorphoses, and a bird may eat it. How do humans behave? A Vietnamese girl is born as a refugee, and a sea pirate may do violence to her. Both the fly and the girl are living in dangerous conditions, and both the bird and the pirate have been conditioned to act out of unreflective hunger and passion. Furthermore, we can see that Nhat Hanh is not being degrading; once again he identifies with them: "I am the child in Uganda," and "I am the twelve-year-old girl, refugee on a small boat." From Nhat Hanh's perspective, it is possible—and, for a Buddhist, necessary—to feel complete empathy for victims of hardship. In his own commentary on these verses, Nhat Hanh says, "I feel the hunger, the misery, the despair those children feel; the identical feelings that are in the hearts of those children are in mine; there is no separation between us."[37] Here we see the extraordinary degree of emotional commitment that William Scott Green raised in defining the parameters of altruism in this volume's introduction.

Nhat Hanh says that the theme of this poem is, "Where is my enemy?" It would be easy to be angry at the arms dealer or the pirate and make them into enemies, but a mindful person—a person aware of the dependently arising, interconnected nature of things—cannot be angry or create enemies because such a person sees that if he or she had grown up in the same social, educational, and economic conditions of the pirate, for example, he or she probably would be that pirate. Realizing this, Nhat Hanh comments, it is not easy to take sides.[38] We should do what a mother does with two fighting children: She doesn't take sides, she tries to make peace. To take sides is to make ourselves strangers, when in reality we are all related—and thus not strangers at all. Here Nhat Hanh returns again to Flower Garland School teachings: "Real efforts for reconciliation arise when we see with the eyes of compassion, and that ability comes when we see clearly the nature of interbeing and interpenetration."[39]

Following a main teaching of both the Zen school to which he belongs and the Theravada school's mindfulness teachings he has so absorbed, Nhat Hanh insists that we be nonjudgmental in our attitudes toward and dealings with the arms sellers and sea pirates of the world. There should be no more condemnation of them than there is of a bird or snake. How can he suggest this? Nhat Hanh's response is that all beings are driven by the same forces: Hunger seeks satiation, passion seeks to attain what is desired. Human ideas of good and bad are meaningless in this context. Furthermore, if we would choose to kill the pirate and merchant dealer for their crimes, "to shoot them would be to shoot us all."[40] This is not only because the arms dealer or pirate could be any one of us if we were born and raised under the same conditions as they were, but also "because all of us are to some extent responsible for this state of affairs."[41]

Once again we are brought back to the teaching of intercausality. Everything that exists comes into being as the result of causes and conditions. These causes and conditions, in turn, are all interpenetrating and interdependent in an endlessly complex way. In this view, everything that happens is related—albeit often in a distant way—to everything else that happens. In this sense, we are all at least partially responsible for the arms merchant and pirate's actions.

Nhat Hanh presses potential altruists to carefully consider ways in which their actions may have directly or indirectly led to harmful results in the world. We must examine violent situations such as war and see the roots of war in the unmindful ways we have been living. Would-be altruists must examine our participation in economic and social systems that deprive others of resources and deepen the gap between rich and poor.[42] We are co-responsible, Nhat Hanh insists, because we have failed to sow enough seeds of peace in others.[43] We must look at things more holistically, seeing that everything we do in our lives has to do with the condition of the world.[44]

This perspective is codified in the Order of Interbeing's Eleventh Mindfulness training: "Aware of the great harm done to our environment, and society, the commitment not to follow a vocation that is harmful to humans and nature." Although this commitment closely follows the classical Buddhist definition of "right livelihood," the vow extends beyond its usual parameters: "Aware of global, economic, political, and social realities, the need to behave responsibly as consumers and as citizens, not investing in corporations that exploit others or deprive them of their chance to live."[45] Commenting on this vow, Nhat Hanh says that even when one follows a vocation that helps one realize full compassion, one still must strive to better understand how one might still be causing harm, even if it is indirect. No individual livelihood can be perfectly right; instead, one should strive to realize a collective right livelihood.[46]

Finally, with respect to the issue of the enemy, the hated other, Nhat Hanh asserts that it never helps to draw a line and dismiss some people as enemies, even those who act violently. Change can be effected only when we approach such people with love. Working for peace out of anger never works.[47]

We also are in no position to judge, Nhat Hanh continues, as long as we live in *samsara*—a world of delusion and unreflective pursuit of our passions. The possibility of change always exists in *samsara*, and a person can go from bad to good, or vice versa. As Todd Lewis discussed in chapter 5 of this volume, Buddhism teaches that beings possess no "self"—no inherently existing, unchanging essence. Thus, no one is essentially good or essentially bad. Nhat Hanh teaches that we must learn to see things even-mindedly, without imposing labels such as "good" and "bad." These labels are relative and can change. For example, Nhat Hanh speaks of a rose and a garbage heap. The rose that is so "good" and "pure" in its current beauty will shortly become garbage when it decays. By the same token, the "bad," "impure" contents of rotting garbage can be turned into fertile ground for growing flowers, vegetables, and fruits.[48]

Does removing judgmental distinctions of "good" and "bad" mean, however, that morality and moral conscience should be ignored? By no means: We have seen the morality of empathetic compassion implicit in Nhat Hanh's identification with both victim and victimizer. Moreover, Nhat Hanh's repeated call at the foregoing poem's beginning and end to "please call me by my true names" is his way of expressing that the one is the many—that he is actually all of the beings included in it:

Please call me by my true names,
so I can hear all my cries and laughter at once,
so I can see that my joy and pain are one. . . .[49]

We cannot simply identify with the boat-girl and affirm her suffering while negating the pirate as "bad." As Sallie King has pointed out, Nhat Hanh attempts to show, through his identification with both the boat-girl and the pirate, that we can and must overcome a confused dualistic attitude toward the complexities of suffering.[50] He teaches that through identifying with both good and bad and through meditative discovery of the impulses underlying one's own "goodness" and "badness," we can finally put such divisive distinctions and categories behind us and go forth with compassion. As the poem says at its end:

Please call me by my true names,
so I can wake up
and open the door of my heart,
the door of compassion.[51]

Sallie King has made another salient point: As a Zen Buddhist and hence a Mahayana Buddhist, Nhat Hanh would regard such compassion as Buddha-nature.[52] Buddha-nature is our true identity, conditioned by understanding and compassion. In Mahayana thought, Buddha-nature is absolutely differentiated from ego-personality, or what is known in Sanskrit as *ahamkara*—literally, "I-maker." The latter lives in and is conditioned by the kind of ethical judgmentalism found in the world of *samsara.*

Buddhism teaches that attachment to the idea of such a "self" as one's true identity is the source of a dangerous, passion-driven self-centeredness that predominates in this world and ultimately can result only in the furthering of personal suffering and harm to others. Only by freeing oneself from this attachment can one realize one's own Buddha-nature. Buddha-nature could be said to be altruistic, in the sense that one who acts from it acts in a spontaneously selfless, kind, and skillful way and acts only with the welfare of others in mind. This way of acting out one's Buddha-nature is the outgrowth of the Mahayanist training of see-ing self and other as nondifferent and its vow to act for the welfare of all beings without self-concern. This is what Mahayana Buddhists mean by compassion. For them, compassion is a goodness higher than ethical dis-crimination. Nhat Hanh teaches that this is the moral condition from which people should act.

Conclusions

To give further attention to the issues raised in Green's introduction, I turn finally to the three questions he poses about altruism and consider how Nhat Hanh's socially engaged Buddhism might respond to them. With regard to Buddhism's main categories of behavior for the welfare of others, I see three broad categories: meditative practice, ethical interac-tion, and teaching.

Buddhism has sets of meditative exercises that go directly to the en-actment of altruism. In Theravada Buddhism, emphasis is placed on a set of practices called the cultivation of sublime attitudes (Sanskrit: *brah-mavihara-bhavana*). There are four such attitudes to be developed: lovingkindness, compassion, sympathetic joy, and equanimity. Accord-ing to the most important doctrinal interpreter in Theravada history, Buddhaghosa, these attitudes are defined as follows: Lovingkindness has the characteristic of devotion to others' welfare, the function of offering welfare, and the effect of counteracting anger; compassion has the char-acteristic of devotion to removing others' suffering, the function of not allowing others' suffering, and the effect of counteracting harmfulness; sympathetic joy has the characteristic of rejoicing in others' well-being, the function of not being envious, and the effect of counteracting dis-pleasure; and equanimity has the characteristic of regarding all beings with even-mindedness, the function of seeing beings equally, and the ef-fect of counteracting lust.[53] These sublime attitudes are cultivated through a progressive series of repeated contemplations in which one identifies oneself equally with all beings—even perceived enemies—everywhere in the world, with a mind that is wide, enlarged, unbounded, and free from ill-will and hatred.[54]

Central to Mahayana Buddhism are sets of meditative exercises that are designed to move one to actively and skillfully employ all conducive means to bringing about—in both oneself and others—the awakening that realizes freedom from suffering. In one such meditation—known as the meditation of "six causes and one result"[55]—one progressively and repeatedly thinks of all fellow beings as unconditionally loving mothers, remembers the kindness of such caring beings, vows to repay that kindness, recognizes all beings as familiar and thus equally deserving of that reciprocation, and aspires to contribute to the ultimate happiness of others by helping to lead them to a liberative awakening. These six reflections result in the actual adoption of the spiritual path that will bring these meditatively cultivated aspirations to fruition. Another Mahayana meditation with similar altruistic aims is called the "exchange of self and others";[56] in essence, it is concerned with reflecting on how both one's own and others' suffering are brought about by one's own selfish orientations and coming to realize the seeming paradox that one's ultimate happiness comes only when one gives up self-interest and is totally given over to bringing about others' happiness.

As a teacher in the unusual Vietnamese tradition—unusual, that is, in the way it combines certain Theravada and Mahayana practices—Nhat Hanh has all these means of developing altruism at his disposal, and his Order of Interbeing indeed employs them. The decision of Nhat Hanh that both altruistic action and meditative preparation would define socially engaged Buddhism has meant that the meditative category of altruistic behavior that has always been a part of Buddhist tradition has remained part of his newly fashioned Buddhism. Furthermore, in combining meditation and activism, Nhat Hanh challenges a vocational dichotomy that often has manifested in Buddhism, in spite of its ideals: the dichotomy of the hermit monk who concentrates on meditation and infrequently interacts with others and the village monk who concentrates on interacting with others and infrequently mediates. Not only does Nhat Hanh's socially engaged Buddhism combine these roles, it also assigns these roles to laypeople. Moreover, Nhat Hanh insists that the central insight gleaned from the mindfulness meditation he emphasizes most—the insight that we exist in dependence on one another—compels one to act for the welfare of others because to do otherwise would only have negative or at best neutral consequences all around.

As for the behavioral category of morality, Buddhism has a wide range of altruistic moral principles regarding action, such as nonviolence in body, speech, and mind and application of lovingkindness and compassion toward others. Again, the Order of Interbeing follows all of these traditional principles; most significant, however, in terms of its new contributions to the ethics of altruism in Buddhism are the Fourteen Mindfulness Trainings and how, with many of these commitments, Nhat Hanh has taken basic Buddhist moral principles and articulated how they can contribute to conflict resolution, uplift of the oppressed and dispossessed, and protection of the environment.

For example, the Fifth Training takes the Buddhist imperative traditionally reserved for monastics, that of nonpossession, and asks that lay members of the Order of Interbeing take it up, with a mind to giving over material resources to persons who have a more immediate need for them.[57] The Eighth and Ninth Trainings take the "right speech" aspect of the path and emphasize how compassionate, nonjudgmental listening and speaking are essential to keeping communications open and resolving *all* conflicts, from the familial to the societal. Furthermore, Nhat Hanh teaches that conflicts can be overcome only with constructive speech that inspires hope and confidence and is free from words that might cause division or hatred. Right speech also entails the conviction and honesty to always speak out about situations of injustice.[58] The Tenth Training continues in this vein, insisting that although one must always be aware of the political consequences of speech, one must always speak the truth without simply weighing these consequences.[59] The Eleventh Training expands on traditional notions of right livelihood, instructing members to not consume things whose production has caused environmental harm or economic exploitation, to not invest in corporations that sometimes cause such problems, and to be mindful that even if one has a vocation that contributes to developing full compassion, one still must strive to be aware of any potential harm one's work might do, however indirect. No individual livelihood can be perfectly right, Nhat Hanh teaches; the goal should be to realize a collective right livelihood.[60]

With respect to the category of teaching, Buddhism traditionally has regarded instructing others in Dharma or Buddhist doctrine to be the highest form of generosity to others because it provides them with a path to eliminating suffering. Nhat Hanh's career shows him to be fully committed to this altruistic behavior. His founding of a university and a school for social services in the face of opposition in Vietnam; his publication of more than 100 books (many in multiple languages); and his ceaseless lecturing and workshops, at Plum Village and throughout the world—all directed to the goal of achieving peace—amply attest to Nhat Hanh's deep commitment to this form of Buddhist altruism.

With respect to Buddhist definitions of "others," Nhat Hanh clearly subscribes to the Buddhist conviction that no one is truly other, and he makes this case by taking some key classical texts and finding a new way of articulating core Buddhist ideas regarding universal interdependence.

BRADLEY S. CLOUGH

According to Buddhist doctrine, all sentient beings—Buddhist or otherwise—are others who deserve compassionate treatment and beneficial aid, and Nhat Hanh stands squarely in this tradition. His long-term work with war victims and refugees, regardless of any marker of "otherness," and his efforts to work with victimizers on the same grounds show Nhat Hanh to be a noteworthy example of ideal Buddhist attitudes toward and interaction with others.

On a related note, William Scott Green, in laying out the four components of his definition of altruism, asserts that the part of the definition referring to "others" carries the implication that the altruist is capable of seeing the object of concern as someone distinct from himself or herself. In his philosophy of socially engaged Buddhism, Nhat Hanh seems to be telling us that although not all beings in the world are exactly the same, the degree to which one can be truly altruistic depends on how much one can see others as ultimately being not distinct but being crucially connected with oneself. In doing so, Nhat Hanh may well push us to rethink—as I hope I have shown in the areas of his thought and activity I investigate in this chapter—both what altruism means and what altruistic behavior entails.

Green's second question asks for an assessment of the meaning of altruistic behavior within a religion. Todd Lewis treats this question well and at some length in chapter 5. From my perspective, behavior is assessed in Buddhism mostly in terms of the impact on the recipient and the motivation of the actor; the two main standards are nonharming and happiness. With respect to impact on the recipient of action, the minimum expectation is that others are not harmed. Maximally, one's actions result in increasing the happiness of others. The type of happiness at which the putative altruist should aim, however, is not what Buddhists would regard as the fleeting pleasures of the world but a deep, lasting happiness that comes from equable compassion and freedom from hatred, delusion, and addictive attachment to the things of this world. This understanding brings us back to the Buddhist emphasis on teaching: The way to best contribute to a person's happiness is to help guide them to a realization of selfless love and an overcoming of enmity, misunderstanding, lust, and greed. Again, Nhat Hanh's well-established participation in this Buddhist project provides us with a living model of this kind of happiness.

On the actor's side of the equation, motivation is central in Buddhism. The operative factor in the Buddhist version of the law of karma is intention. Positive outcomes stemming from one's actions depend to a great extent on the motivation of the actor. Referring to Buddhism's sublime attitudes, a classical Buddhist commentary says that "loving-kindness is the *state of desiring* (my emphasis) to offer happiness and welfare with the thought, 'may all beings be happy'.... Compassion is the *state of desiring* (my emphasis) to remove suffering and misfortune, with the thought, 'may they be liberated from these sufferings.'"[61] From Buddhism's beginnings, karma or action has denoted wholesome or unwholesome volitions (Pali: *kusala-* and *akusala-cetana*) and the concomitant mental states that arise from them, and "right intention" has been one of the factors of this religion's path to nirvana. In short, actions motivated by generosity, lovingkindness, and clarity of mind result in good conditions for self and other, and those motivated by what Buddhists call the three poisons of greed, hated, and delusion bring about harmful results. Of course, a person's motivations often are mixed. The degree to which any action—even a generally well-intentioned one—is tainted by any of the three poisons is the degree to which the benefit of that action to self and other is lessened. Nhat Hanh's emphasis on the purpose of the Buddhist *sangha* or community being compassionate and understanding, rather than acting for personal gain or profit, demonstrates that he accepts fundamental Buddhist teachings about karma and in this case sees no need to rearticulate them.

When I assert that Nhat Hanh accepts the Buddhist notion of karma, a certain important qualification should be added with respect to a key issue raised in chapter 5: *punya* or merit. Notably, within the Zen tradition of which Nhat Hanh is a product there is a critique of adherents whose practice focuses on merit-gaining. This critique is evidenced by a well-known episode in one of the key foundational myths of East Asian Zen. In the episode, the patriarch Bodhidharma—the figure whom tradition credits with bringing Zen from India to East Asia—is approached by a king who proudly tells him of the various good deeds he has done and then asks the venerable master what merit he has earned. Bodhidharma replies, "No merit whatsoever." If one follows this dialogue to its end, one sees that the character of Bodhidharma is portrayed as attempting to eliminate reification of concepts into false absolutes that become sources of passionate attachment. More immediately, however, the part of the dialogue cited above contains the lesson that performing good actions with merit as the primary goal will result only in continued entanglement in a cycle of suffering (Sanskrit: *samsara*).

Green's last question asks if the religion creates contexts in which it is possible that acting for the welfare of others might entail negative consequences for the actor. As part of their definition of generosity, some classical Buddhist texts include willingness to give up one's life, if it means that one could protect others from harm. The guiding principles and actions of Nhat Hanh's Order of Interbeing since its inception clearly have to do with the possibility of being intentionally generous in precisely this way. The order's principles state that one must be willing to speak out and act against injustice, even if doing so might threaten one's personal safety. In their struggles for peace, Nhat Hanh and his followers have entered war zones to rescue villagers, have been exiled for speaking and writing about the conduct of oppressive leaders, and have put their lives on the line to bring boat people to safety. According to a system (the law of karma) in which well-intentioned deeds bear good future results, is the end of such actions of ultimate benefit to the actor? The answer is yes, of course; I would argue, however, for a definition of altruism as action in which the *overriding motivation* is immediate benefit to others, not to oneself.

Of the world's various Buddhisms, East Asian Zen arguably pays the least attention to the law of karma and future benefits. Yet even if one disputes this claim, Nhat Hanh's main teaching clearly is what one might call imminent nirvana—maintenance of a constant state of peaceful awareness in the present moment, with no attachment to future outcomes. With this ideal, along with care for others, as the main concerns regarding action—even if the action turns out to be beneficial to the actor in the future—I would argue that Nhat Hanh's Buddhism, to use Jacob Neusner's language, yields a doctrine and practice of altruism. The value, then, placed on altruism in Thich Nhat Hanh's socially engaged Buddhism is very high indeed. This high value is inspired, as I hope I have shown, by an important classical text and the commentarial writings of the Flower Garland School—one of the most influential schools of interpretation in Buddhist history.

Notes

1. Nancy K. Morrison and Sally Severino, "Attuning Consciousness: The Origins of Altruism," paper presented at conference on "Altruism in the World Religions," Bard College, Annandale-on-Hudson, New York, November 17, 2004.
2. Although Thich Nhat Hanh is nominally a Zen master, a closer look at his background reveals that he was steeped in the unique Buddhism of Vietnam, which embraces not only Zen but another Mahayana form, Pure Land Buddhism, and Theravada Buddhism—especially its teachings on mindfulness meditation.
3. The Lam Te Zen School is the Vietnamese branch of the Lin-chi (Chinese) or Rinzai (Japanese) Zen school.
4. Thich Nhat Hanh, *Being Peace* (Berkeley, Calif.: Parallax Press, 1987).
5. Ibid., 95.
6. Ibid., 98–99.
7. Thich Nhat Hanh, *Peace Is Every Step: The Path of Mindfulness in Everyday Life* (New York: Bantam Books: 1991), 91.
8. Ibid.
9. Ibid., 100.

10. A relevant book in this respect is Nhat Hanh's manual of how to employ mindfulness practices in the context of wartime service: *The Miracle of Mindfulness: A Manual of Meditation,* rev. ed. (Boston: Beacon Press, 1975). Also pertinent is *Being Peace,* his manual for Western peace activists.
11. Thich Nhat Hanh, "Ahimsa: The Path of Harmlessness," in *Buddhist Peacework: Creating Cultures of Peace,* ed. David W. Chappell (Boston: Wisdom Publications, 1998), 157.
12. Ibid.
13. Ibid.
14. Nhat Hanh, *Peace Is Every Step,* 99.
15. Francis Cook, *Hua-yen Buddhism: The Jewel Net of Indra* (University Park: Pennsylvania State University Press, 1997), 67–68.
16. Ibid., 68.
17. Ibid., 2.
18. This description of the "Great Barn" analogy is greatly indebted to the discussion in Cook, *Hua-yen Buddhism,* 14.
19. Nhat Hanh, *Being Peace,* 86–87.
20. Nhat Hanh, *Peace Is Every Step,* 96.
21. Thich Nhat Hanh, *Love in Action: Writings on Nonviolent Social Change* (Berkeley, Calif.: Parallax Press, 1993), 107–8.
22. Thich Nhat Hanh, "The Individual, Nature, Society," in *The Path of Compassion: Writings on Socially Engaged Buddhism,* ed. Fred Eppsteiner (Berkeley, Calif.: Parallax Press, 1995), 41.
23. Nhat Hanh, *Being Peace,* 88.
24. Nhat Hanh, "The Individual, Nature, and Society," 42.
25. Nhat Hanh, *Being Peace,* 89–90.
26. Ibid., 90.
27. Thich Nhat Hanh, *Interbeing: Commentaries on the Tiep Hien Precepts* (Berkeley, Calif.: Parallax Press, 1987), 17.
28. Nhat Hanh, *The Miracle of Mindfulness,* 95.
29. Ibid., 103.
30. Nhat Hanh, *Peace Is Every Step,* 111.
31. Thich Nhat Hanh, "Please Call Me by My True Names," in Eppsteiner, *The Path of Compassion,* 47.
32. Nhat Hanh, "Ahimsa," 156.
33. Thich Nhat Hanh, "Please Call Me by My True Names," 38.
34. Nhat Hanh, "Ahimsa," 155.
35. Nhat Hanh, "The Individual, Nature, and Society," 43.
36. Nhat Hanh, *Love in Action,* 108.
37. Nhat Hanh, *Being Peace,* 62.
38. Nhat Hanh, "Please Call Me by My True Names," 31.
39. Nhat Hanh, *Peace Is Every Step,* 118–19.
40. Nhat Hanh, *Being Peace,* 62.
41. Ibid.
42. Nhat Hanh, "Please Call Me by My True Names," 41.
43. Nhat Hanh, "Ahimsa," 156.
44. Thich Nhat Hanh, *Peace Is Every Step,* 111.

45. Nhat Hanh, *Being Peace*, 101.

46. Ibid., 97–98.

47. Nhat Hanh, "Ahimsa," 156.

48. Nhat Hanh, *Peace Is Every Step*," 96–97.

49. Nhat Hanh, *Love in Action*," 109

50. Sallie B. King, "Thich Nhat Hanh and the Unified Buddhist Church of Vietnam: Nondualism in Action," in *Engaged Buddhism: Buddhist Liberation Movements in Asia,* ed. Sallie B. Queen and Christopher S. Queen (Albany: State University of New York Press, 1996), 341.

51. Nhat Hanh, *Love in Action*, 109.

52. King, "Thich Nhat Hanh and the Unified Buddhist Church of Vietnam," 341.

53. Buddhaghosa, *Visuddhimagga*, Harvard Oriental Series no. 41, ed. Henry Clark Warren (Cambridge, Mass.: Harvard University Press, 1950), ix 93–108.

54. *Digha Nikaya* i 250–51.

55. Mahayana tradition traces this practice to Asanga (in his *Bodhisattvabhumi*), who is believed to have received it from the bodhisattva Maitreya.

56. Mahayana tradition traces this practice to Shakyamuni Buddha, from whom it passed through the bodhisattva Manjushri to Shantideva. The extant source that contains the source for this practice is the perfection of meditation (*dhyana-paramita*) chapter (particularly verses 120–54) of Shantideva's *Bodhicharyavatara*.

57. Nhat Hanh, *Being Peace*, 92.

58. Ibid, 95.

59. Ibid, 96–97.

60. Ibid, 97.

61. Buddhaghosa, *Paramatthajotika*, vol. 1 of *Sutta-Nipata Commentary being Paramatthajotika II*, ed. Helmer Smith (London: Pali Text Society, 1916), ii 128; emphasis added.

Chapter 7

Altruism in Japanese Religions: The Case of Nichiren Buddhism

Ruben L. F. Habito

A widely acclaimed study notes an underlying principle that "operates as perhaps the most vital common religious denominator" among the various representatives of Japanese religions.[1] This group of religions includes traditional Shinto and Buddhism, as well as the new religious movements that have arisen since the twentieth century. The principle is termed *genze riyaku*, or the pursuit of worldly benefit—described as "a normative and central theme in the structure and framework of religion in Japan—sought through numerous ritual practices, symbolized by various religious objects such as talismans and amulets, and affirmed in doctrinal terms in various religious organizations as well as through textual traditions."[2] In this context then, pursuing the question of how the notion of altruism figures in the organizational, textual, ritual, ethical, and other dimensions of Japanese religions would appear to be a misguided or misplaced endeavor because this theme goes headlong against the stream of what is described as "the common religion of Japan."

Recognizing the prevalence in Japanese religions of this pursuit of worldly benefit, which one might identify with a kind of "egoism," nevertheless the question of the possibility of altruistic attitudes, actions, and themes in religious and cultural expressions of Japan remains pertinent. Hence, a thorough investigation of manifestations of altruistic attitudes and actions in Japanese religions, with critical and constructive reflection on their significance in light of the overall tendency toward the pursuit of worldly benefits, remains an open task.

This chapter is an initial attempt toward such an overarching task, focusing on one representative of Japanese religions. I address the question of how the notion of altruism figures in Nichiren Buddhism, as a religious framework that grounds and actively promotes sociopolitical engagement.

The thirteenth-century Japanese Buddhist prophet Nichiren (1222–1282) and his followers through the centuries up to our time are known for their religious message that believers should take an active role in the sociopolitical arena. In the medieval and premodern periods of Japanese history, communities of Nichiren Buddhist adherents undertook courses of action stemming from religious decisions that put them in conflictual relationship with ruling authorities, resulting in their persecution and repression by the government. In pre–World War II Japan, a movement known as "Nichirenism" (*Nichiren-shugi*) provided religious rationale for a group of intellectuals espousing and supporting the government's nationalistic and expansionist policies. Ironically, in the same context Nichiren's thought also served as an inspiration for some Buddhists who resisted or opposed the Japanese government's rightist and militarist tendencies—a political stance that led to their arrest, incarceration, and execution.

In the current Japanese scene, a major political party in coalition with the ruling Liberal Democrats, the New Komeito party, has come into prominence with slates of candidates and platforms backed by the Soka Gakkai, a religious group inspired by Nichiren's Buddhist teaching; this group now also has communities of followers in different parts of the world. This group also has been described as an example of socially engaged Buddhism—among the many that can be so identified in the world today.[3] Other internationally known groups of Nichiren followers include the Nipponzan Myōhōji priests and nuns—who chant the august title of the Lotus Sutra in Japanese to the beat of their celestial drums at peace marches and rallies in troubled areas of our globe—and the Rissho Kosei-kai, which sponsors a prestigious annual award (the Niwano Peace Prize, named for its founder) for persons dedicated to the cause of peace in different parts of the world.

In the first section of this chapter I present a brief outline of the historical context of Nichiren's engagement in the sociopolitical realm, describing the religious grounding of such an engagement as seen in Nichiren's own writings. In the second section of the chapter I lay out key elements in the religious vision and teaching of Nichiren Buddhism, describing first the view of ultimate reality that is the centerpiece of this teaching and then the religious practice prescribed toward realization of ultimate reality thus conceived.[4] In the third section I consider the adversities Nichiren experienced in the course of propagating his religious message and examine the stance he took in situations of adversity and persecution in the context of religious practice.[5] Having presented key features of Nichiren Buddhism as a religion, in the remaining sections of the paper I consider the notion of altruism and examine its viability in the case of Nichiren Buddhism, offering reflections on the questions raised by William Scott Green in the introduction to this book.

Religious Basis for Sociopolitical Engagement

A central motif in Nichiren's religious career was his emphasis on the salvific efficacy and the supremacy of the Lotus Sutra among all Buddhist scriptures. His own engagement in the sociopolitical arena began at the age of thirty-eight, when he presented a treatise to the ruling authorities titled "On Establishing Correct Teaching and Securing Peace in the Land" (*Risshō Ankoku-ron*). This work begins with the following description of the conditions of the time: "In recent years, there are unusual disturbances in the heavens, strange occurrences on earth, famine and pestilence, all affecting every corner of the empire and spreading throughout the land. Oxen and horses lie dead in the streets, the bones of the stricken crown the highways. Over half the population has already been carried off by death, and there is hardly a single person who does not grieve."[6]

Nichiren describes a situation beleaguered by natural disaster as well as social chaos, leading to widespread suffering among the populace. In lamenting the situation, Nichiren also presents his analysis of the causes that led to this malaise: "I have pondered the matter carefully with what limited resources I possess, and have looked a little at the scriptures for an answer. The people of today all turn their backs upon what is right: to a person, they give their allegiance to evil. This is the reason that the benevolent deities have abandoned the nation and departed together, that sages leave and do not return. And in their stead devils and demons come, and disasters and calamities occur."[7]

In Nichiren's view, the protective powers and guardian deities have abandoned Japan and its people because they are displeased at the erroneous religious teaching that is allowed to proliferate among the people. This "erroneous teaching" to which Nichiren refers is the Pure Land doctrine propagated by Honen (1122–1212) and his followers. In Honen's time this doctrine won the adherence of more and more people who, in the chaos of the period, sought solace and salvation from an unstable and highly vulnerable state of life. Pure Land Buddhism centers on the devoted recitation of the name of Amida Buddha, the Buddha who reigns in the Western Paradise and has promised to save all who call on his name from this world of suffering and take them to his Land of Bliss.

For Nichiren, this form of religious practice was tantamount to blasphemy and spiritual treason, as well as a serious breach of filial piety, on several counts. First, devotion to Amida Buddha was a blatant slight to Shakyamuni, the Lord of the Dharma, sovereign over all the dharma realms. In Nichiren's Buddhology, which was based on the teaching of the Lotus Sutra, Amida was only one among the multitudes of emanations deriving from Shakyamuni, the Lord of Dharma. Hence, to pass over Shakyamuni and profess devotion to Amida was an inversion of the hierarchy. Second, Pure Land devotion sidestepped the Lotus Sutra—which Nichiren regarded as the King of all sutras—and therefore was based on a heretical doctrine. Third, seeking salvation in the Western Paradise of Amida was thereby an act of abandonment of this earthly realm, proclaimed in the Lotus Sutra and thus regarded by Nichiren as the realm that belonged to Shakyamuni, the Lord of Dharma—a realm meant to be transformed into Lotus Land.

What, then, was the "correct teaching" espoused by Nichiren to assure peace and security of the land? It was nothing other than the teaching of the Lotus Sutra, which proclaims the One Vehicle of deliverance for all sentient beings; the sovereign rule of Shakyamuni, Lord of Dharma, over the entire universe; and the way of the bodhisattva, a path of dedicated service for the well-being of others and toward the establishment of this earthly realm as the Lotus Land, reclaiming it as the domain of Shakyamuni.

In Nichiren's understanding, Shakyamuni, Lord of Dharma, is supreme Sovereign, demanding allegiance and fealty; exalted Teacher, imparting the truth that will deliver all sentient beings from suffering and thus calling forth gratitude; and all-compassionate Parent of all sentient beings concerned with the ultimate well-being of all his children, calling forth a response of filial piety. Thus, practicing a form of religious devotion that ignored Shakyamuni was an act of treachery, disloyalty, blasphemy, and ultimate breach of filial piety.

Nichiren's foray into the political domain was based on his conviction that the key to alleviating the suffering being wrought upon the people in his time lay in a change of heart among the entire populace—beginning with the political and military rulers, down to every inhabitant of the country—that called for them to set aside their misled adherence to false doctrine and practice and to turn to the correct teaching of and practice prescribed by the Lotus Sutra. The political and military authorities were in a privileged position to effect this change of heart, by prohibiting religious practices and forms of devotion deemed erroneous and, as a corollary, by actively promoting and promulgating correct religious teaching and practice. In concrete terms, these leaders could ban Pure Land Buddhist devotion and espouse Lotus teaching and practice as public policy.

This policy change, in short, was Nichiren's formula for saving the nation from the natural disasters and the social and political chaos of the time. He presented this plan formally to the government authorities and strongly urged them to adopt it as their own on behalf of the entire country. Needless to say, this proposal fell on deaf ears; it also evoked hostility toward Nichiren and his band of followers on the part of the ruling authorities, and predictably, that of the many Pure Land adherents of the time as well. Throughout his career, Nichiren made repeated attempts to convince government and military officials of the cogency of his message, especially as external threats (impending Mongol invasions) and internal turmoil (rebellion of some factions among the ruling classes) continued to plague the nation and the people. Nichiren understood and

duly proclaimed these events as having been predicted in Buddhist scriptures, as a consequence of the people's turning to false doctrine. These
pronouncements only heightened the animosity of rulers and religious
leaders against Nichiren and his followers.

This hostility and animosity translated into persecution and harassment, which in turn convinced Nichiren and his community of followers
all the more of the validity and authenticity of their religious message (as
I describe in a subsequent section).

Intertwined sociological, political, religious, and other factors came
into play in the ways Nichiren's followers interacted with the societies of
their time throughout Japanese history. Nichiren's own life and example—
as well as his teaching, handed down through his many writings—provided the inspiration for his followers through the ages to live their religious vision marked by engagement in the social and political domain.

At the core of this vision is the task of transforming this earthly
realm—a realm of suffering and dissatisfaction, a realm of conflict and
chaos—into the Lotus Land: a land of contentment and joy, a land of
peace and harmony. This Lotus Land would be a land where the Lord-
ship of Shakyamuni is acclaimed by all, his Fatherhood duly acknowledged by all beings—who are now able to regard one another as brothers
and sisters and children of the same parent and thus can live compassionately toward one another.

The religious vision of Nichiren, grounded in the teaching of the
Lotus Sutra, would not divert a devotee's attention from the tasks of this
world to seek some form of solace or reward in another world or in the
afterlife. It is a vision that intrinsically calls for engagement with this
earthly realm, toward its ultimate transformation.

The Religious World of Nichiren Buddhism: Realizing Lotus Land

View of Ultimate Reality: Dharmic Realm and Lord of Dharma

For Nichiren, the supreme reality that encompasses the entire universe is
none other than the world of the Lotus Sutra. In the background of his
understanding of this world is the exposition by the Chinese T'ien T'ai
Master Chih-I (538–597 CE), who articulated the various implications of
Lotus teaching in his many writings.

A key insight that Nichiren derived from Master Chih-I's interpretation of the Lotus Sutra is that of the mutual interpenetration of the ten
worlds. In this view, each of the ten realms of sentient beings that in-
habit the universe—that is, hell-dwellers, hungry ghosts, titans or fighting
spirits, animals, humans, heavenly beings, hearers-of-the-word (śrāvakas),

solitary sages (*pratyekabuddhas*), bodhisattvas, and Buddhas—contains all of the other nine within its own being.

Each of the ten realms of sentient beings, which contains all of the other nine, in turn is contained in each of the ten "suchnesses," or modes of existence—adding up to 1,000 realms. These realms, in turn, are manifested in the three dimensions of past, present, and future—making 3,000 realms altogether. Master Chih-I's grand insight into reality involves the affirmation that each thought-moment we experience contains all 3,000 realms. In short, each moment of thought is a manifestation of the entire universe characterized as a kaleidoscope of 3,000 realms mutually interpenetrating one another.

This insight into reality, described as the doctrine of 3,000 realms in a single thought-moment (*ichinen-sanzen*), underlies Nichiren's understanding of the teaching of the Lotus Sutra. This insight can be regarded as an unfolding of the doctrine of interdependent origination described in early Buddhist scriptures and further developed in early Mahayana Buddhism as the notion of Emptiness (*śūnyatā*). Chinese thinkers went on to give positive conceptual formulations to this unwieldy notion of Emptiness that were more palatable to the practical East Asian mentality; Master Chih-I's system is one such formulation.

Thus, ultimate reality is understood as a dharma realm of 3,000 mutually interpenetrating realms that is manifested fully in each thought-moment as experienced by sentient beings. To realize this reality is to be liberated from the delusion of a separate self and consequently to be freed from the constricting effects of such a deluded notion—which is at the root of the three poisons of greed, anger, and ignorance.

In each thought-moment, one realizes an intimate interconnectedness with all sentient beings. Realizing that there is no such thing as a separate self, one comes to recognize as well that there is no such thing as an "other" that is separate from oneself.

Another feature of Nichiren's view of ultimate reality that derives from the teaching of the Lotus Sutra refers to the central role of Shakyamuni, Lord of Dharma—depicted in the sutra as the Father of all sentient beings in this earthly realm.

I, too, being father of the world
Who heals all misery and affliction...
I, ever knowing all beings,
Those who walk or walk not in the Way,
According to the right principles of salvation
Expound their every Law
Ever making this my thought:
"How shall I cause all the living

To enter the Way supreme
And speedily accomplish their buddhahood?"[8]

This Buddha, the Lord of Dharma, is no longer the historical figure of Gautama but one who has attained enlightenment in eons past and now dwells in a timeless realm. This eternal Buddha has entered earthly history and has taken the form of Gautama but also continues to exist beyond historical time, moved by compassion to undertake actions in this earthly realm to liberate sentient beings—his own children—from their situations of suffering. "The Life Span chapter reads: 'It has been immeasurable, boundless hundreds, thousands, ten thousands, millions of nayutas of kalpas since I in fact attained Buddhahood.' The Shakyamuni within our lives is the eternal Buddha since time without beginning, who obtained the three bodies more than numberless major world system dust particle kalpas ago."[9]

At the center of Nichiren's religious vision, then, is this all-wise and all-compassionate Shakyamuni, Lord of Dharma, Father of all sentient beings, who continues to manifest different kinds of skillful means to liberate his children from their situations of suffering. At the service of this all-wise and all-compassionate Father are multitudes of bodhisattvas—literally, "beings on the path of awakening"—who dedicate themselves in their given historical locations toward fulfilling the task of the all-compassionate One. In some writings Nichiren appears to regard himself as such a being—that is, one of those bodhisattvas who have sprung up from the earth, depicted in the Lotus Sutra, as emissaries of Shakyamuni, Lord of Dharma. In later writings Nichiren appears to take on the vantage point of Shakyamuni himself, Lord of Dharma, regarding himself as parent, teacher, and guide to sentient beings in his country, Japan, whom he regards with compassion and to whom he offers himself in service, toward the opening of their eyes and toward the transformation of this earthly realm into the Lotus Land.

In sum, Nichiren's view of ultimate reality presents two facets. One facet is captured by the phrase "3,000 worlds in a single thought-moment"—a vision of the mutual interpenetration of all beings, whereby each and every sentient being in this universe is understood as containing within itself all other beings and is realized in every thought-moment experienced by each one. Another facet is seen in the dynamic action of Shakyamuni, Lord of Dharma, who looks at all sentient beings in this earthly realm as his own children and manifests skillful means toward their liberation from suffering. This recognition of all sentient beings as children of the all-wise and all-compassionate One places each sentient being in an intimate circle of life shared with one another and with all, grounded on being children of the same Parent.

Taking both of these facets of ultimate reality into account, from Nichiren's religious perspective one regards the world of sentient beings as "not other" to one's own self, as belonging to the wondrous realm of interpenetration of the 3,000 worlds whereby one situates one's own "identity," and as intimately connected to oneself in sharing the same life and "identity" as children of the all-wise and all-compassionate Father of all sentient beings. In either case, one realizes "identity" that is devoid of an "alterity."

Religious Practice in Nichiren Buddhism

Religious practice understood as the way toward realization of ultimate reality can be described under two aspects: a "self-oriented" or individual aspect and an "other-oriented" or social aspect. The former has to do with "arriving at" this realization of ultimate reality, and the latter can be described as "departing from" or "emerging from" this realization.

Proclaiming the liberative power of the Lotus Sutra for all beings, especially the "foolish and ignorant beings of this Age of the Latter Days of Dharma,"[10] Nichiren enjoins all sentient beings to simply receive and keep the Lotus Sutra with a stance of faith and devotion. The concrete way to express this stance of receiving and keeping the Lotus Sutra is in chanting its august title. In Japanese, this chant is intoned as "*Nam Myōhō Renge kyō*" (Homage to the Sutra of the Wondrous Dharma of the Lotus Flower). "Showing compassion for those unable to comprehend the gem of the doctrine of the three thousand realms in a single thought-moment, the Buddha wrapped it within the five characters (of *Myōhō Renge kyō*) with which he then adorned the necks of the ignorant people of the latter age."[11]

Chanting this august title enables the devotee to partake of the merit and salvific power contained in the sutra and make one's very own and to continually unpack in one's daily life this gem of the doctrine of the 3,000 realms in a single thought-moment. This chant is the prescribed mode of religious practice in its individual aspect, which thereby enables the devotee to experientially realize one's interconnectedness with all sentient beings in the universe.

The other-oriented, or social, aspect of religious practice involves enjoining individuals around oneself to receive the Lotus Sutra with faith and devotion and actively going out to correct views held by others in matters of ultimate reality and religious practice. The devotee of the Lotus Sutra, in short, is called to be an emissary who proclaims the liberative power of the sutra to others, as Nichiren himself did. A corollary of this task of being an emissary of the Lotus Sutra is that of maintaining and expressing one's critical stance vis-à-vis all teachings and ways of practice deemed misguided or erroneous. This latter feature has placed Nichiren and his followers throughout history into situations of opposition and conflict with other groups who espoused different religious viewpoints. The Lotus devotee's motivation for engaging in this task of propagating this devotion to others comes into question. The following passage elucidates Nichiren's own view of the matter. "When all people throughout the land enter the one Buddha vehicle and the Wonderful Dharma alone flourishes, because the people all chant *Nam Myōhō Renge kyō* as one, the wind will not thrash the branches nor the rain fall hard enough to break clods. The age will become like the reigns of Yao and Shun. In the present life, inauspicious calamities will be banished, and the people will obtain the art of longevity. When the principle becomes manifest that both persons and dharmas 'neither age nor die,' then each of you, behold! There can be no doubt of the sutra's promise of 'peace and security in the present world.'"[12]

In short, acceptance of the Lotus Sutra by all people—with concomitant acknowledgment of Shakyamuni, Lord of Dharma, as Parent, Teacher, and Sovereign and giving him due filial devotion, gratitude, and respectful obedience—will bring about the realization of peace and security in this earthly realm. Everyone will recognize one another as members of one family, all children of the same all-wise and all-compassionate Father, Shakyamuni, the Lord of Dharma. Suffering will be alleviated, death and disease will be overcome, and all people will live in the Lotus Land with peace and joy.

Another way of describing the structure of religious practice in Nichiren Buddhism is by way of the Three Mystic Dharmas, outlined in a treatise said to have been written by Nichiren from his retirement in Mt. Minobu toward the end of his career. These "three great mystic dharmas" (*sandai-hihō*) consist of first, chanting of the august title of the Lotus Sutra as described above (*daimoku* in Japanese); second, visualization of Shakyamuni, Lord of Dharma, flanked by hosts of other buddhas and bodhisattvas in his cosmic locus at Eagle Peak, made present through a calligraphic representation enshrined at a sacred place (*go-honzon* in Japanese); and third, establishment of a sacred altar as a locus of actualization of Buddhist precepts (*kaidan* in Japanese, also translated as "ordination platform"). The first and second Dharmas require no further elaboration. The third of the Three Mystic Dharmas, however, has remained controversial for Nichiren's followers through the ages, generating differing interpretations on its social and political implications.

When the Dharma of the ruler becomes one with the Dharma of the Buddha, the Buddha-Dharma accords with the Dharma of the ruler, when the ruler and his ministers all uphold the Three Great

Mystic Dharmas, and the past relationship between King Utoku and the monk Kakutoku is again realized in the future in this impure and evil Latter Age of the Dharma, then surely an imperial edict and shogunal decree will be handed down, to seek the most superlative site, resembling the Pure Land of Eagle Peak, and there to erect the ordination platform. You have only to await the time.[13]

The controversy revolves around the issue of the relationship between the religious realm and the political realm—represented by the terms "Dharma of the Buddha" and "Dharma of the ruler," respectively. Without going into the details of this longstanding debate, with its manifold levels of nuance, the point at issue is the nature of the political mission of Nichiren's followers, especially vis-à-vis the imperial system of Japan. One side of the debate looks forward to the conversion of the ruler—that is, the emperor (*Tennō*: literally, "Heavenly Ruler")—who will then proclaim the rule of Dharma, ushering in a new era of peace and prosperity. Nichiren Buddhist adherents who aligned themselves with emperor-centered nationalistic and militaristic policy before and during World War II read the foregoing passage about the third Mystic Dharma in a way that tended to identify Japanese national interests and imperialistic design as the path to realization of the Lotus Land, with the Japanese emperor regarded as the new *cakravartin*, or Dharma-wheel-turning Ruler who will bring about this new order.

On the other side, there were Nichiren adherents who saw the great danger in this alliance with, and subservience to, the imperial system, proclaiming that the Dharma of the Buddha should be upheld above the Dharma of the ruler. In their reading, the "ordination platform" is not to be identified with an imperially established and officially designated location; it should be seen as a locus of actualization of the Dharma, made manifest wherever a devotee of the Lotus Sutra brings its teaching to bear in one's life and activity in this earthly realm. This Dharma can occur in chanting the august title of the sutra, in an act of devotion before the sacred calligraphic image, or in activities related to propagating the Lotus teaching in different social and political contexts. Adherents who affirmed the supremacy of the Buddha's Dharma over imperial Dharma in this way were accused of *lèse majesté* and regarded as traitors, and many of them were arrested and incarcerated during the turbulent wartime years. For such persons, whose religious convictions brought them in direct conflict with national policy and state interests and who were therefore persecuted and made to suffer in this wake, Nichiren's own accounts of his suffering and persecution served as inspiration, strengthening them in their resolve.

ALTRUISM IN JAPANESE RELIGIONS

Persecution and Political Harassment:
Religious Significance

As an outcome of his activities in propagating the message of the Lotus Sutra—which included making formal demands for certain kinds of decisions and action on the part of ruling authorities, as well as criticizing what he regarded as "erroneous teachings" and misguided religious practices—Nichiren drew the ire and resentment of many people, especially those in positions of political and religious power in his society. This conflict led to persecution and harassment against himself and his then-small band of followers.

Nichiren gives an account of this facet of his life:

Who is it who is cursed and spoken ill of by the populace? Who is the priest who is attacked with swords and staves? Who is the priest who, because of the Lotus Sutra, is accused in petitions submitted to the courtiers and warriors? Who is the priest who is "again and again banished," as the Lotus Sutra predicted? Who else in Japan besides Nichiren has fulfilled these predictions? . . .
Let me show you phrase by phrase how the text applies to me. "They may be despised," or as the Lotus Sutra says, "People will despise, hate, envy, or bear grudges against them"—and in exactly that manner I have been treated with contempt and arrogance for over twenty years. "They may be cursed with an ugly appearance," "They may be poorly clad"—these too apply to me. "They may be poorly fed"—that applies to me. "They may seek wealth in vain"— that applies to me. "They may be born to an impoverished and lowly family"—that applies to me. "They may be persecuted by their sovereign"—can there be any doubt that the passage applies to me? The Lotus Sutra says, "'Again and again we will be banished,'" and the passage from the Parinirvana Sutra says, "They may be subjected to various other sufferings and retributions." [These passages also apply to me.][14]

This passage indicates how Nichiren's experiences of persecution and harassment not only failed to weaken his resolve to continue his mission or deter him from his mission; on the contrary, these experiences confirmed him in the authenticity and religious significance of his continuing engagement in propagating the Lotus Sutra. These events enabled him to experience the truth of the Lotus Sutra, through a "bodily reading" (*shikidoku*) of scriptures. This term is used among Nichiren's followers to indicate actualization in one's own life of what is proclaimed in the sutra, as Nichiren relates in the foregoing passage.[15]

149

Throughout history, many of Nichiren's followers experienced similar situations of adversity as a result of their religious activities. Like Nichiren, they were not dissuaded or deterred from the pursuit of the tasks enjoined upon them on the basis of their religious vision; instead, these experiences of adversity reinforced their conviction of the genuineness of the path they had taken and led them to an ever-deeper religious experience of the truth of the Lotus Sutra.

The Notion of Altruism and Nichiren Buddhism

I now return to the initial question posed in this study on altruism and religion: How does altruism figure within the religious framework of Nichiren Buddhism? Unpacking this general question into more concrete terms, William Scott Green's formulation suggests three questions: first, in this religious tradition, as presented in its texts (specifically the Lotus Sutra and the writings of Nichiren) and in its historical development, "What are the major categories of behavior for the welfare of others? What does the religion mean by 'others' both doctrinally and historically?" Second, "How does the religion assess the meaning of behavior for the welfare of others? For instance, does it assess such behavior in terms of its impact on the recipient, in terms of the action itself, in terms of the motivation or intention of the actor, or some combination of the above?" Third, "Does the religion create a context in which it is possible that intentional action for the welfare of others can have only a neutral or negative consequence on the actor?"

On the first point, the view of ultimate reality in Nichiren Buddhism serves as the backdrop for a response. The two aspects of ultimate reality calling our attention are the doctrine of "3,000 worlds in a single thought-moment" and the notion of Shakyamuni, Lord of Dharma, the Father of all beings.

With regard to the former aspect, a conscious subject understands itself from an ultimate perspective as wrapped within a web of mutual interconnection and interpenetration with all sentient beings. In light of this grand vision of the universe as an interconnected web wherein each one is enveloped and each one finds its proper place within the whole, there is no such thing as an autonomous or separate self; thus, there also is no such thing as "other." This conscious subject that thinks of itself as such—that is, as a conscious subject that is separate from others—is at best a provisional entity, based on an illusion or, rather, a delusion. To see through this delusion is to realize one's true nature—that is, Buddha nature. Buddha nature is no other than this infinite interconnected web, manifesting itself concretely in each and every thought-moment in an individual's life.

With regard to the latter aspect, all sentient beings are understood as children of Shakyamuni Buddha, Lord of Dharma, and therefore are identified as members of the same Buddha family. This reality constitutes our nature as Buddha-nature—that is, as children of the Buddha who has proclaimed the One Vehicle of liberation for all. In this context, as children of the same Buddha-family, all "other" beings are intimately part of my own being, kin to myself; thus, "their" welfare is inseparably linked with "mine."

This vision of familial interconnection can be regarded as the ground for activation of the power of compassion—literally, "suffering-with." The notion of compassion in Buddhism derives from two terms: *mettā*, and *karuṇā*. The former, often translated as "lovingkindness," is expounded in the well-known *Mettā Sutta*, with the image of the heart and mind of "a mother toward her only child," which each one is enjoined to cultivate toward all sentient beings. The term *mettā*, then, refers to this intimate kinship between mother and child that grounds behavior that seeks the well-being of one's kin as one's very own. The image of Shakyamuni, Lord of Dharma, as Father of all beings then resonates with this circle of intimate kinship that generates attitudes and acts toward the well-being of one's kin—no longer considered as "other." The term *karuṇā* refers to solidarity in suffering, seeking its alleviation. Again, attitudes and acts in this regard derive from this understanding of intimacy and kinship, in feeling and experiencing the pain and suffering of the "other" as one's very own.

In Nichiren Buddhism, then—in ways that also resonate with other forms of Buddhism—the notion of the "other" is superseded by an all-inclusive notion of ultimate reality as interconnected, wherein one realizes intimate kinship with all beings, moving one to assume attitudes and take actions grounded in compassion. An important religious event in the life of a given individual, then, is one's awakening to this ultimate reality, enabling one to see through the delusion of one's separate self. This awakening, in turn, is precipitated by, occasioned by, and realized in religious practice.

The response to the second question, on the meaning of attitudes and acts vis-à-vis the "other," likewise flows from this vision of ultimate reality and can be seen in greater focus in the light of the religious practice prescribed in this tradition.

As I note above, the main form of religious practice in Nichiren Buddhism is repetitive chanting of the august title of the Lotus Sutra, *Nam-myōhō-renge-kyō*. Through this act of vocally enunciating this august title, the salvific power of the sutra is activated, and the devotee is enveloped in this interconnected realm whereby the 3,000 worlds that represent the entire universe are made manifest in the here and now, embodied in the being of the chanter. In this moment of chanting, the individual self of the chanter is merged with the realm of the interconnected universe, and the chanter experiences a dissolution of the "egoic self," with the concomitant manifestation of the 3,000 worlds in this single moment of thought rapt in the chant of *Nam-myōhō-renge-kyō*. In short, this act of chanting dissolves the barrier between "self" and "other," bringing about the manifestation of a realm of reality that goes beyond the dualism of self and other.

Thus, the religious practice of chanting can be considered as an action that overcomes the self–other duality, as a gateway to the realization of a nondual realm. This form of religious practice in itself may not be considered as "behavior on behalf of others" because it is first and foremost an act that leads an individual to an experiential realization of ultimate reality. Its *de facto* outcome in bridging the barrier between "self" and "other," however, predisposes an individual practitioner to see "others" no longer as such (that is, as "others") but intimately connected to one's very own being.

Nichiren himself expounded on this religious act of chanting the august title, in the context of his view of ultimate reality, as efficacious not only in bringing about the realization of Lotus Land in the earthly realm but also as evoking auspicious power that can heal ailments and bring about worldly benefit. This aspect of chanting has been underscored among Nichiren's followers through the ages and has been presented as a way of winning adherents to the practice. As it has been handed down and understood among many devotees of this practice through history and up to the present, this aspect of generating worldly benefit has taken prominence as having primary significance. In this context, the act of chanting, taken as a means toward attaining worldly gain, also can be and has become a tool of the egoic self in realizing its own narrow goals, rather than bringing a practitioner to a mode of awareness freed from the dualistic notions of self versus other.

Religious practice in Nichiren Buddhism has an inherent other-oriented aspect: The imperative of conveying the truth of the Lotus Sutra to others is an important aspect of the sutra's own teaching. The experience of one's interconnectedness with all reality, opened to the devotee in and through chanting of the august title, leads one to seek actualization in society of what one has experienced inwardly. In short, the devotee is impelled by this very experience to go out and proclaim the Lotus Sutra's message to people, seeking to bring them to an acceptance of and devotion to the Lotus Sutra.

The political dimension of the Nichiren Buddhist's religious practice follows from the recognition that the "social" and the "political" are inseparable. Nichiren was acutely aware of the power of the political domain in influencing the lives of the people in his society and times and therefore sought directly to influence this domain toward actualization of his religious vision. This attitude reflects a recognition that other religious communities, whose message centers on an otherworldly kind of salvation, may be less forthcoming.[16]

The question, however, is whether such action that leads the Nichiren Buddhist toward engagement in the sociopolitical realm comes out of what we can understand as "an altruistic motivation"—that is, something that is done out of care and concern for the welfare of "the other" (to take this term in its practical usage, the theoretical problem regarding its viability in the Nichiren Buddhist vision of reality notwithstanding).

Nichiren's treatise *On the Establishment of Correct Teaching and Securing the Peace of the Land* (*Risshō Ankoku ron*), which launched him into sociopolitical involvement, begins with a passage (cited above) that comes out of his deep care and concern for the sufferings and travails of the people in the society of his time. In this treatise, Nichiren also describes how he "pondered the matter carefully ... and searched the scriptures for an answer" that might throw light on this situation.[17] A straightforward reading of this treatise would lead us to affirm an altruistic motivation behind his religious quest. In short, seeking to alleviate the suffering of the people around him, Nichiren looked into their causes and, seeking light from Buddhist scriptures, arrived at an answer: The truth was not being served because erroneous teaching proliferated and the Lotus Sutra was not given its due as the supreme teaching with universal salvific power. Given this "answer" that Nichiren arrived at through reading and reflection on scriptures, his vision of "what is to be done" was simply a concomitant of his religious vision: "Let everyone acknowledge the supreme teaching of the Lotus Sutra, and all will be well."

Of course, one might offer the critique that this perspective was a simplistic view of things and (from a Western, post-Enlightenment perspective) point out that Nichiren failed to appreciate the complexities of the sociohistorical conditions of his time. Further investigation of and reflection on how Nichiren followers in contemporary times—in Japan as well as in other parts of the world where they now have active communities engaged in the issues of their respective societies—have pursued or would pursue this question, in terms of their reading of Nichiren's text as a primary religious resource and in terms of their own understanding of the grounds of their sociopolitical engagement, is called for.[18]

Hermeneutical and sociohistorical issues duly acknowledged as ongoing tasks, in any case, the claim of an "altruistic motivation" as underlying the entire religious project of Nichiren Buddhism is certainly supportable by the texts (i.e., Nichiren's writings). One also could approach Nichiren's text from a different, unsympathetic perspective, however—with the observation that he could have been merely "using" the situation of social chaos and political upheaval that was bringing tremendous suffering to the people as a "means" for conveying his religious message of the supremacy of the Lotus Sutra. If one takes such a stance at the outset, one's reading of Nichiren's account of the sufferings of the people would be colored by a tinge of cynicism, taking his writings not so much as indications of his compassionate or altruistic concern but as instruments for religious purposes.

Such a perspective might be maintained in reading Nichiren's inaugural treatise *Risshō Ankoku ron* in isolation, or even in conjunction with other treatises in which Nichiren addresses the social and political crisis facing the nation and calls for a return to "correct teaching." Careful reading of other writings, however—notably the numerous letters he sent to individuals or small groups of followers throughout his career, especially those composed during his years of retirement at Mt. Minobu—would topple such an unsympathetic view of Nichiren's motivations. These letters reveal a heart and mind overflowing with care and compassion, seeking the well-being and ultimate realization of all people, beginning with the ones with whom he was in direct contact.

A passage written the year before Nichiren's death reveals this heart and mind of compassion that propelled him throughout his entire religious career:

> Now, since the twenty-eighth day of the fourth month of the Kenchō year (1253) until now, the twelfth month of the third year of Kōan (1280), for a period of twenty-eight years, Nichiren has devoted his life to none other than this cause: to do all that is possible to put these seven or five characters of (*Nam*) *Myōhō-renge-kyō* into the mouths of all the sentient beings of the country of Japan. It is just as a mother, in her compassionate love, would do all that is possible to put milk into the mouth of her infant child.[19]

This passage, together with many others in the Nichiren corpus, offers a glimpse of Nichiren's primary concern—which is the ultimate well-being of all, beginning with those in his own country, Japan. For him this state of ultimate well-being can come about only as one awakens to the salvific truth of the Lotus Sutra and thereby realizes one's true nature as a child of Shakyamuni, Lord of Dharma. One thereby lives in Shakyamuni's constant presence in communion with all other beings in the universe, who also are children of the same Father and have come to acknowledge this reality as they together chant the words *Nam-myōhō-renge-kyō*, the august title of the Lotus Sutra, bringing about the Lotus Land in this very earthly realm.

Nichiren's virulent accusations against political and religious leaders included proclamations that they would "fall into the deepest hells" for their errant actions, especially for misleading the people down the same path of perdition. It is important to note that the notion of "hell" in the Buddhist worldview involves not an irrevocable, eternal state but a realm of intense suffering with different forms, depending on the nature and gravity of the evil actions performed by the individual during a previous lifetime. In this worldview, through the sufferings one undergoes in the hellish realms, one can exhaust the negative karma accrued in previous lifetimes and thereby be reborn in another mode within the tenfold cycle of sentient beings—and thus be given another chance toward ultimate realization of one's inherent Buddhahood. In Nichiren's view, being consigned to hellish realms did not constitute an eternal destiny; it could be precisely an occasion to acknowledge the error of one's previous ways, leading to a new awakening that would usher in the path to ultimate realization. Thus, Nichiren's invectives against "errant ones" are not necessarily rejection of these persons from his field of care and concern; instead, they can be regarded as harsh punitive measures taken by a mother or father toward an erring child for the latter to come to a change of heart.

Nichiren's involvement in the sociopolitical issues of his time clearly was an outgrowth of his deep care and concern for the ultimate well-being of the people of his society. His goal was not so much social or political reform as such but a change of minds and hearts on the part of social, political, and, of course, religious leaders, in a way that would usher in a new social order marked by peace and security—the realization of Lotus Land in this earthly realm.

In this framework, the term "compassion" may aptly characterize the underlying dynamism of Nichiren's actions. In light of his view of ultimate reality, "altruism" in its strict sense of "concern for and action toward the well-being of others without regard for oneself" would be inexact. Nichiren's overarching concern is realization of the Lotus Land, which would entail the ultimate well-being of all in a way that has transcended the self–other duality.

The motivations underlying the actions of Nichiren's followers throughout history as they engaged in the sociopolitical issues of their own times, by following Nichiren's outward example, also cannot simply be presumed to be the same as the founder's; thus, this issue also calls for further examination. Of course, a similar compassionate concern also may have been present, but various historical actions taken by Nichiren's followers must be evaluated on their own terms. For example, with regard to the confrontative attitudes and actions taken by Nichiren's followers versus political and religious figures of their respective times, there may have been elements of self-righteousness: an absolutization of one's religious standpoint with a concomitant denigration of all other religious views, a sense of superiority that leads to a paternalistic or patronizing stance against other religious communities or teachings. Attitudes and acts that are based on such attitudes clearly are on the opposite end of altruism. A religious motivation in itself cannot be identified or equated with an altruistic stance.

With regard to the third point in Green's set of questions, "neutral or negative consequences" of one's actions that befall the actor in the context of the religious goals in Nichiren Buddhism are not necessarily a direct indication of an altruistic state of mind. In Nichiren's own testimony, the adversities and experiences of suffering and persecution he experienced as a consequence of his actions in propagating devotion to the Lotus Sutra were construed as confirmation of the genuineness of his message because such negative repercussions were presaged in the Lotus Sutra itself for those propagating its doctrine—indicating the controversial nature of the sutra itself from its inception and the tumultuous times in which it was composed. Thus, the Lotus Sutra's social and historical context mirrored Nichiren's own, and he underwent a profound religious experience as an outcome of his sufferings on behalf of the Lotus Sutra. His followers were opened to similar religious experiences of confirmation of their actions as they encountered these "negative consequences."

In short, acceptance of these negative outcomes, concretely—persecution, harassment, chastisement, or disapproval by society in general of one's actions—does not necessarily confirm an altruistic state of mind. Certainly it can be a manifestation of a magnanimous spirit that is willing to sacrifice life and limb for the realization of one's ultimate goal—as for Nichiren himself and undoubtedly for many of his followers who also experienced trials and tribulations in their religious careers. It also can be simply self-reinforcement, however, of a religious perspective that remains on the level of the egoic self.

Conclusion

This examination of Nichiren Buddhism presents an ambivalent picture of the role of altruism (strictly defined in Green's terms) within the religious framework of this tradition. The tradition's view of ultimate reality—seen from one angle as a realm of interconnectedness of all beings in the universe experienced in a devotee's earthly life in a single thought-moment—draws one into a realm that overcomes the self–other duality. From another angle, it conveys the ultimate identity of all sentient beings as children of the one Buddha. Thus, it invites adherents to experiential realization of a realm that has overcome the dualistic opposition of "egoism" and "altruism," a realm whereby one acknowledges that the good of one is at the same time the good of each and every "other."

Nichiren Buddhism's prescribed forms of religious practice—on the self-oriented level as the chanting of the august title of the Lotus Sutra and on the other-oriented level as the endeavor to propagate the teachings of the Lotus in society—can be undertaken as acts that liberate one from the egoic self. On the other hand, these practices also may be experienced as reinforcements of this egoic self. Likewise, experiences of adversity and suffering as an outcome of one's religious practice in the sociopolitical realm can be manifestations of a magnanimous spirit that transcends one's egoistic interests, but they also can be a reconfirmation of one's own religious perspective that does not necessarily take one beyond the egoic level.

In this chapter I have alluded to features of Nichiren that call for further reflection, including the perennial question of the relationship between the religious and political domains and the relationship between the this-worldly dimension and the otherworldly dimension in a religious worldview. More detailed examination of these questions, in the context of comparative analysis with other religious traditions, can yield fresh insights that can throw light on our understanding of religion in human life and society.

In considering Nichiren Buddhism as one example of a Japanese religious tradition, I have noted, from several angles, the ambivalence—or perhaps, more boldly, the inutility or inapplicability—of the "egoism versus altruism" polarity that belongs to common parlance in Western philosophical and psychological discourse, whereby the latter is valued over the former. There is a need for a more expanded notion that would overcome this dualistic opposition of egoism versus altruism, whereby the "other" would be understood as an inherent aspect of the "self," and "identity" in itself includes "alterity," and vice versa.

Notes

1. Ian Reader and George J. Tanabe, *Practically Religious: Worldly Benefits and the Common Religion of Japan* (Honolulu: University of Hawaii Press, 1998), 23.
2. Ibid., 14.
3. Christopher Queen and Sallie B. King, *Engaged Buddhism: Buddhist Liberation Movements in Asia* (Albany: State University of New York Press, 1996).
4. The twofold (self-oriented and other-oriented) aspect of Nichiren Buddhist practice relates to the second question raised by William Scott Green in the introduction to this book: "How does the religion assess the meaning of behavior for the welfare of others? For instance, does it

assess such behavior in terms of its impact on the recipient, in terms of the action itself, in terms of the motivation or intention of the actor, or some combination of the above?"

5. This section references Green's third question: "Does the religion create a context in which it is possible that intentional action for the welfare of others can have only a neutral or negative consequence on the actor?"

6. *The Writings of Nichiren Daishonin* (hereafter WND), trans. Gosho Translation Committee (Tokyo: Soka Gakkai, 1999), 6.

7. Ibid., 7.

8. Bunno Kato et al., *The Threefold Lotus Sutra* (Tokyo: Kosei Publishing, 1988), 256.

9. WND, 365.

10. Ibid., 376.

11. Ibid.

12. Translation in Jacqueline Stone, *Original Enlightenment: The Transformation of Japanese Buddhism* (Honolulu: University of Hawaii Press, 1999), 291–92; WND, 392.

13. Translation in Stone, *Original Enlightenment*, 289.

14. WND, 278, 281.

15. Ruben L. F. Habito, "Bodily Reading of the Lotus Sutra: Understanding Nichiren's Buddhism," in Ruben L. F. Habito and Jacqueline Stone, "Revisiting Nichiren." Special Issue of *Japanese Journal of Religious Studies* 26. nos. 3–4 (1999): 281–306.

16. The principle of "separation of church and state," which comes out of the American historical experience and is a viable principle in setting certain distinctions and clarifying ground rules in the relationship between the state or the political domain and the church or the religious domain, has tended to be interpreted in one-sided ways and calls for further reflection in light of the historical experience of religious communities in different cultures throughout the world. In any case, the relationship between the religious and political dimensions of human existence is a matter that calls for continuing reflection in different religious and historical contexts.

17. WND, 7.

18. Informal conversations I have had with several Western-born members of the Soka Gakkai International—perhaps the most dynamic and influential among the different groups of Nichiren Buddhists in our day—have indicated acute appreciation of this question and ongoing task involving a "hermeneutics of Nichiren's texts" in the communities of professed adherents.

19. *Showa Teihon Nichiren Ibun*. Showa Revised Critical Edition, Nichiren's Writings (Tokyo: Rissho Daigaku Nichiren Kyogaku Kenkyusho, 1989), vol. 2, p. 1844, lines 2–4 (translation by the author).

Chapter 8

Altruism in Classical Hinduism

Richard H. Davis

T he *Mahabharata* is a massive tale of war. Its immense, complex narrative relates an internecine struggle between two sets of cousins that comes to involve the entire ruling class of India and leads to its near-extermination. War, we are often told, is one of the great tests of human character—the mortar and pestle by which theories of human motivation and action are ground down and examined. The lessons of war are not limited to the battlefield. Over the centuries Hindus have repeatedly looked to the narratives and discourses of the *Mahabharata* to reflect on their own lives and their own ethical and religious quandaries.

Historians and archeologists postulate that some kind of "Bharata War" took place in northern India around 900 BCE and that this battle provided the starting point for oral recitations by bards associated with warrior clans, who retold the glorious deeds of great warriors in that battle over succeeding generations. These recitations are not what have been preserved and passed down to us, however. Sometime during the Sunga period, between 200 and 100 BCE, oral traditions of the great war were collected, composed, and turned into a cohesive text. This composed text remained open, evidently, to interpolations for several centuries more, until sometime during the Gupta period (300–450 CE), when an authoritative written draft effectively closed the text.[1]

Over the long intervening period between the originating event and the Sunga and Gupta redactions of the *Mahabharata*, a great deal changed in India, and the text reflected those changes. The original war took place in a small area of northern India—near the present-day capital of the Republic of India, Delhi—among seminomadic pastoral clans. The retelling of this war in the *Mahabharata*, by contrast, reflects a sedentary and urbanizing culture spreading itself through most of the subcontinent, a class-based social system, and a monarchical form of political organization. The composed *Mahabharata* is not simply a reflection of its society, however. The *Mahabharata* is often called "encyclopedic" to highlight its comprehensive scope; unlike an encyclopedia, however, which aims to reflect the existing state of knowledge about the world or some subset of it, the *Mahabharata* aims to call a new world into being. In its deliberative and discursive style, the text presents arguments for a new model of "brahmanic" kingship, a new mode of social organization, and a new form of devotional theistic Hinduism. Much of what we think of as classical Hinduism finds its earliest written expression in this expansive epic work.

Over the course of the *Mahabharata's* composition, there also had occurred great changes in moral concepts, subsumed under the key ethical term *dharma*. These changes involved shifts in attitudes toward violence and war. In reconsiderations of *dharma* and the propriety of violence, we can see a case in classical Hinduism for altruism in the sense of selfless, other-directed, beneficial action.

In this chapter I consider questions of war, violence, *dharma,* and the motivation for action as they are addressed in two of the most important non-narrative, discursive sections of the *Mahabharata*: Krsna's counsel to Arjuna in the *Bhagavad Gita* (a portion of Book 6) and Bhisma's teachings to Yudhisthira in the *Santiparvan* (Book 12). I show how these two advisers to the Pandava heroes present arguments for a form of "generalized altruism" that can accommodate the selective use of violence and how Krsna both supports this conception and complicates it with an innovative call for "devotional altruism."

Two Scenes

In a valuable introductory discussion for a new translation of Books 11 and 12 of the *Mahabharata* (hereafter abbreviated as *MBh*), James Fitzgerald refers to the *Bhagavad Gita* (hereafter abbreviated as *BhG*) and the *Santiparvan* as discursive "bookends" to the narrative account of the war itself.[2] At the center of the epic are eighteen days of battle, recounted in great detail in Books 6 through 10 of the *Mahabharata*. As with so many wars in human history, from the Peloponnesian War to World War II and beyond, the Bharata War (at least in its epic retelling) involves a rapid escalation in duplicity, treachery, ferocity, and sheer brutal destructiveness.[3] No doubt the older oral legends the bards told of the Bharata War featured glorious triumphalist praises of the battlefield prowess and courageous deeds of the warriors. The presentation of war in the composed *Mahabharata* maintains some of these laudatory accounts, but the mood within which they are framed is altogether different. It is a story of wartime victory suffused with regret, sorrow, and overwhelming grief.[4]

Nowhere is this clearer than in the book that immediately follows the war: Book 11, called the "Book of the Women."[5] After the final day of battle the blind king Dhrtarastra leads the women of Hastinapura, capital of the defeated Kauravas, out to the battlefield. As these wealthy, protected women of an urban court, usually so refined and gentle, leave their seclusion, they wail and shriek like ospreys. They burn like beings on fire with grief, anxiety, and rage. They hurl accusations at the victorious

Pandava prince Yudhisthira, and the queen, Gandhari, curses Krsna, whom she believes to have brought on the war, even though she recognizes him to be a god. At the battlefield these pampered women stumble about in the mire and gore looking for the bodies or body parts of their fathers, husbands, brothers, and sons; they must fight off the carrion-eating crows, jackals, and goblins who have arrived en masse at the combat to gorge on the slaughter. Queen Gandhari, who narrates much of this scene, pauses in her description to anticipate with bitter irony the triumphalist bardic poetry that will later eulogize these corpses: "Clever bards would celebrate them in the wee hours of every night with the very best songs of praise and flattery. Now the best of women, tormented with pain—women in an agony of grief and pain—mourn them wretchedly, o tiger of the Vrsnis" (MBh 11.16.41–42).[6]

In her juxtaposition of bardic panegyric of dead warriors with the existential grief of the warriors' women, Gandhari epitomizes the transformation in the moral complexion of war that has occurred in the composed Mahabharata. No longer glorious or celebratory, the epic now portrays war as a tragic necessity.

The tragic view of war leads the principal actors in the story to deep doubts about their motivations and extensive reflection on their actions. Although this reflection is spread throughout the Mahabharata, issues of motivation, action, duty, and consequence are most directly reconsidered in the two discourses that form bookends to the war books. To gain a full sense of the impact of these sections of the epic, it is necessary to describe the two scenes.

Immediately before the first battle is to begin, the two opposing armies face one another on the field of Kuruksetra:

There were berserk men there, clutching their weapons—10,000 standards commanded by champions. There were 5,000 elephants, all the chariot trains, footmen, and commanders, carrying bows and swords and clubs by the thousands in front and by the thousands in back. The other kings were largely stationed in this sea of troops where Yudhisthira himself was positioned, with thousands of elephants, tens of thousands of horses, thousands of chariots and foot soldiers, relying on which he marched to attack Duryodhana Dhrtarastra. Behind followed hundreds of thousands and myriads of men, marching and shouting in thousands of formations. And in their thousands and tens of thousands the happy warriors sounded their thousands of drums and tens of thousands of conches (MBh 5.197.17–19).

The foremost Pandava warrior, Arjuna, requests that his charioteer, Krsna—who also is his friend and brother-in-law—drive him onto the field between the two armies so he can survey the enemy array. What Arjuna sees there catalyzes all his anxieties and doubts about the impending war. Opposite the Pandava side Arjuna sees not only his cousins the Kauravas but also his grandfather, uncles, and teachers. To fight his own family, Arjuna realizes, will violate a central tenet of his code of conduct: family loyalty—a principle of *dharma*. His body trembles and his bow slips out of his hand. He speaks in despair to Krsna:

> I see no good to come from killing my family in battle. I do not wish victory, Kesava, nor kingship and pleasures. . . . The very men for whose sake we want kingship, comforts, and joy, stand in line to battle us, forfeiting their hard-to-relinquish lives. Teachers, fathers, sons, grandfathers, maternal uncles, fathers-in-law, grandsons, brothers-in-law, and other relatives-in-law—I do not want to kill them, though they be killers, Madhusudana, even for the sovereignty of the three worlds, let alone earth (*BhG* 1.31–35).

Arjuna can see no beneficial outcome that could possibly warrant the terrible transgression he sees in the prospect of killing his own kinsmen.

Krsna's task, then, is to persuade Arjuna to overcome his qualms and fight. Arjuna's reservations are not a simple matter of cowardice, though Krsna does accuse him of that. Because Arjuna sees his objection to this battle in terms of *dharma*, Krsna must bring war within the framework of ethical action. He must articulate moral reasons for Arjuna to fight that are compelling enough to overcome Arjuna's legitimate repugnance toward the slaughter of his own kinsmen. Arjuna's dilemma is the initial moral concern of the *Bhagavad Gita*, although Krsna expands his topic considerably beyond the original charge. Ultimately Krsna does convince Arjuna, who goes on to fight relentlessly over the ensuing eighteen days of battle and is crucial to the victory of the Pandavas.

At the conclusion of the war, nearly all the teachers and kinsmen Arjuna saw on the first day of battle have been slain. Almost the entire class of warriors has been exterminated in the terrible slaughter. One estimate holds that five million warriors die in the course of the battle. The Kaurava women come onto the field with their searing laments, and the corpses are burned in immense crematory fires. The few surviving Pandavas remain near the battlefield for thirty days because they have been polluted by their contact with death; then they enter Hastinapura in a tattered, triumphant procession. Throughout the aftermath of battle, the eldest Pandava, Yudhisthira, has been wracked with grief, guilt, and apprehension. He repeatedly threatens to renounce the kingship that has accrued to him, and others repeatedly must convince him not to abandon his duty. When the warriors enter the capital, Yudhisthira hears a voice from the crowd, speaking as if to give voice to his own inner doubts:

> All these brahmins have entrusted me to speak for them [claims the protestor Carvaka], and they say "Curses upon you, sir, a wicked king who slaughtered his own kin! What good can there be in your ruling the kingdom, son of Kunti, since you have completely erased your own kinsmen? And once you have caused the killing of your elders, death would have been better for you than surviving" (*MBh* 12.39.25–27).[7]

Yudhisthira allows himself to be consecrated as king, but the demons of his guilt cannot be washed away so easily. Finally, at the insistence of Krsna, Yudhisthira goes for fuller counsel to his great-uncle Bhisma.

Bhisma had sworn a lifelong vow of celibacy to assist his father Santanu in marrying a fisher-woman, so he had no direct offspring. Nevertheless, he became the court patriarch and honorary royal "grandfather" at Hastinapura, and both the Kauravas and Pandavas (all grandchildren of Bhisma's brother) considered him a wise adviser. The Kauravas chose him as military commander for the war, and Bhisma dutifully served in that capacity even though his sympathies lay with the other side. Bhisma led the Kauravas for the first nine days of battle, but on the tenth Arjuna—employing a deception that Bhisma himself had recommended the Pandavas use against him—gave him a mortal wound. The warrior pierced Bhisma with a multitude of arrows. On account of his previous self-restraint, however, Bhisma had acquired the power to choose his own moment of death. With hundreds of arrows protruding from his body and cushioning him off the ground Bhisma lay through the remainder of the battle and its aftermath. There, on a bed of arrows on the battlefield of Kuruksetra, Yudhisthira seeks him out.

Although Bhisma is near death he still has enough acumen and stamina to transmit his full knowledge to Yudhisthira. Moreover, Bhisma does so at considerable length. His teachings in the *Santiparvan* and *Anusasanaparvan* cover more that 37,900 lines of text—roughly equivalent in length to the Christian Bible.[8] At the center of Bhisma's teachings, detailed and prolific as they are, is his aim to persuade Yudhisthira to accept his duty as consecrated king. As with Krsna's advice to Arjuna, Bhisma seeks to convince Yudhisthira to act. To do so Bhisma must reconcile for Yudhisthira the task of kingship, which requires the use of force and violence, with the concept of *dharma*. To rule effectively and wholeheartedly, Yudhisthira must be convinced that his actions as sovereign will accord with *dharma*.

What, then, is *dharma*? Consideration of this term—a key concept in the *Mahabharata* and many other classic Hindu works—brings us back to the key term of this book: altruism.

Two Dharmas

Dharma derives from the Sanskrit root *dhr*, to uphold, maintain, support. It may be broadly rendered as that which upholds or supports the order of things. The cosmos generally operates according to orderly principles, Hindus believe, and these are principles of *dharma*. Yet *dharma* also pertains to the realm of human activity, and once we descend from cosmic order to the human, determining *dharma* becomes a more problematic enterprise. Any Sanskrit-English dictionary will provide a long list of translational approximations: decree, statute, law, practice, observance, duty, right, righteousness, virtue, morality, religion, good works, code of conduct, and many more. This profusion of translations does not mean that Indians were unable to decide. *Dharma* was a crucial term of public discourse—too important to be left uncontested. Therefore, every school of thought and persuasion articulated its own perspective on *dharma*. The Buddhists and Jains designated their heterodox teachings as *dharma*, as did the various orthodox traditions we now call Hindu.

Dharma also changed over time. One of Fitzgerald's valuable insights is to separate two distinct senses of *dharma* as it is used in the *Mahabharata*. Although these two senses are juxtaposed in the text, they can be distinguished as earlier and later in historical origin.

The first and chronologically earlier sense of *dharma* involves self-interested action that is efficacious in a broad and often nonempirical manner. "Dharma is something one does," Fitzgerald writes, "which then unfailingly connects one to an important good, or goods, that do not lie completely within the reach of normal human effort, such as victory, glory, future prosperity, or a good afterlife."[9] This notion of *dharma* is best seen in the early brahmanic or Vedic theory of sacrifice—the preeminent form of ritual practice in early Hinduism. According to this view, a sacrificial action (*karman*) should be undertaken by an agent out of a desire (*kama*) for some benefit or fruit (*phala*) that will result from that action. An unusually potent action, sacrifice can attain for its performer not only "empirically visible" (*drsta*) results but also "empirically invisible" (*adrsta*) outcomes—that is, far-reaching results such as future prosperity or heaven that do not have any immediately discernible relationship to the action itself. This instrumentalist view of *dharma*, then, emphasizes the importance of goal-directed action in which the principal beneficiary is the actor.

Well before the composition of the *Mahabharata* during the Sunga dynasty, another sense of *dharma* circulated in northern India. As Fitzgerald puts it, "The newer concept of dharma often replaces personal self-interest with a devaluation of one's particular being affiliated with a sense of connectedness to all others and a concomitant sense of kindness towards others."[10] The new view seems to have developed in part from various religious teachings in the period 600–200 BCE that broadly sought some state of transcendence or liberation (*moksa, nirvana*) from the cycle of death and rebirth through a variety of practices such as meditation, gnostic insight, and asceticism. Fitzgerald speaks of this movement as a "broad, heterogeneous 'discourse of yoga'" involving brahmanic thinkers, peripatetic yogis, and those who placed themselves outside the orthodox fold, such as Buddhists and Jains.[11] Others have termed it a "renunciatory movement" because many of the practices required that one remove oneself from ordinary social roles to pursue salvation.

Within the yogic or renunciatory analysis, desire (*kama*) is identified not just as a motivater of action but also as one of the primary forces that maintains the individual in a state of continuing bondage. Self-interested action leads to invisible results, just as the sacrificialists averred, but these results are precisely what keep one enmeshed in a world process that is now identified as full of suffering. Breaking out of this process therefore requires disciplines (*yoga*) that enable the seeker to break the grip of self-interest. Such disciplines include cultivation of nonviolence (*ahimsa*) toward others, physical acts of austerity and self-abnegation, meditations aimed at withdrawal of one's attachments to the sensory world, and cultivation of insight that erases boundaries between self and others.

Clearly this second perspective on *dharma*, in its stance against self-interested action, brings us closer to the senses of altruism in modern Western usage surveyed by William Scott Green in the introduction to this book. After reviewing several definitions and discussions of the term "altruism," Green suggests that we understand it to refer to "intentional action ultimately for the welfare of others that entails at least the possibility of either no benefit or a loss to the actor." Yet there is one central difference between Green's definition and Fitzgerald's second understanding of *dharma*. Renunciation (*sannyasa*) involves intentional removal of oneself from normal family and social roles, as the site of desire and self-interested activity. Renunciatory ethics emphasizes avoidance of desire-based action, but this attitude could take the form of avoiding *all* action. Altruism is preeminently a matter of action intended to benefit others. There is no such thing as altruistic inaction.

The *Mahabharata* is an activist text. Although it acknowledges at considerable length the tragic repercussions of (improper) actions and endorses the values and efficacy of renunciation (for certain persons, in certain circumstances), it repeatedly and forcefully asserts the importance of action in the shared social world. In fact, both bookend discourses respond to the threats made by principal actors in the *Mahabharata* not to act. Arjuna initially decides not to fight on the battlefield of Kuruksetra, and Yudhisthira is tempted not to rule in Hastinapura after the Pandava victory. In both cases their advisors—Krsna and Bhisma, respectively—are called on to convince the protagonists to act, to fulfill their duties.[12] To do so Krsna and Bhisma must show how the duties Arjuna and Yudhisthira are to carry out—the warrior's duty to fight, the sovereign's to rule—and the harsh incumbent actions these duties entail do not contradict the kinder, gentler sense of *dharma* spelled out in renunciatory ethics. In a sense, the advisors must persuade Arjuna and Yudhisthira that acting as a warrior or a king can be a form of generalized altruism. Krsna and Bhisma recommend actions that, in a phrase found throughout the *Mahabharata*, "take delight in the welfare of all beings."[13]

Bhisma's Teachings on Kingship

I treat Bhisma's discourse before that of Krsna, even though it occurs later in the *Mahabharata,* because Bhisma's teachings to Yudhisthira offer a better starting point with regard to the issues of action and motivation. These teachings cover many subjects, but of greatest interest in this context is Bhisma's initial discussion of the principles of kingship. On the first day of instruction Yudhisthira presents Bhisma with his personal dilemma: "Those who know *dharma* hold that kingly rule is the very highest *dharma*, but I think it is a great burden" (*MBh* 12.56.2).[14] Yudhisthira's great need is for Bhisma to clarify the fundamental principles of the *dharma* of kings.

Bhisma responds by emphasizing first the importance of energetic human activity. The king must act, and act vigorously. Renunciation, Bhisma suggests, is not a viable option for one destined to be king. Royal action, he continues, includes opposing anyone who opposes you—even your teacher or friend. Here Bhisma clearly addresses the great dilemma that the Pandavas faced in the war, when they did face teachers and friends and relatives as opponents, and he condones their actions as part of the *dharma* incumbent on those who would rule.

At the same time, Bhisma also praises the virtues of gentleness and self-restraint: "The king who is endowed with good qualities and good character, who is self-controlled and gentle, who follows *dharma*, who has conquered his senses, and who is handsome and broad-minded never falls from Royal Splendor" (*MBh* 12.56.19). Here Bhisma speaks in the idiom of renunciatory ethics, with its emphasis on self-restraint and unselfishness. "A king should always follow the same *dharma* a pregnant woman does. Hear the reason, great king, that makes this desirable. A pregnant woman forsakes the lover who pleases her heart and devotes herself to the welfare of her baby. Undoubtedly the king who follows the *dharma* should always do the same, o most splendid of the Kurus—renouncing his own pleasure, he should do whatever benefits the world" (*MBh* 12.56.44–46). In Bhisma's analogy, the pregnant woman becomes a paradigm for altruism because she forsakes actions that would bring her pleasure or personal gratification to devote herself to the welfare of another—her baby. The altruistic *dharma* of a king similarly lies in renouncing personal aims in favor of seeking to "benefit the world"—that is, all creatures under his sovereign protection. There is one difference, however. The pregnant woman has a single specific recipient for her altruistic conduct, whereas the king's conduct is aimed more generally for the benefit of all. A gentle and self-restrained king, Bhisma adds, comes to be trusted by his subjects "as if he were the Himalayas" (*MBh* 12.57.29). Like mountains, gentle kings are beneficial to all.

Bhisma recognizes that although self-restraint and gentleness may endear the king to the kingdom, these personal qualities do not suffice in a world full of threats. A king who is always gentle will come to be ignored, so it is necessary to exercise force. Gentle *and* harsh—behave in both ways, Bhisma advises. The king should direct his rod of punishment (*danda*) at those who pose a threat to the settled order of society. This use of force will lead to protection (*raksana*), and Bhisma regards protection as the central task of kingship. "Protection," he says, "is the preservation of the world" (*MBh* 12.57.43). The king's selfless provision of protection for all provides the social order within which subjects may pursue their own interests. Bhisma quotes an aphorism of Sukra Bhargava in support of this teaching: "Get a king first, then a wife, then wealth. If the world has no king how can one have a wife? How wealth?" (*MBh* 12.57.41). Energetic activity, personal self-control and self-restraint, gentleness and selective violence, and protection are the key tenets in Bhisma's instruction on the *dharma* of kingship.

On the second day, Yudhisthira begins the session with a question about the beginnings of kingship. Where did kingship come from? How is it that one human, who is demonstrably made up of all the same physical constituents as others, comes to be elevated over all others? Bhisma answers Yudhisthira's inquiry with an origin tale about the first king, Prthu, which exemplifies many of the points he has previously made and provides further amplification.

In the Krta Age long ago, says Bhisma, there was no king and no ruling authority. All creatures guarded each other in accord with *dharma*, so there was no need for a governing authority. Over time, however, humans became weary and began to neglect their sacrifices and other meritorious deeds. Once they began to omit these virtuous acts they started to come under the sway of greed and desire. With the rise of human greed, society fell into disorder, and *dharma* disappeared. The gods became terrified. They went to their leader—Brahman, grandfather of the world—to ask for assistance. Because humans had stopped offering sacrifices, the gods themselves were deprived of their usual sustenance. Brahman promised to consider the problem and do something to alleviate the gods' fear.

Brahman's first response was to create a corpus of teachings, 100,000 lessons long, concerning *dharma* and all other topics necessary to human conduct. He passed this massive text to other gods, who abridged it into more concise forms suitable to the limited attention and shorter lifespan of humans. The gods then asked the god Visnu to create a being "worthy to be superior to other mortals," who could bring order to human society (*MBh* 12.59.94). Visnu's first creation was Virajas, a being of "dazzling fiery energy." Virajas was not interested in kingship, however; he wished to devote himself to the practice of renunciation. Virajas's son and grandson likewise had no inclination toward protecting society, and both pursued ascetic paths. Finally Virajas's great-grandson Ananga showed a proper disposition for a king. However, Ananga's son Atibala, though also adept in ruling, came to be dominated by his senses, and Atibala's successor Vena proved to be altogether ruled by his own passions and hatred. As a result, he behaved toward his subjects without any of the constraints of *dharma*. In this rapidly deteriorating situation it became necessary for brahmin seers to intervene. They killed King Vena with blades of sacrificial grass.

The brahmins now tried their hands at creating a king. First they churned the right thigh of Vena's corpse. From the thigh emerged an ugly little man who looked like a charred post. The brahmins tried to restrain this botched creation, but the man ran off into the mountains where the barbarians live. Next the brahmins churned the right hand of Vena, and this time they met with better success. A brilliant being emerged: Prthu, who looked like Indra, king of the Vedic gods. He appeared already armed with sword and bow, and already knew the Vedas. Prthu asked the gods what he should do, and they advised him: "Do without hesitation whatever is *dharma*, having restrained yourself—having forsaken your likes and dislikes, acting the same toward every person, having put desire and anger and greed and pride far off and away. Keeping *dharma* in view at all times, you must restrain forcibly any man in the world who strays from *dharma*" (*MBh* 12.59.110–12). Prthu agreed to become king, if the brahmins would serve as his assistants. The gods consecrated him as king, and, Bhisma concludes his tale, this paradigmatic king "made *dharma* supreme in the world" (*MBh* 12.59.122).

Bhisma's story of Prthu and his unsuccessful predecessors situates kingship as a response to human moral failure. Human immorality also affects the gods. In the golden age, no governing authority is required because all creatures spontaneously enact their proper duties; when weariness sets in and allows desire and greed to gain a foothold among humans, however, it provokes a crisis for the gods, who depend on the sacrificial offerings of humans. The gods make the first step toward instituting kingship. According to Bhisma, however, Brahman in his wisdom first creates codes for proper conduct and only then sets in motion the instantiation of a king. Principles of royal *dharma*, Bhisma suggests, exist prior to the person of the king.

When the time comes to create the occupant of kingship, even the god Visnu cannot get it right. In the string of royal failures one sees the two great dangers facing human kings. If they are too virtuous they may renounce kingship altogether, like Virajas and his first two offspring. On the other hand, if they are self-interested they will be susceptible to their own greed and desire, and they are likely to abuse their own powers. The brahmins finally succeed with Prthu, who combines a militant preparedness—he is born wearing armor—with a self-abnegating commitment to the general welfare. Just as important is this new ruler's reciprocal commitment to the brahmins who have churned him into being.

Throughout Bhisma's teachings, then, lies an emphasis on altruistic personal characteristics in the person of the king. In accord with the gentler sense of *dharma*, the king must act not out of self-interest and not on his own behalf but on behalf of all creatures—or at least all subjects under his own protection. Bhisma also recognizes, however, the ambiguous position of the king. To protect his subjects the king must be willing to exercise violence. According to renunciatory ethics, violence is inherently detrimental to the highest attainments. Royal violence may be necessary to maintain the social order, but the king who is responsible for maintaining order is left in a compromised position from the point of view of religious salvation.[15]

Classical Hindu texts such as the *Mahabharata* envision several ways of resolving the king's dilemma, and Bhisma subsequently discusses some of them in his final discourse. One way is simply to acknowledge a moral separation between the class of warriors and rulers (*ksatriya*) and that of religious specialists, the brahmins. In this view, only brahmins are qualified to practice the most rigorous forms of *dharma*, and only brahmins therefore can be expected to attain religious transcendence. Another solution is to divide an individual's life into stages (*asrama*). According to this perspective, worldly engagement during the householder stage of life (*grhastha*) may be followed by retirement from social obligations—designated as the forest-dwelling (*vanaprastha*) and renunciatory (*sannyasin*) stages of life. During the latter stages, the retiree may assiduously practice renunciatory values and disciplines and seek a final liberation. The *Mahabharata* implicitly endorses this resolution in its narrative: After listening to Bhisma's teachings, Yudhisthira goes on to rule in Hastinapura for thirty-six years; then he renounces the throne, installs his grandnephew Pariksit as royal successor, and leads his brothers and wife on a religious pilgrimage to heaven.

Krsna's Teachings on War, Duty, and Devotion

Krsna presents a more radical solution to the warrior's dilemma in his teachings to Arjuna before the battle. Recall that Krsna's teachings are provoked by Arjuna's refusal, at the very onset of battle, to fight. Arjuna does not intend to reject all violence. He has been trained all his life as a warrior, after all. It is the prospect of killing his own kinsmen and teachers that he finds intolerable. Yudhisthira has voiced the same complaint: "How can war be waged with men we may not kill? How can we win if we must kill our gurus and elders?" (*MBh* 5.151). Arjuna regards the situation as a conflict between two claims of *dharma*. On one hand, his duty as a member of the warrior class (*ksatriya-dharma*) is to fight in proper battles. On the other hand, loyalty to family (*kula-dharma*) precludes his fighting against members of his own family and clan. According to Arjuna, people may act against *dharma* either out of greed for personal gain or out of confusion about one's proper duty in a particular situation. Arjuna renounces any desire for gain in the war to come. However, he says, his mind is confused about what *dharma* is, and he appeals to Krsna for guidance.

There is a simple answer to Arjuna's dilemma. Krsna states it succinctly: "Look to your *dharma* and do not waver, for there is nothing more salutary for a baron (*ksatriya*) than a war in accord with *dharma*" (*BhG* 2.31). In a hierarchy of obligations, Krsna ranks the duty of a warrior as higher than that of family, just as Bhisma assures Yudhisthira after the war that a king must act against even family members who oppose him. In a sense, the old *ksatriya* codes of clan loyalty and honor have brought on this war, and Krsna and Bhisma seek to articulate broader, more universal ethical principles that will supplant the fractious warrior ethos.

For Krsna, clearing up *dharma*-confusions is only a starting point, however. He quickly raises another topic that has to do with "cutting away the bondage of the act" (*BhG* 2.39). Although Arjuna has not explicitly stated this issue as a concern, Krsna intuits his unstated objection. In effect, Arjuna proposes a renunciation of action, while Krsna is urging him to act as a warrior. Won't this act inevitably lead to karmic consequences? Won't it necessarily create further bondage for Arjuna? Krsna recognizes that to make his case for fighting persuasive, he must acknowledge and counteract the renunciatory argument. He must show Arjuna a way to act in the world that will not engender further bondage.

To make his case, Krsna distinguishes two modalities of action. In sacrifice, as the Vedic ritualists understand it—and in all goal-directed action—a desire (*kama*) for some end leads to a suitable intentional action (*karman*), which leads to a result or fruit (*phala*) of that action. As the renouncers have argued, however, this desiderative act also generates some karmic residue or bondage that enmeshes the actor in the continuing world-process. Krsna does not dispute this renunciatory analysis. Sacrifice undertaken in this spirit does indeed lead to bondage. He asserts, however, that there is another way of acting that does not engender bondage. If one acts without any interest in the fruit of the action, he states, one cuts away the bondage of the act: "Your entitlement (*adhikara*, duty, responsibility) is only to the rite (*karman*, action), not ever at all to the fruits (*phala*). Be not motivated by the fruits of acts, but also do not purposely seek to avoid acting. Abandon self-interest, Dhanamjaya, and perform the acts while applying this single-mindedness" (*BhG* 2.47–48).

In effect, Krsna redefines renunciation. Renunciation is not a matter of abandoning action—which Krsna later points out is not possible anyway. Rather, renunciation is a matter of abandoning attachment to the fruit of action. Action undertaken without any interest in the result or fruit to be gained—truly disinterested action—allows one to act *in* the world and not bind oneself further *to* the world.

Throughout the *Bhagavad Gita*, Krsna illustrates the notion of disinterested action in numerous ways. For example, early in his teachings he ridicules Vedic sacrificers who perform their ritual "inspired by desires, set upon heaven." Their way of acting brings on rebirth, robs them of their minds, and leaves them addicted to pleasures and power (*BhG* 2.42–46). Yet later he praises many different types of sacrificial actions. Why the change? In the latter cases, Krsna emphasizes, the acts are done without regard to result: "All the *karman* of one who acts sacrificially dissolves when he is disinterested and freed, and has steadied his thoughts with insight" (*BhG* 4.23).

How, then, does one act in this way? It cannot be easy to act altogether without self-interest. Arjuna asks Krsna just what a person who is disinterested and free, with thoughts steadied by insight, would look like: "What describes the man who stands in concentration (*sthitaprajna*),

Kesava? What does the one whose insight is firm say? How does he sit? How does he walk?" (*BhG* 2.54).

Krsna goes on to describe the one who stands in concentration. The *sthitaprajna* gradually withdraws his senses from their sensory objects, like a tortoise withdrawing its limbs. He feels neither craving for pleasure nor distress when adversity strikes. He experiences no preference for anything but equanimity toward all that comes his way: "When he experiences the objects with senses that neither love nor hate and are under his control, and thus has himself under control, he attains to serenity. In a state of serenity all his sufferings cease, for in one whose mind is serene, singleness of purpose is soon fixed" (*BhG* 2.64–65). In effect, the *sthitaprajna* is someone who incorporates the renunciatory disciplines of yogic withdrawal and gnostic insight to attain a mental state of equanimity. Krsna reserves his highest praise, however, not for the renouncer who withdraws and abstains from worldly action but for the "renouncer" who continues to fulfill his role in society, without attachment to the fruits of his actions. The actions of a *sthitaprajna* may appear outwardly to be the same as those of someone who is attached and self-interested, but the *sthitaprajna's* actions are done "only to hold the world together." Freed from all self-interest, the one whose insight is firm acts for the benefit of all beings.

To this point Krsna's argument for Arjuna's active engagement in battle parallels the argument Bhisma offers for Yudhisthira's kingship after the battle, with one additional twist. In Krsna's new theory of action, the worldly actor doing his duty (*dharma*) with a disinterested mentality, acting only for the good of the world, does not retain any detrimental karmic consequences. Generalized altruism, if done in the proper state of mental equanimity, is liberating.

Krsna has one more big twist to turn, however. Throughout his discourse, beginning with enigmatic hints and brief references, Krsna points to his own divinity. As he continues he begins to make bolder and more audacious assertions, until he claims to be the highest Supreme God. Finally, in chapter eleven, when Arjuna requests visible confirmation of this statement, Krsna presents himself in his supernal aspect as an all-encompassing Absolute. He is God, simultaneously immanent and transcendent.

The disclosure of Krsna's identity has consequences for the discussion of action. Krsna illustrates this point with yet another perspective on sacrifice. If Krsna is truly the Absolute, then all the elements of sacrifice may be identified with Krsna. As he puts it, "I am the rite, I am the sacrifice, I am the libation to the ancestors, I am the herb, I am the formula (*mantra*), I am the butter, I am the fire, I am the offering" (*BhG* 9.16). The wisest method of sacrifice in such a dispensation, therefore, is to direct one's sacrifice straight to Krsna. Of course, some people may continue to offer sacrifices to other deities, but these sacrifices will be less effective. In fact, Krsna continues, the important thing is not the quantity or quality of the offering itself but the mentality and understanding with which any offering is given: "If one disciplined soul proffers to me with love a leaf, a flower, fruit, or water, I accept this offering of love from him. Whatever you do, or eat, or offer, or give, or mortify, Kaunteya, make it an offering to me, and I shall undo the bonds of *karman*, the good and evil fruits" (*BhG* 9.26–27).

Krsna's new theological self-revelation adds a new angle to the issue of disinterested action. To this point in the narrative, Krsna has argued that one should seek to act without attachment to the fruit of action, and he has suggested various renunciatory disciplines that will help one to attain this mental equanimity. Now he suggests another way to gain detachment: through devotion (*bhakti*) toward Krsna himself. Krsna advocates *bhakti* as a new form of disciplinary practice (*yoga*), alongside the disciplines of knowledge (*jnana-yoga*) and action (*karma-yoga*). By devoting one's thoughts and actions toward Krsna, making Krsna the desire (*kama*) and fruit (*phala*) of all one's activities, one can attain detachment from one's own self-centered desires. In fact, compared with other methods *bhakti* is more accessible, more direct, and more efficacious: "I am equable to all creatures [says Krsna], no one is hateful to me or dear— but those who share (*bhajanti*) me with love (*bhakti*) are in me and I am in them. Even a hardened criminal who loves (*bhajate*) me and none other is to be deemed a saint, for he has the right conviction; he soon becomes law-minded (*dharmatman*) and finds peace forever" (*BhG* 9.29–30). The method of *bhakti* is not restricted to brahmins, renouncers, or religious specialists. It also is available to women and members of lower classes— as well as to hardened criminals.

This revelation places Krsna's urging of Arjuna to fight in a new light as well. Arjuna should fight without personal interest in any fruits of the action, still, but now he should consider that his action is a form of devotion to Krsna. Doing his duty as a warrior is following Krsna's directive. Krsna powerfully reinforces this verbal teaching by offering his friend, at Arjuna's request, a vision of his Supreme Form (*parama-rupa*). In this vision Arjuna sees an overwhelming, ferocious figure, dazzling as the light of a thousand suns, with countless weapons, multitudes of eyes and bellies, and endless mouths bristling with fangs. Arjuna sees all the warriors and kings on both sides in the war as they are sucked into Krsna's flaming mouths, like mountain rivers flooding toward the ocean. Understandably, Arjuna finds this fearsome vision of his erstwhile friend and charioteer deeply unsettling, and he tells Krsna he does not comprehend. Krsna answers first by revealing his larger purpose and then reiterates his directive to Arjuna.

I am Time grown old to destroy the world,
Embarked on the course of world annihilation:
Except for yourself none of these will survive,
Of these warriors arrayed in opposite armies . . .
I myself have doomed them ages ago:
Be merely my hand in this, Left-handed Archer!
Slay Drona and Bhisma and Jayadratha,
And Karna as well as other fine warriors—
My victims—destroy them and tarry not!
Wage war! You shall trounce your rivals in battle! (*BhG* 11.32–34)

Arjuna should regard his acts as a warrior in the impending battle as an extension or instrument of Krsna's divine will.

Krsna's discourse in the *Bhagavad Gita* pushes generalized altruism—or devotional altruism, as it becomes—to its limit. Krsna's self-revelation to Arjuna as a limitless being consuming the warriors of both sides fits with a larger eschatological dimension of the *Mahabharata*. In this view the Bharata War is not simply the tragic outcome of human greed and antagonism among India's *ksatriyas* but also a necessary purging of the warrior class—a "sacrifice of battle," in Alf Hiltebeitel's apt phrase—to clear the ground for the establishment of a new political order that is based on superior principles of *dharma*, which will be instituted with Yudhisthira's consecration.[16] Actions that appear from an ordinary perspective to be highly inimical to the welfare of others (such as killing them) may be seen from the higher perspective offered by Krsna as a form of devotional altruism directed to the agent who controls the world-process and acts for the benefit of all creatures.

Worldly Warriors

In the *Mahabharata*, both Bhisma and Krsna speak to protagonists who have central roles to play in the events of the epic, and both urge their listeners to play those roles vigorously. Renunciation of worldly action is not a legitimate option, in the view of these advisers. Both advocate action in accord with *dharma*, and both take pains to specify what *dharma* involves—specifically the *dharma* of the *ksatriya* class of warriors and rulers. Yet Hindus have always seen in these discourses lessons about proper action that are more broadly applicable to all humans who are responsible for their own actions.

Both teachers emphasize that their auditors should pursue their own duties without self-interest. This vision of *dharma* entails action not for oneself but "for the benefit of all creatures," without any expectation of reward. I refer to such action as generalized altruism because the teachers leave the category of "all creatures" broad and undifferentiated. They do not disqualify anyone from the beneficence of the dutiful *ksatriya* on the basis of religious affiliation or other criteria. Bhisma does emphasize, however, that brahmins are especially worthy of royal favor—a common theme in the literature of *dharma*.

The altruistic directives of *dharma*—that kings act for the benefit of all—faces a problem with regard to the issue of violence. Both Yudhisthira and Arjuna suffer qualms when they are called to exercise violence, and both advisors acknowledge that the royal duty of protection requires that the king may have to employ the rod of punishment against those who threaten the social order. Although violence may have negative karmic repercussions for the one who perpetrates it, Bhisma assures his royal pupil that this action is a necessary part of a king's duty. Krsna takes this assurance one step further. If performed in a truly disinterested manner, without personal attachment to the fruit of action, he claims, not even violence engenders karmic bondage. A proper mentality neutralizes karmic consequences.

Krsna provides several recommendations for how a worldly warrior may gain the ability to act with such equanimity. Many of his suggestions draw on the gnostic insights and ascetic disciplines promulgated by the various renunciatory orders in early classical India. He also presents a new method: that of devotion or *bhakti* to God—namely, to Krsna himself. By making Krsna the motivating basis of one's actions, one may remove self-interest. Action undertaken out of devotion to Krsna, though not motivated by any attachment to the fruits of that action, in fact constitutes the most effective means of gaining the highest religious state. Action based on Krsna-*bhakti* has positive salvific results. From this perspective, Krsna is able to urge Arjuna into a gruesome, all-destroying war as a matter of devotional altruism, with the assurance that the war actually is an expression of divine will.

Hindus in the modern world have wrestled repeatedly with the implications of Krsna's teachings. Within the political setting of British colonial control, some Indian nationalist leaders saw in Krsna's call for vigorous and militant action a rationale for armed resistance on behalf of the Motherland, Bharat Mata. Others, such as Mohandas Gandhi, sought to interpret the theistic and violent aspects of the *Gita* as allegorical. Gandhi emphasized the call for altruistic action for the betterment of humanity and particularly prized Krsna's description of the *sthitaprajna* as offering a method for disciplined and effective action in the world. With regard to Krsna's command that Arjuna fight, however, Gandhi regarded this question as an interior struggle that each of us must conduct within ourselves.[17]

Conclusion

Within the two discourses of the *Mahabharata*, representing a classical Hindu perspective on action (*karman*) and its consequences, the key term throughout is *dharma*. The teachers Bhisma and Krsna characterize *dharma* as a particularized duty that is incumbent on a person, and both seek action in accord with *dharma* as most conducive to the welfare of others. In these teachings, the category of "others" most often is treated in its most general sense, as indicated by the common phrase, "take delight in the welfare of all beings." Indeed, both Bhisma and Krsna justify violent action against even persons closely related to the actor, if that is what *dharma* requires.

Whereas in the *Santiparvan* Bhisma assures Yudhisthira that even violence toward some persons may be necessary to assure the common good, in the *Bhagavad Gita* Krsna takes up the more difficult question of intention. He urges Arjuna to give up any attachment to the fruits of his action. Only by acting without any self-regarding motivations, Krsna asserts, can one avoid the "bondage of the act." Here Krsna refers to a common premise of classical India, which holds that all intentional action entails some "unseen" consequences that bind one to continued existence both in this lifetime and in future lives. Krsna introduces the possibility that if action is truly detached from any concern with the consequences for oneself, it may not cause additional bondage to continued existence. This detached action ultimately can lead to the highest state— understood as *moksa,* or liberation from all bondage to the cycle of recurrent life. Therefore, in Krsna's view, action devoid of all selfish interest and conducive to the welfare of others paradoxically benefits the selfless actor in the highest degree. Although he urges Arjuna to act without any concern for the consequences, beneficial or otherwise, he holds out an ultimate reward for such seemingly altruistic action.

Notes

1. I adopt the sequential view of stages of composition for the *Mahabharata*, as presented by translators J. A. B. Van Buitenen and James L. Fitzgerald; see James L. Fitzgerald, *The Mahabharata, Volume 7: Book 11, The Book of the Women, Book 12, the Book of Peace, Part One* (Chicago: University of Chicago Press, 2004), xvi. One may compare the hypothesis of a briefer compositional process, as effectively argued in Alf Hiltebeitel, *Rethinking the Mahabharata: A Reader's Guide to the Education of the Dharma King* (Chicago: University of Chicago Press, 2001). Following Fitzgerald, I emphasize the intentional and rhetorical character of the compositional process—particularly the Sunga period redaction—against earlier scholarly views, which postulated a "grab-bag" notion of composition.

2. Fitzgerald, *The Mahabharata*, 139. I acknowledge Fitzgerald's interpretive work as the most important background to this chapter. See also James L. Fitzgerald, "The Great Epic of India as Religious Rhetoric: A Fresh Look at the Mahabharata," *Journal of the American Academy of Religion* 51, no. 4 (1983): 611–30 and idem, "India's Fifth Veda: The Mahabharata's Presentation of Itself," in *Essays on the Mahabharata*, ed. Arvind Sharma, Brills' Indological Library, vol. 1 (Leiden, The Netherlands: E. J. Brill, 1991), 150–70, for a general introduction to key themes in the *Mahabharata*.

3. See Fitzgerald, *The Mahabharata*, xxiv–xxxi, for a brief recounting of the war books. W. J. Johnson, *The Sauptikaparvan of the Mahabharata: The Massacre at Night*, Oxford World's Classics (Oxford: Oxford University Press, 1998), offers an accessible translation of Book 10, which contains some of the most gruesome actions of the war.

4. Fitzgerald, "The Great Epic of India," and J. A. B. Van Buitenen, "Introduction," in *The Bhagavadgita in the Mahabharata* (Chicago: University of Chicago Press, 1981), 3–4, both point to this shift in tone.

5. Fitzgerald, *The Mahabharata*,29–76

6. This translation is from Fitzgerald, *The Mahabharata*,56. All subsequent translated passages are drawn from J. A. B. Van Buitenen, *The Mahabharata* (Chicago: University of Chicago Press, 1973–1978); Van Buitenen, *The Bhagavadgita*; and Fitzgerald, *The Mahabharata*.

7. The speaker here is Carvaka, a demon disguised as a brahmin. The text makes clear that Carvaka in fact does not speak for the brahmins of Hastinapura, for they immediately disown Carvaka's criticism and praise Yudhisthira the victor.

8. Van Buitenen, *The Mahabharata*, xxiii, refers to it as "the longest deathbed sermon on record."

9. Fitzgerald, *The Mahabharata*, 104.

10. Ibid.

11. Ibid., 110.

12. Fitzgerald, *The Mahabharata*, develops the compelling argument that these discourses, and the composed *Mahabharata* as a whole, constitute a brahmanic response to the paradigm of Buddhist kingship exemplified by the Mauryan emperor Asoka. Although I accept this historical argument, it is beyond the purposes of this chapter.

13. I owe this observation to Norvin Hein, who catalogs and analyzes more than fifty instances of the phrase in the epics *Mahabharata* and *Ramayana* in Norvin Hein, "Epic *Sarvabhute Ratah*: A Byword of Non-Bhargava Editors," *Annals of the Bhandarkar Oriental Research Institute* 67 (1986): 17–54.

14. I adopt the translation of Fitzgerald, *The Mahabharata*, 295, but retain *dharma* rather than his translational equivalents (here, "Law").

15. See Jan Heesterman, *The Inner Conflict of Tradition: Essays in Indian Ritual, Kingship, and Society* (Chicago: University of Chicago Press, 1985), on this dilemma facing royal *dharma*.

16. Alf Hiltebeitel, *The Ritual of Battle: Krishna in the Mahabharata* (Ithaca, N.Y.: Cornell University Press, 1976).

17. See Robert N. Minor, *Modern Indian Interpreters of the Bhagavadgita*, SUNY Series in Religious Studies (Albany: State University of New York Press, 1986), for an excellent collection of essays exploring various modern Hindu interpretations of the *Bhagavad Gita*. Gandhi's responses to the *Gita* may be found in M. K. Gandhi, *Discourses on the Gita*, trans. Valji Govindji Desai (Ahmedabad, India: Navajivan Publishing House, 1960 [1930–1933]), and idem, *The Bhagavadgita* (New Delhi: Orient Paperbacks, 1989). For a sensitive discussion of Gandhi's interpretive strategies, see Bradley Clough, "Gandhi, Nonviolence, and the Bhagavad-Gita," in *Holy War: Violence and the Bhagavad Gita*, ed. Steven J. Rosen (Hampton, Va.: Deepak Heritage Books, 2002), 59–80.

Chapter 9

Altruism in Chinese Religions

Mark Csikszentmihalyi

"Toil for the good of the people" (*wei renmin fuwu*) was one of the central slogans of the Maoist period of Chinese history, leading up to and including the Cultural Revolution (1966–76). Because Maoism defined itself in opposition to traditional culture—especially to Confucianism—the rhetoric of that period in Chinese history was committed to a view in which the foundation of traditional culture was an expression of the ideology of the slave-owning class. Although the attempt by Mao to induce people to act in the interest of others owes much to the European tradition of Marx and Engels, by defining this imperative in opposition to Confucianism Mao was contributing to a longstanding Chinese debate about the proper object of moral action.[1] Twenty-four centuries earlier, prior to the Chinese discovery of Europe, the radical thinker Mozi rejected the Confucian dictum that one should act partially toward one's kin.

Followers of Mozi and Confucius have debated about the correctness or selfishness of acting partially towards one's in-group—whether bound by kinship, geography, or ties of fealty—since the fourth and third centuries BCE in China. Confucians emphasized the virtue of "filial piety" (*xiao*), which promoted special care by children for their parents. In criticizing this care as leading to inequitable distribution of resources, both Mohists (i.e., the followers of Mozi) and Maoists held that Confucianism was not just partial but that this partiality resulted in behavior that was selfish and immoral. The similarity between these two critiques establishes a connection between the early debate over Confucian partiality and that over the imperative to act for the welfare of others in Europe.

This connection, however, does not mean that Confucian partiality and egoism are the same, nor that Mozi's doctrine of "impartial caring" (*jian'ai*) is a form of altruism. I argue that there are important parallels between "universal caring" and altruism, as well as between the historical moment of the nineteenth-century rejection of traditional religious justifications for moral action and Mozi's rebellion against an ethic that accepted the inequalities inherent in traditional social structures. Because the later Confucian tradition draws on the post-Mozi writer Mencius and his doctrine of "extending" (*tui*) one's originally partial feelings of kindness (*en*), however, it generally has sought to mediate between points of view that might be considered egoistic and altruistic. The influential synthesis of Mencius and its later development by Song Dynasty neo-Confucians provide a solution to the conflict that I call "graduated altruism." By highlighting this solution, I hope to draw two important facets of the history of Chinese religions back into the general discussion of altruism: the role of the metaphor of parental nurture in the conceptualization of altruism and the way in which attempts at naturalizing moral capacities leads into the discussion of altruism-like ideals.

Altruism and "Impartial Caring" in the *Mozi*

Comparing categories across languages, cultures, and historical eons is at the very core of religious studies, and critical scrutiny of this task is particularly important for western scholars whose focus falls outside the Abrahamic traditions. In exploring a nineteenth-century European term such as altruism, there is a range of possible approaches one might take in making comparisons. On one hand, one could choose a particular aspect of the term as the salient feature and search for it in the target culture. In the case of altruism, that feature might be concern for the well-being of others, rejection of selfishness or egoism, or willingness to sacrifice one's own interests. The result is somewhat underdetermined because "altruism in the sense of concern for others" is likely to be found in any culture, but its relation to a more complete sense of altruism would still require scrutiny. On the other hand, the approach outlined by William Scott Green, using the multifaceted definition of Kristen Renwick Monroe, is more comprehensive in that it attempts to generalize the major features of a robust definition of altruism. In the broadest sense, altruism is defined as "action intended to benefit another, even when such action risks potential sacrifice to the well-being of the actor."[2] The risk in this case is overdetermining the meaning of altruism because this definition requires that cross-cultural translations of terms such as "other," "sacrifice," and "well-being" be brought together in a particular way.[3] In the context of traditional Chinese religion, then, using the latter approach to comparison is not simply a matter of finding a likely term that is a translation of "altruism" but a matter of engaging that term's constituent parts.

The distinction that is most basic to the concept of altruism is the difference between self and other. There is a long tradition of distinguishing between "Eastern" and "Western" conceptions of the self, but in this case such distinctions are too essentialized to be of much use. From the perspective of the "Western" self, the nineteenth-century invention of the term *altruism* occurred in an atmosphere that in many cases was influenced by Asian religions—or, at the least, by the consciousness of them as alternatives to more familiar traditions. Arthur Schopenhauer (1788–1860), whose *Die Welt als Wille und Vorstellung* (1819) argues that liberation from the will may only result by transcending the limitations of individuality imposed by the ego, was strongly influenced by the *Upanishads* introduced to him by Friedrich Majer. Although the writings of Auguste Comte (1798–1857) reveal no such explicit influence, the humanist impulse that underpinned Comte's positivist approach was a product largely of rejection of religious epistemology.[4] Likewise, many descriptions of the "Eastern" self, such as the famous work of Hajime Nakamura, draw particularly on conceptions of self that are influenced by Buddhism. Although Buddhist notions of altruism certainly are an important part of any consideration of Chinese religions, historically they are different from those of indigenous Chinese religions.[5] For this reason, in this chapter I focus on conceptions of self and the problem of altruism in Chinese religions outside of Buddhism—although of course Buddhism exerted a strong influence on other religions after it came to China in the first century CE.[6]

If we look at Chinese religions as having competing visions of self and other, an attempt at generalizing moral sentiments in a way that is similar to altruism is found in the writings of the *Mozi*. The *Mozi* is a composite text associated with the late fifth century and early fourth century BCE figure Mo Di, although much of the text is thought to derive from the "Mohist" schools of the fourth through second centuries BCE. This text develops a social theory that is based on the need to conserve and equitably distribute resources. This theory is best described as consequentialist in the sense that it is a system in which the moral rightness of an act is determined solely by the goodness of the act's consequences. Significantly, however, goodness is defined at the level of society as a whole, not in terms of the individual or the clan. For this reason, there is no moral self in the *Mozi*; the sole consideration of whether one should act is the effect of the action on the wealth, population, and order of the society. The text explicitly rejects affiliations that are at the core of the concept of self associated with Confucius.[7] In particular, it calls into question the assumption that the virtues of *xiao* (filial piety) and *zhong* (loyalty) may be maximized only by serving one's own parents more than other parents or one's ruler more than other rulers.

The *Mozi*'s doctrine of *jian'ai* holds that resource allocation is maximized by application of the principle that "one must treat one's friend's body as if it were one's own, and one must treat one's friend's parent as if he or she were one's own."[8] The followers of Mo Di believed that in an ideal society, there would no longer be an unequal distribution of resources caused by favoritism based on affiliation with friends, family, or community. Chapters 14–16 of the *Mozi* bear the title "Impartial Caring."

Chapter 14 directly addresses the issue of self and other: "If it were truly the case that the people of the world cared for each other impartially, then one would care for others (*ren*) as one cares about one's own self (*shen*). Could there still be unfilial persons? If one looked upon one's father as one looked upon oneself, how could one be unfilial?"[9]

This view of self and other requires that, for the purposes of action that bears on the distribution of resources, the fundamental parent-child relationship should not be taken into account. Similarly, it argues that the virtues of parental kindness (*ci*) and sibling concern (*di*) also would be served best by acting without regard to the very affiliations on which these terms are based. So, too, the *Mozi* claims, would treating others' homes and persons as one's own eliminate burglary and theft—and treating others' states as one's own would put an end to war.

In the limited senses of eliminating self-interest as a direct guide for action and replacing it with the welfare of others, the *Mozi*'s conception of impartial caring is altruistic. One important aspect of the *Mozi*'s scheme rules it out as altruistic, however, in the stricter definition offered by Green. That aspect is the additional motivation for other-directed action provided by automatic retribution for immoral action through the agency of "ghosts and spirits" (*guishen*). The *Mozi* assures its readers that good deeds (as defined in its consequentialist calculus) will be rewarded just as bad deeds will be punished. As with several of the other traditions examined in this volume, then, the followers of Mozi promoted actions of universal benefit to others but also provided a redundant system to motivate people to act in that way for what might be regarded as selfish motives. This "selfishness" might be contrasted with the partiality implicit in the virtue of filial piety, which for Confucians was more than simply a guide for action in the context of family.

Filial Piety and the Classification of Others

At the core of the worldview of Confucius (Kongzi, trad. 551–479 BCE), as expressed in the *Analects* (Lunyu, literally "Considered Discussions"), is the idea that others should not all be treated the same way. Most basically, special consideration is due one's parents—a partiality regarded as reflecting the special nurturing one's parents have already provided. For the early Confucians, however, this special consideration was the model for the type of inductive moral reasoning at the core of their ethical system. Filial piety was the archetype for the ritual relationship one has with other members of society.

The central place of filial piety for early Confucians is illustrated by the identification of filial piety as central to the ritualization process. According to *Analects* 2.5, Master Meng Yi asked Confucius about filial piety, and Confucius answered that one should "never go against [the rites]." Then one of his disciples prompted this explanation of his answer:

> Fan Chi asked: "What do you mean by that?"
> The Master said: "During their lives, serve them according to what is ritually proper. When they are dead, bury them according to what is ritually proper, and sacrifice to them according to what is ritually proper."[10]

Indeed, filial piety may be regarded as the model for a person's ritual relationship with others, but because filial piety is in some sense prior to the others it is of particular importance. Indeed, proper performance of filial piety by a ruler is proof of his virtue and can lead to corresponding virtuous behavior on the part of his subjects. *Analects* 2.20 explains how a ruler who is mature will have subjects who are reverent, and a ruler who exercises filial piety and parental kindness will have loyal subjects.

We may immediately draw two important contrasts with the *Mozi*'s impartial caring. First, whereas the *Mozi* was concerned exclusively with the distribution of material goods, the *Analects* is concerned with attitudes and action in a ritual context that does not necessarily involve material goods. From a philosophical perspective, this distinction reflects the difference between a consequentialist approach and a virtue ethics approach. Second, although the *Analects* emphasizes sacrifice on the part of the actor for the good of the parent, it does not generalize this attitude to all others.[11] It is possible to regard this type of sacrifice as a limited form of altruism or, more likely, a form of egoism in which the self includes one's parents and children.

Although filial piety plays a major role in the *Analects*, it would be inaccurate to say that it continued to play a pivotal role for all Confucians. Yet there is no question that it did for some. For example, the third or second century BCE *Classic of Filial Piety* (*Xiaojing*) was directly associated with Confucius and his disciple Zengzi throughout much of Chinese history. The *Classic of Filial Piety* portrays filial piety as the necessary attitude behind successful interaction between father and son, ruler and subject, or any other relationship based on hierarchy. Confucius tells his disciple Zengzi why this is so: "Of those things Heaven and Earth have given birth to, humans are the most valuable. Of all the things that humans do, none is greater than filial piety. Of the kinds of filial piety, none is more significant than sacrificing to Heaven."[12]

Honoring one's parents is only one expression of filial piety in the *Classic of Filial Piety*, but sacrifice to previous generations, and thereby to Heaven, is more important. Nonbiological filiation also is crucial, and chapters 2 through 6 of the *Classic of Filial Piety* detail filial behavior for different rungs on the feudal ladder, from emperor down to commoner. Yet although filial piety plays a major part in popular Confucianism and has played an important historical role in some strands of the history of the religion, its eclipse as a central facet of Confucian ethics is evident in the focus on the virtue of "benevolence" (*ren*), which in some ways may be regarded as a legacy of the *Mozi*'s "impartial caring."

Graduated Altruism in the *Mencius*

The later Confucian tradition owes quite a bit to the version of altruism found in the *Mozi*, however, because its development did not stop with the *Analects*. A significant reform of the early Confucian idea that filial piety was the source of virtuous behavior took place in the works of Mencius (Meng Ke or Mengzi, c. 380–c. 290 BCE), who sometimes was known as the "second sage" (*yasheng*). In the fourth and third century BCE text *Mencius*, the virtue of benevolence takes on some of the generalized features of altruism because of the influence of the *Mozi*. The *Mencius* assumed a central role in the Confucian canon in the Song dynasty, so this form of graduated altruism became a central feature of Confucian ethics throughout most of the traditional period.

The *Mencius* explicitly distances itself from the position of the *Mozi*, which it portrays as one of two doctrinaire positions that attack Confucian hierarchies. *Mencius* 3B9 laments the fact that the doctrines of Yang Zhu and Mo Di "fill the empire":

> If the Ways of Yang and Mo do not decline and the Way of Kongzi does not hold sway, such evil theories will delude the people and block the path to benevolence and righteousness. Once the path to benevolence and righteousness is blocked, beasts will devour humans, and humans will devour each other. So I am deeply anxious and rise to protect the theories of the former sage and proscribe Yang and Mo. . . . Whoever can dispute and proscribe Yang and Mo is a follower of the sage.[13]

The *Mencius* reports that the theories of the early Confucians were not nearly as popular as those of Yang Zhu and Mo Di. Mo Di's views are examined above; Yang Zhu's have been characterized as a form of "egoism." Indeed, in the description of these doctrines in *Mencius* 7A26, these views sound like egoism and altruism: "Yangzi's principle is 'each one for himself' (*weiwo*). If he had to cut a single hair in order to benefit the empire he would not do it. Mozi's principle is 'impartial caring.' If he had to injure himself from head to toe in order to benefit the empire he would."[14]

Although the *Mencius* rejects both of these paths, it also goes on to reject a path that steers the middle course between these actions. It introduces this third position, that of an otherwise unknown figure named Zimo: "Zimo hews to the center. While hewing to the center is close to the right course, hewing to the center fails to make use of one's sense of balance, and in this way is like taking either extreme. What I detest is those who take the extreme, because they are thieves of the Way. They hold to one, and in doing so abandon a hundred others."[15]

The *Mencius* argues that both Yang Zhu and Mo Di take profit (*li*) as the basis of their decisions about action and in this way are doctrinaire. By imposing an external standard of morality on people, they fail to rely on innate dispositions and faculties such as a sense of balance (*quan*) that are the proper seat of moral decision making.[16] Here a basic difference between the Confucian and non-Confucian views of the good is apparent. The Confucian view rejects the act-based ethical structure of both Yang and Mo and instead focuses on cultivation of character.

The internalist appeal of the *Mencius* effectively changes the basis of Confucian ethics from one grounded in traditional patterns of behavior to a set of internal ethical dispositions that must be developed for a person to become a moral actor. The primary disposition is to benevolence—an innate aspect of all people. The *Mencius* introduces the notion of "extending" (*tui*) the natural feelings one has for family members to all people and argues that the process of moral self-cultivation entails learning to extend compassion from one's in-group outward, eventually reaching all people.

Again, from an ordinary language viewpoint, the goal is a form of altruism, but it may be arrived at only by developing tendencies that manifest themselves initially as partiality toward certain people at the expense of others. An alternate formulation is that one learns to expand the definition of self until it encompasses all others, and one arrives at a position that is similar to the *Mozi*. The historian Gu Jiegang (1893–1980) argued that many of the doctrines of "kingly government" (*wangzheng*) in the *Mencius* derived from the *Mozi* and that they were geared to promotion of the good of the people over that of the aristocracy. As a result, Gu wrote, "Mengzi was not purely a disciple of Kongzi, but rather he reconciled the two schools of Kongzi and Mozi."[17] Indeed, the *Mencius* begins with the notion of natural partiality to family as espoused by the early Confucians and then argues for a gradual widening of one's in-group, ending with a generalized form of compassion. It is important to note that the rejection of a uniform imperative about profiting the world in *Mencius* 7A26 aligns the text against strict considerations of utility as found in the *Mozi*.

In 1190 Zhu Xi (1130–1200) published a commentary on the four books called *Collected Commentaries on the Sentences and Sections of the Four Books* (*Sishu zhangju jizhu*)—the *Analects*, the *Mencius, Great Learning*, and *Doctrine of the Mean*. Because of Zhu's intellectual stature, his reliance on the concept of "extension" cemented the ideal of graduated altruism, as found in the *Mencius*, as a cardinal part of Confucian ethics. Even the earliest twentieth-century reformer Liang Qichao (1873–1929) regarded China's weakness as its deficiency in political theory. For this reason, Liang was critical of some of the Confucian legacy and turned to pragmatic works such as the Warring States *Guanzi* and those of the Song Dynasty writer Wang Jinggong.[18] Liang's radical reformism had a place for filial piety, which he considered one of three basic sources of morality, growing out of a basic concern for the future.[19]

The integration of filial piety into Liang's reformism is an outgrowth of later Confucian arguments about the universal benefits of partial caring. One dominant mode of argument was that strengthening the family unit benefits everyone because networks of partial relationships are the optimal guarantee of social welfare. As in many premodern societies, affiliation groups were regarded as the key to mutual benefit across society in the same way that a rising tide lifts all ships. By contrast, later social reformers were drawn to ideas of economic equality that valued economic work units over traditional family units. As I discuss at the outset of this chapter, in the Socialist period of the People's Republic of China beginning in 1949, this type of critique of Confucianism as partial and therefore inequitable—as seen in the *Mozi*—was revived. This view rejected the notion of innate moral dispositions and, like the *Mozi*, sought to improve the material situation of the state through adoption of general principles for action.

Conclusion

It is possible to compare Chinese religions to two different versions of altruism. The first is altruism as a historical instance, traced back to Comte and his contemporaries. The second is the attempt to define altruism outside of history, with all the inevitable normative resonances that such an effort produces. As with many of the chapters in this book, the requirement that altruistic actions must have no benefit for the actor poses a challenge to the Chinese system that at first most resembles altruism—that of the *Mozi*. The reason no Chinese tradition is altruistic in the strict sense is that the narrow definition incorporates elements of different ethical systems. First, it employs the notion of material welfare—an aspect of an ethics that emphasizes the results of actions and concern about the aggregate effect on the entire society. Yet it also uses the notion of intention—a vestige of the ethics of motive and character in which good actions undertaken for the wrong reasons should not be considered truly good. The latter worldview historically has been tied to a much broader definition of welfare that recognized values such as conversion or helping others attain nirvana, cultivating one's own character, or improving one's postmortem conditions. The hybrid character of the definition of altruism was present in its historical formulation and in attempts to generalize it. I suggest that this hybrid nature is part of the reason the scriptural traditions of the great religions do not precisely fit into the definition.

Probing the relationship between altruism and Chinese religions has uncovered some unique aspects of the Chinese case, as well as some suggestive similarities. Perhaps the most cogent characterization of Chinese theories analogous to egoism and altruism, *Mencius* 7A26, ultimately advocates a particular Confucian alternative to both theories. Perhaps the reason the graduated altruism of the later Confucians was so much more influential than the purer view of the *Mozi* had to do with widespread acceptance of the importance of filial piety in Chinese society. Particular affection and an obligation to provide materially for one's parents was even accepted by modern critics such as Liang Qichao, recapitulating the way the *Mozi*'s rejection of filial piety was mediated through the compromise position of the *Mencius.*

Although the solution of graduated altruism is uniquely developed in the Chinese tradition, this aspect of the Chinese approach to altruism underlines the role of the metaphor of parental nurture in the conceptualization of altruism. This issue is especially interesting in light of David Sloan Wilson and Elliott Sober's question in *Unto Others: The Evolution and Psychology of Unselfish Behavior*: Do people have other-directed ultimate desires? This question is difficult because psychological approaches are limited by their inability to gauge ultimate causes, so apparently altruistic behaviors are always subject to (sometimes convoluted) egoistic explanations. In chapter 10, "The Evolution of Psychological Altruism," the authors use a model of biological and cultural evolution and the example of parental care to argue that hedonism is maladaptive compared to a redundant system in which altruistic actions arise from altruistic ultimate desires reinforced by egoistic ultimate desires. The resulting "motivational pluralism" is a plausible method of "getting parents to take care of their children" and "getting members of a group to take care of each other."[20] Both the underlying metaphor and the structure of their solution exhibit similarities with the compromise in the *Mencius.*

Although the *Mencius* does not justify altruism on the basis of biological or evolutionary adaptive advantages, it shares another interesting parallel with European conceptions of altruism. The *Mencius* is a part of a fourth- and third-century move to naturalize the virtues by locating them in particular organs of the body. The location of the *Mencius*'s virtues in the body's inner organs is made explicit in the *Historian's Records* (*Shiji*, circa 100 BCE), where benevolence is located in the spleen.[21] By contrast, Dr. Franz Joseph Gall's system of phrenology located benevolence in "the middle of the frontal bone in front of the coronal suture."[22] Comte's reliance on Gall to show that virtues such as benevolence were part of human nature is very similar, then, to the way the *Mencius* argues that dispositions to benevolence are incipient in the body. Both are part of attempts to naturalize moral capacities that lead into the discussion of altruism-like ideals.[23] Both also are responses to systems that locate the origins of morality outside the human body.

These similarities shed light on some of the moves made by the *Mozi* and Comte in attempting to expand the range of the object of other-directed moral actions. They also suggest that underlying the comparison between these various historical instances is a shared moment of generalization. Both the *Mozi* and Comte sought to take an ideal of other-directed action embedded in a tradition's social structure or cosmology and justified in terms of that tradition and generalize that action on the basis of a consequentialist justification. We should not be surprised, however, that the specifics of their result are not the same.

Notes

A version of this chapter was presented on November 17, 2004, at the "Altruism in World Religions" conference at Bard College. The author would like to thank the organizers of the conference, the participants for helpful questions and comments, and Johanna Klotz, the student interlocutor.

1. Other parallels between traditional Chinese ethics and those of the Cultural Revolution have been pointed out in Benjamin Schwartz, "The Reign of Virtue: Some Broad Perspectives on Leader and Party in the Cultural Revolution," in *Party Leadership and Revolutionary Power in China,* ed. John Wilson Lewis (Cambridge: Cambridge University Press, 1970).
2. William Scott Green, "Altruism and the Study of Religion: Preliminary Questions," introduction to this volume, drawing on Kristen Renwick Monroe, "Explicating Altruism," in *Altruism and Altruistic Love: Science, Philosophy, and Religion in Dialogue,* ed. Stephen G. Post et al. (Oxford: Oxford University Press, 2002): 106–22.
3. The most common pitfall of such comparisons is the "recipe fallacy," in which one attempts to generalize each aspect of a phenomenon in a familiar culture and then uses the resulting checklist to hunt for a corresponding phenomenon in another culture. The problem is that although each generalized aspect may be intelligible and present in the target culture, nothing ensures that such aspects are bound together in anything like the same complex as in the original culture. This fallacy occurs in applying nonreductive

definitions of religion or generalizations of a particular phenomenon, such as William James's definition of mysticism. It also arises when one takes a particular ideal out of a dialogue in one culture and finds like characteristics in other cultures.

4. Comte's emphasis on "altruism" as the basis of a secularized version of Christian ethics reflects his positivist assumption that theology is a mode of knowledge that reflects an imperfect version of natural principles. The turn to natural principles—where nature is conceived of as transcending culture—was a response in part to the consciousness of other cultures. John Stuart Mill (1806–1873) wrote that the chief benefit he derived from Comte's thought was an understanding of the "peculiarities of an era of transition of opinion" that caused him to look forward to a future "so firmly grounded in reason and in the true exigencies of life that they shall not, like all former and present creeds, religious, ethical, and political, require to be periodically thrown off and replaced by others"; see *Autobiography of John Stuart Mill* (New York: New American Library, 1964), 126–27. In a similar vein, René König argues that "Comte asserted the relativism of moral ideas—that they vary with different cultures and social systems—in opposition to the notion that norms are rooted either in divine revelation or in a general spiritual order, separate from social life and untouched by it"; see René König, "Auguste Comte," in *International Encyclopedia of the Social Sciences*, ed. David Sills (New York: Macmillan Co. and The Free Press, 1968), 201–6, at 202.

5. In the history of Chinese religions, one of the primary sources of conflict between Confucianism and Buddhism was a product of their different conceptions of self and the individual's proper relation to family. Fan Ning (339–401 CE) argued against Buddhist cosmology when he wrote that the spirit disappeared at death. One of the primary criticisms of Buddhism by Tang Dynasty essayist Han Yu (768–824 CE) was that the monastic renunciation of family contravened the Chinese virtue of filial piety (*xiao*).

6. See especially chapter 7 in this volume, as well as Ruben L. F. Habito, "Compassion out of Wisdom: Buddhist Perspectives from the Past toward Human Future," in Post et al., *Altruism and Altruistic Love*, 362–75.

7. A provocative collection of essays on Chinese conceptions of self is W. Dissanayake, R. T. Ames, and T. P. Kasulis, eds., *Self as Person in Asian Theory and Practice* (Albany: State University of New York Press, 1988). I have written about the problem of nonbelievers in Confucianism in Mark Csikszentmihalyi, "Confucianism," in *God's Rule: The Politics of World Religions*, ed. Jacob Neusner (Washington, D.C.: Georgetown University Press, 2003), 213–32. There, I argue that Confucianism's conception of self and other significantly changed when it began to self-consciously define itself as a tradition in competition with Taoism and Buddhism in the sixth century CE.

8. Chapter 16 of *Mozi xiangu* (Zhuzi jicheng edition; Beijing: Zhonghua, 1954), 4.73. The translation of *jian'ai* as "impartial caring" is Philip J. Ivanhoe's and may be contrasted to the less accurate "universal love" of Burton Watson. See Philip J. Ivanhoe, *Ethics in the Confucian Tradition* (Indianapolis: Hackett, 2002).

9. Chapter 14 of *Mozi xiangu*, 4.68.
10. Cheng Shude, ed., *Lunyu jishi* (Beijing: Zhonghua, 1990), 81–83.
11. Keith Knapp's work on filial piety stories includes unbelievable stories of self-sacrifice on the part of filial children. See Keith Knapp, "New Approaches to Teaching Early Confucianism," *Teaching Theology and Religion* 2, no. 1 (1999): 45–54.
12. *Xiaojing*, chapter 9.
13. Jiao Xun, ed. *Mengzi zhengyi* (Beijing: Zhonghua, 1987), 13.456–62.
14. Ibid., 27.915–20.
15. Ibid.
16. For a discussion of *quan*, see chapter 3 of Mark Csikszentmihalyi, *Material Virtue: Ethics and the Body in Early China* (Leiden, The Netherlands: Brill, 2004).
17. *Handai xueshu shilue* (Beijing: Zhonghua, 1998), 32. Reversing this reasoning, Hsiao Kung-chuan (Xiao Gongquan) noted similarities between the *Mozi*'s impartial caring and benevolence, arguing that Mozi was originally a Confucian. See Hsiao Kung-chuan, *A History of Chinese Political Thought*, vol. 1 (Princeton, N.J.: Princeton University Press, 1979).
18. Liang Qichao et al., *Zhongguo liu da zhengzhi jia* (Taipei: Zhongzheng, 1964), 1 and 16.
19. Chester Tan. *Chinese Political Thought at the Start of the Twentieth Century* (New York: Anchor , 1971), 39.
20. Elliot Sober and David Sloan Wilson, *Unto Others: The Evolution and Psychology of Unselfish Behavior* (Cambridge, Mass.: Harvard University Press, 1998), 326.
21. *Shiji* 4.1236.
22. The ninth edition of the *Encyclopedia Britannica* notes that Gall "noticed a rising on the head of the highly-commended servant of a friend, as well as on a benevolent schoolmate who nursed his brothers and sisters when they were ill" (Edinburgh: Adam and Charles Black, 1885), vol. 18, 845.
23. Comte locates altruistic impulses not in divine grace but in the anterior region of the brain, "where there are distinct organs for the sympathetic impulses and the intellectual faculties"; Auguste Comte, *The Catechism of Positive Religion*, trans. Richard Congreve (London: Kegan Paul, 1891), 176. I am indebted to an unpublished article by Thomas Dixon for this quotation.

Epilogue

William Scott Green

To many people in contemporary American life, altruism—the ideal of selfless concern and care for the other—appears to be a distinctively religious value. Because all religions teach the importance of caring for others in one fashion or another, it seems to follow that religion should be the natural soil in which the seeds of human altruism can grow. This anthology probes that supposition.

The working definition the authors use for altruism derives from the writings of contemporary scholars in various fields that employ the term. Under this working definition, altruism is "intentional action ultimately for the welfare of others that entails at least the possibility of either no benefit or a loss to the actor." The definition does not claim to be normative or prescriptive or to state a truth about the world. Its modest aim is to establish a set of criteria that give altruism a meaning that distinguishes it from different kinds of other-regarding behavior. These criteria allow us to test the category's usefulness. If we do not know what we are looking for, we cannot know if we find it.

As the introduction to this volume makes clear, our common purpose was to see if altruism is a useful and appropriate category for the academic study of religion. Does altruism provide a distinctive perspective, raise questions otherwise unasked, or freshly illuminate aspects of religion? In short, does altruism make religion more intelligible by exposing it in a way that no other category does or has? Does it add value to our academic work?

In typical academic fashion, the answer seems to be both no and yes: "no" because there is broad agreement among the contributors to this volume that the contemporary understanding of altruism used for this experiment either does not apply or is otherwise unsuited to the classical materials of the religions under study; "yes" because, in the process of deciding the "no," the chapters in this anthology collectively reveal the resources for benevolence, charity, and human caring in the foundation texts of the religions they study. Whether those resources ever would have been collected in one place without this effort is anybody's guess.

As the working definition shows, the variable that distinguishes altruism from other modes of care and concern for the other is the element of loss to the actor, of self-sacrifice. The idea that one can serve others without benefit and only at a cost to oneself seems to give altruism its ethical punch, so to speak—to make it morally exciting and notable. Of the questions posed to the contributors, therefore, the most important probably was, "Does the religion create a context in which it is possible that intentional action for the welfare of others can have only a neutral or negative consequence on the actor? Is it possible for action on behalf of others to have no beneficial consequence for the actor?" The question does not limit the notion of "beneficial consequence" to this-worldly rewards; it can include all the otherworldly rewards a religion promises.

In general, the contributors found that this question did not correspond well to the religions they study. The reason, as Jacob Neusner explains in the case of rabbinic Judaism, is that contemporary altruism operates with categories different from religion:

> Altruistic conduct is difficult to locate in the classical statements of law and theology of Judaism because the category-formations of that Judaism—with their emphasis on human obligation to carry out the divine will, with reward or punishment the consequence of obedience or rebellion—make no provision for a critical role of unselfish, unrewarded behavior that benefits others at a cost to oneself. Altruism so defined is asystemic and antisystemic because it turns virtuous conduct into supererogatory action, while the commandments govern: Greater is the action of one who is commanded and acts than the one who is not commanded but acts, in context, to carry out a virtuous deed.

In a similar vein, Bruce Chilton observes that in early Christianity, "concern for the other carries with it a reward from God that cannot be enhanced, and is only undermined, by the anticipation of benefit in this world." The theme of what seems to be unavoidable reward for selfless behavior appears in Hinduism as well. Richard Davis explains that in Hinduism, because of the karmic system, even selfless action for others produces inevitable benefit for the actor. He points to a teaching of the God Krsna in the Hindu epic the *Mahabharata* that action devoid of all selfish interest and conducive to the welfare of others paradoxically benefits the selfless actor in the highest degree. Although Krsna urges Arjuna to act without any concern for the consequences, beneficial or otherwise, he holds out an ultimate reward for such seemingly altruistic action.

Similarly, Todd Lewis argues that Buddhism cannot be said to be altruistic. Lewis points out, however, that some exemplary Buddhist figures, whose "seeds of karma have been 'burnt up,'" did live lives of genuine suffering in the service of others.

EPILOGUE

Th. Emil Homerin doubts the appropriateness of altruism for Islam because "God has promised in the Qur'an to reward every good deed done by any person." Homerin reaches what may be a general conclusion of the applicability of contemporary altruism to religion:

> If the possibility of heavenly and/or spiritual reward for an action disallows it from being altruistic, it is difficult to see how altruism could be "a useful and appropriate category for the academic study of religion." In this case, altruism would appear to be a secular, not religious, category.

There are other problems with the category as well. The contemporary definition of altruism makes assumptions about the nature of a "self" and "others," but these modern categories do not translate well into either Greco-Roman philosophy, as Robert Berchman observes, or, as Reuben Habito shows, Nicheren Buddhism. Mark Csikszentmihalyi points to yet another mismatch. He suggests that contemporary altruism's focus on "material welfare" and "intention"—which he regards as standing in tension with one another in their conception of "welfare"—explains its general awkward fit with the world's major religious traditions.

The conclusion seems obvious: Contemporary altruism is too culturally bound and historically shaped to serve as a major tool for the study of religion. It violates many, if not most, of the categories of the religions considered here, and it therefore is not a strongly effective approach to the work of description and comparison of which the academic study of religion is composed. A constructive element of this outcome is recognition that secular and religious worldviews really can be incompatible, and communication between them demands much work.

Although contemporary altruism seems not to find a home in the world's major religions, the results of this study are far from entirely negative. The inappropriateness of contemporary altruism to these religions does not mean that they are bastions of selfishness. The contrary is the case. The discrete studies in this volume display in wonderful detail how benevolence and charity operate within the values and structures of the religions studied. Whether in the Talmud's story of Mr. Five-Sins, Jesus' parables, the tale of Shaykh Abû ʿAbd Allâh, the teachings of Pali Buddhist texts, the discipline of Nicheren, the teachings of Krsna, the ideal of friendship in Greco-Roman philosophy, or the "graduated altruism" of the *Mencius*, every tradition represented in this volume exhibits the important extent to which active concern for others stands within its system and represents fundamental categories of meaning. Some of these examples bear some resemblance to contemporary altruism, and some do not; as several of the contributors point out, however, only by a rigid secular calculus is benevolence less benevolent because the actor benefits. Without question, religions are major forces for other-directed human behavior. That such behavior operates within a transcendent or eternal framework does not diminish its impact or lessen its capacity to improve the human condition.

Contributors

Alan J. Avery-Peck is Kraft-Hiatt Professor of Judaic Studies and chair of the Department of Religious Studies at the College of the Holy Cross, Worcester, Massachusetts. He is most recently a coauthor with Jacob Neusner of *The Routlege Dictionary of Judaism* (Routlege, 2004). He is an editor and coauthor of *The Encyclopedia of Judaism*, second edition (Brill, forthcoming), and *The Blackwell Companion to Judaism and The Blackwell Reader in Judaism* (Blackwell, 2000). He is also editor of the annual journal *The Review of Rabbinic Judaism: Ancient, Medieval and Modern* (Brill).

Robert Berchman is professor of philosophy and religious studies at Dowling College and senior fellow at the Institute of Advanced Theology at Bard College. His recent books are *Porphyry's Against the Christians* (Brill, 2005), *In the Glance of the Logos: Essays in Later Ancient Philosophy* (Brill 2005), editor of *Mediators of the Divine: Horizons of Prohecy, Divination, and Theurgy in Mediterranean Antiquity* (Scholars Press, 1998), and as coeditor of *Plato Redivius* (University Press of the South, 2005).

Bruce Chilton is the Bernard Iddings Bell Professor of Philosophy and Religion at Bard College. His most recent books are *Rabbi Jesus: An Intimate Biography* (Doubleday, 2000), *Redeeming Time: The Wisdom of Ancient Jewish and Christian Festal Calendars* (Hendrickson, 2002), *Rabbi Paul: An Intellectual Biography* (Doubleday, 2004), and *Mary Magdalene: A Biography* (Doubleday, 2005).

Bradley S. Clough is associate professor of history and the Abdulhadi H. Taher Chair of Comparative Religion at the American University in Cairo. He is the author of *Noble Persons' Paths: Diversity and Controversy in Early Indian and Theravada Buddhist Soteriologies* (Motilal Banarsidass Publications, 2005); "A Modern Theravada Buddhist Meditation Controversy" in *Sri Lanka Journal of the Humanities*, vol. 30, nos. 1 and 2 (2005); and "Gandhi the Rama-bhakta" in the *Journal of Vaishnava Studies*, vol. 12, no. 2 (spring 2004).

Mark Csikszentmihalyi is associate professor of East Asian Languages and Literature at the University of Wisconsin-Madison. His publications include *Material Virtue: Ethics and the Body in Early China* (Leiden: Brill, 2004), and "Confucianism: An Overview" and "Confucianism: The Classical Canon" in *Encyclopedia of Religion*, 2nd ed. (Gale, 2005).

Richard H. Davis is professor of religion and Asian studies at Bard College. He is the author of *Ritual in an Oscillating Universe: Worshiping Siva in Medieval India* (Princeton, 1991) and *Lives of Indian Images* (Princeton, 1997), and editor of *Images, Miracles, and Authority in Asian Religious Traditions* (Westview, 1998) and *Iconographies of the Nation in India* (Orient Longman, 2005).

William Scott Green is Dean of the College and professor of religion, Philip S. Bernstein Professor of Judaic Studies at the University of Rochester. His recent publications are "Stretching the Covenant: Job and Judaism," in *Review and Expositor*, vol. 99, no. 4 (fall 2002); "Realistic Expectations: The Limits of Theological Negotiation," in *When Judaism and Christianity Began: Essays in Memory of A. J. Saldarini* (E. J. Brill, 2004); and coeditor (with Jacob Neusner and Alan Avery-Peck) of *Judaism from Moses to Muhammed* (E. J. Brill, 2005).

Ruben L. F. Habito is professor of world religions and spirituality and associate dean for academic affairs at Perkins School of Theology, Southern Methodist University. His publications include *Experiencing Buddhism* (Orbis, 2005), and *Living Zen, Loving God* (Wisdom, 2004).

Th. Emil Homerin is professor of religion in the Department of Religion & Classics at the University of Rochester. Among his many publications are *From Arab Poet to Muslim Saint* (2nd revised edition, Cairo: American University Press, 2001), his anthology of translations, *Ibn al-Fârid: Sufi Verse & Saintly Life* (Paulist Press, 2001), and several chapters on Islam in *The Religious Foundations of Western Civilization* (Abingdon Press, 2005).

Todd Lewis is professor in the Religious Studies Department at The College of the Holy Cross. His books include *Popular Buddhist Texts from Nepal: Narratives and Rituals of Newar Buddhism* (2000), *The Himalayas: A Syllabus of the Region's History, Anthropology and Religion* (1995), and the coauthored textbook *World Religions Today* (2005).

Jacob Neusner is research professor of theology and senior fellow of the Institute of Advanced Theology at Bard College, a member of the Institute of Advanced Study, Princeton; life member of Clare Hall, Cambridge University; and senior visiting fellow of the Institute of Advanced Study at the University of Bologna. He holds seven honorary doctorates and is author of many books.

Acknowledgments

This book emerged from a conference at Bard College on altruism in world religions—a project of the Institute of Advanced Theology. An undergraduate seminar was devoted to the study of papers prepared for the conference (not all of which are reproduced here). The book was planned as a distinct statement in the context of the academic study of religion, including theology. The conference included papers on the social science study of altruism and the psychiatric approach to the same topic. In addition, the seminar featured a film interpreted in context by Bard College film professor John Pruitt. A special word of thanks goes to the social scientists and scholars of medicine and psychiatry who participated in the conference and showed the assembled scholars of religion in the humanities framework of text and interpretation a completely different approach to learning. Thus, a variety of approaches to the topic set forth our reading of the issue. We defined the book in its own terms, however; it is not a record of what was said at the conference. The editors aspire to contribute to the academic study of religion: comparison and contrast.

The conference was sponsored by the Templeton Foundation through the Institute for Research on Unlimited Love—Altruism, Compassion, Service, in collaboration with the president of the Institute, Stephen G. Post, of Case Western Reserve Medical School in Cleveland, Ohio. The conference was ably managed by Emily Darrow of the Institute of Advanced Theology. Dean Michele Dominy represented Bard College in welcoming the participants. In these and other ways, Bard College complemented the support of the Institute. The editors, who organized and chaired the conference, express their thanks to Bard College as well as the Institute for Research on Unlimited Love—Altruism, Compassion, Service, for making the work possible.

Index

Abû ʿAbd Allâh Muhammad, 82–84, 85
ʿAdawîyah, Râbiʿah al-, 80
Alexander the Great, 105
almsgiving (zakât/sadaqah), 71–79
altruism, Green's definition of, ix–xiii,
    191–94; and Chinese religions, 180–81,
    182, 186–88; and Christianity, 65–66; and
    classical Buddhism, 108–9; contempo-
    rary altruism, 192–94; and contemporary
    Buddhism, 115, 116–17, 128, 134–36; and
    Greco-Roman philosophy, 2, 3, 23–26;
    and Green's three questions for study,
    xiii; and Hindu dharma, 165; and Islam,
    67, 74, 84; and Nichiren Buddhism, 150;
    and Thich Nhat Hanh's socially engaged
    Buddhism, 115, 116–17. See also under
    individual religions
Amida Buddha, 141–42
Analects (Confucius), 182–83
Aqiba, 58
Aristotle: on friendship, 4–9, 10–13, 20,
    22–23; list of virtues, 49
Aryadeva, 88
Ashoka, 105–7
Avalokiteshvara, 99–100, 119–20
Avery-Peck, Alan, 84. See also Judaism, classical

Bannâ', Hasan al-, 79
Batson, C. Daniel, xii, 2
Berchman, Robert M., 115, 193. See also
    Greco-Roman philosophy
Bhagavad Gita, 162, 170–74, 176
bin Ladin, Usâmah, 79
Bodhicaryāvatāra, 97–98
Bodhidharma, 135
Brooks, Roger, 39, 41
Buddhacarita, 92
Buddhaghosa, 106, 131
Buddhism, classical, 88–114, 192; and
    altruism in cross-cultural definition,
    88–89; anātman doctrine, 92, 111n10;
    arthacaryā, 88–89; and the Ashokan
    paradigm, 105–7; and Buddhist texts,
    93–100; civilization as altruistic
    endeavor, 100–101; doctrinal guidelines
    for living, 91; and Green's questions
    about altruism, 108–9; and the healing
    arts/medicine, 103; hierarchy of altruism,
101–2; and impermanence, 92; and
    indigenous Chinese religions, 181, 189n5;
    and interdependence, 92; karma,
    collective, 102–3; karma and its
    implications, 90–91, 102–3, 109; kingship
    and altruism, 102–3, 105–7; Mahāyāna
    and altruism, 102–3, 105–7; Mahāyāna
    bodhisattva doctrine, 97–98; Mahāyāna
    Buddhism in China, 107–8; Mahāyāna
    meditation traditions, 99–100;
    Mahāyāna sources and tradition, 95–100;
    and merit recipients (merit-gaining),
    101–2, 135; monasteries and missionary
    altruism, 104; monasteries as altruistic
    centers, 100–104; and origins of Buddhist
    tradition, 89–90; and samsāra, 90, 102;
    Theravada sources and tradition, 93–95;
    and universality of suffering, 92
Buddhism, contemporary (socially engaged),
    115–38; acknowledging violence, 126–27,
    129; and Buddhist definitions of "others,"
    133–34; compassion and Buddha-nature,
    130–31; defining socially engaged
    Buddhism, 116; and dependent co-arising
    (intercausality/interbeing), 118, 120–21,
    123–26; goal of achieving prajna
    (liberating insight/understanding), 120;
    and Green's definition of altruism, 115,
    116–17, 128, 134–36; and Mahayana
    meditative exercises, 132; mindfulness
    and Nhat Hanh's socially engaged
    Buddhism, 118–20, 132; and motivation/
    intention in Buddhism, 134–35; and the
    natural world, 126–28; Nhat Hanh's
    altruistic work, 116–18; Nhat Hanh's
    "Please Call Me by My True Names,"
    123–28, 130; Order of Interbeing, 116,
    117–18, 124, 129, 132–33, 135–36; Order of
    Interbeing's Mindfulness Trainings,
    117–18, 124, 129, 132–33; and punya
    (merit-gaining) in Zen tradition, 135;
    and taking responsibility, 125–26, 129;
    teachings of the Flower Garland School,
    120–25, 128; and Theravada sublime
    attitudes, 131–32; and vocations, 129
Buddhism, Nichiren. See Japanese religions
    (Nichiren Buddhism)
Buddhist Pure Karma Society, 108
Burkert, Walter, 19, 20